BABE RUTH

BABE RUTH

A BIOGRAPHY

WAYNE STEWART

BASEBALL'S ALL-TIME GREATEST HITTERS

GREENWOOD PRESS
WESTPORT, CONNECTICUT • LONDON

Library of Congress Cataloging-in-Publication Data

Stewart, Wayne, 1951–
  Babe Ruth : a biography / Wayne Stewart.
      p.   cm. — (Baseball's all-time greatest hitters)
  Includes bibliographical references and index.
  ISBN 0–313–33596–6 (alk. paper)
  1. Ruth, Babe, 1895–1948.   2. Baseball players—United States—Biography.   I. Title.
II. Series.
  GV865.R8S754   2006
  796.357092—dc22   2006009755

British Library Cataloguing in Publication Data is available.

Library of Congress Catalog Card Number: 2006009755
ISBN: 0–313–33596–6

First published in 2006

Greenwood Press, 88 Post Road West, Westport, CT 06881
An imprint of Greenwood Publishing Group, Inc.
www.greenwood.com

Printed in the United States of America

The paper used in this book complies with the
Permanent Paper Standard issued by the National
Information Standards Organization (Z39.48–1984).

10 9 8 7 6 5 4 3 2 1

To my wife Nancy and our sons Scott and Sean,
and to the memory of my parents
Owen (O.J.) and Margaret Stewart

CONTENTS

Contents

SERIES FOREWORD

The volumes in Greenwood's "Baseball's All-Time Greatest Hitters" series present the life stories of the players who, through their abilities to hit for average, for power, or for both, most helped their teams at the plate. Much thought was given to the players selected for inclusion in this series. In some cases, the selection of certain players was a given. **Ty Cobb**, **Rogers Hornsby**, and **Joe Jackson** hold the three highest career averages in baseball history: .367, .358, and .356, respectively. **Babe Ruth**, who single-handedly brought the sport out of its "dead ball" era and transformed baseball into a home-run hitters game, hit 714 home runs (a record that stood until 1974) while also hitting .342 over his career. **Lou Gehrig**, now known primarily as the man whose consecutive-games record Cal Ripken Jr. broke in 1995, hit .340 and knocked in more than 100 runs eleven seasons in a row, totaling 1,995 before his career was cut short by ALS. **Ted Williams**, the last man in either league to hit .400 or better in a season (.406 in 1941), is widely regarded as possibly the best hitter ever, a man whose fanatical dedication raised hitting to the level of both science and art.

Two players set career records that, for many, define the art of hitting. **Hank Aaron** set career records for home runs (755) and RBIs (2,297). He also maintained a .305 career average over twenty-three seasons, a remarkable feat for someone primarily known as a home-run hitter. **Pete Rose** had ten seasons with 200 or more hits and won three batting titles on his way to establishing his famous record of 4,256 career hits. Some critics have claimed that both players' records rest more on longevity than excellence. To that I would say there is something to be said about longevity and, in both cases, the player's excellence was the reason why he had the opportunity to keep playing, to keep tallying hits for his team. A base hit is the mark of a successful plate appearance; a home run is the apex of an at-bat. Accordingly, we could hardly have a series titled "Baseball's All-Time Greatest Hitters" without including the two men who set the career records in these categories.

Joe DiMaggio holds another famous mark: fifty-six consecutive games in which he obtained a base hit. Many have called this baseball's most unbreakable record. (The player who most closely approached that mark was Pete Rose, who hit safely in forty-four consecutive games in 1978.) In his thirteen seasons, DiMaggio hit .325 with 361 home runs and 1,537 RBIs. This means he *averaged* 28 home runs and 118 RBIs per season. MVPs have been awarded to sluggers in various years with lesser stats than what DiMaggio achieved in an "average" season.

Because **Stan Musial** played his entire career with the Cardinals in St. Louis—once considered the western frontier of the baseball world in the days before baseball came to California—he did not receive the press of a DiMaggio. But Musial compiled a career average of .331, with 3,630 hits (ranking fourth all time) and 1,951 RBIs (fifth all time). His hitting prowess was so respected around the league that Brooklyn Dodgers fans once dubbed him "The Man," a nickname he still carries today.

Willie Mays was a player who made his fame in New York City and then helped usher baseball into the modern era when he moved with the Giants to San Francisco. Mays did everything well and with flair. His over-the-shoulder catch in the 1954 World Series was perhaps his most famous moment, but his hitting was how Mays most tormented his opponents. Over twenty-two seasons the "Say Hey Kid" hit .302 and belted 660 home runs.

Only four players have reached the 600-home-run milestone: Mays, Aaron, Ruth, and **Barry Bonds**, who achieved that feat in 2002. Bonds, the only active player included in this series, broke the single-season home-run record when he smashed 73 for the San Francisco Giants in 2001. In the 2002 National League Championship Series, St. Louis Cardinals pitchers were so leery of pitching to him that they walked him ten times in twenty-one plate appearances. In the World Series, the Anaheim Angels walked him thirteen times in thirty appearances. He finished the Series with a .471 batting average, an on-base percentage of .700, and a slugging percentage of 1.294.

As with most rankings, this series omits some great names. Jimmie Foxx, Tris Speaker, and Tony Gwynn would have battled for a hypothetical thirteenth volume. And it should be noted that this series focuses on players and their performance within Major League Baseball; otherwise, sluggers such as Josh

Gibson from the Negro Leagues and Japan's Sadaharu Oh would have merited consideration.

There are names such as Cap Anson, Ed Delahanty, and Billy Hamilton who appear high up on the list of career batting average. However, a number of these players played during the late 1800s, when the rules of baseball were drastically different. For example, pitchers were not allowed to throw overhand until 1883, and foul balls weren't counted as strikes until 1901 (1903 in the American League). Such players as Anson and company undeniably were the stars of their day, but baseball has evolved greatly since then, into a game in which hitters must now cope with night games, relief pitchers, and split-fingered fastballs.

Ultimately, a list of the "greatest" anything is somewhat subjective, but Greenwood offers these players as twelve of the finest examples of hitters throughout history. Each volume focuses primarily on the playing career of the subject: his early years in school, his years in semi-pro and/or minor league baseball, his entrance into the majors, and his ascension to the status of a legendary hitter. But even with the greatest of players, baseball is only part of the story, so the player's life before and after baseball is given significant consideration. And because no one can exist in a vacuum, the authors often take care to recreate the cultural and historical contexts of the time—an approach that is especially relevant to the multidisciplinary ways in which sports are studied today.

Batter up.

ROB KIRKPATRICK
GREENWOOD PUBLISHING

Acknowledgments

To Julia Ruth Stevens, Babe's daughter, and her son Tom for invaluable help and to Linda Ruth Tosetti, Babe's granddaughter, who closes her e-mail with "Ruthian regards," for her enormous help.

Thanks also to the Lorain Public Library with a special nod to Larry Plank; to author Kelly Boyer Sagert; to Gregory Schwalenberg, the curator of the Babe Ruth Museum and Mike Gibbons, the museum's executive director; and to Rob Kirkpatrick for assigning this project to me and John Wagner for his immeasurable help with the book.

CHRONOLOGY

1895   George Herman Ruth is born to parents Kate and George Ruth on February 6 in Baltimore, Maryland.

1902   Ruth is sent away to St. Mary's Industrial School for Boys, where he is listed as "incorrigible."

1914   Jack Dunn of the minor league Baltimore Orioles signs Ruth to a professional contract. He homers in his first professional appearance. Ruth later is purchased by the Boston Red Sox, debuting with them and ultimately earning $2,500. After the season, he marries Helen Woodford.

1915   Ruth clobbers his first home run, taking Jack Warhop deep. Ruth also displays his pitching skills, winning 18 contests.

1916   Ruth becomes a 20-game winner and leads the league with his 1.75 earned run average. He also wins his first World Series start, working 13 straight scoreless innings in a 14-inning, 2-1 win, the longest complete game in Series history.

1917   The United States enters World War I, but Ruth, as a married man, is given a deferment, and once more wins over 20 games (24-13).

1918   For the first of 12 times, Ruth leads his league in home runs with a modest 11. With 13 wins, he is still considered to be a pitcher, but over 95 games (72 in the field) he racks up his most at-bats to date, 317.

1919   Ruth's days as a pitcher end as he slugs 29 homers, a new season record, and homers in every American League park, a first.

1920   The announcement of Ruth's sale to the Yankees is made as a new era begins. For the first of eight times he leads the American League in runs and for the first of six times he tops the league in runs driven in.

1921   The "Bambino" swats 59 home runs, up from 54 the previous year, again shattering his own record. He also hits his first World Series home run in his first Series as a Yankee.

1922   Ruth's first big setback occurs when he is suspended for illegal barnstorming.

1923   Ruth christens Yankee Stadium with a homer in the first game ever played there.

1925   Ruth suffers from "the bellyache heard around the world," afflicted by an intestinal abscess that requires surgery. Later, his manager, Miller Huggins, suspends Ruth indefinitely. By year's end he plods through a miserable season, playing only 98 games with just 25 home runs.

1926   Ruth crushes three homers in Game 4 of the World Series versus the St. Louis Cardinals.

1927   Ruth explodes with a new record, 60 homers, and the Yankees sweep the Pirates in the year of the "Murderers' Row."

1928   On October 9, Ruth again connects for three homers in the Series, again at the expense of the St. Louis Cardinals.

1929   Helen Ruth perishes in a fire; Ruth remarries, taking Claire Hodgson as his wife. On August 11, he blasts his 500th homer, which comes off pitcher Willis Hudlin.

1932   For the 14th and final season, Ruth alone out-homers at least one entire major league team. In Game 3 of the World Series versus Cubs hurler Charlie Root, Ruth gestures with his right hand as he reportedly predicts he would hit a home run. This has become known as the famous "Called Shot."

1933   Ruth plays in the first-ever All Star Game and becomes the first player to hit an All Star Game homer.

1935   The Boston Braves acquire Ruth from the Yankees. On May 25, he drills three home runs in a game but bows out on May 30. He ends his 22-year career with 714 homers and a slew of records.

1936 Along with Walter Johnson, Ty Cobb, Christy Mathewson, and Honus Wagner, Ruth becomes a charter member in the National Baseball Hall of Fame.

1938 On June 18, Ruth accepts a coaching job that was to run for the rest of that season with the Dodgers; he was destined never again to coach or to fulfill his dream of managing in the majors.

1947 Commissioner Happy Chandler declares April 27 to be "Babe Ruth Day."

1948 On June 13 in New York, Ruth says goodbye to Yankee fans as the team honors Babe by retiring his uniform jersey on the 25th anniversary of the opening of Yankee Stadium. On August 16, Ruth loses his battle to throat cancer. He dies at the age of 53 in New York.

1961 Ruth's season record for homers falls to Roger Maris.

1974 Ruth relinquishes his career home run record to Hank Aaron, who goes on to hit 755.

INTRODUCTION

Born in Baltimore to hard-working saloon keepers, and raised mainly in an institution that was incorrectly believed by many to be an orphanage, George Herman Ruth experienced a youth that was not exactly cheerful. Had it not been for baseball, Ruth would have been a shirt maker. However, he learned the game early on, readily showing he could play any position and drill any pitcher's offerings great distances. Destiny had something else in mind for this boy.

The mean streets of the Baltimore waterfront district produced a rough and raw Babe Ruth. One imagines that if young Babe were around today, he'd pop up on the *Jerry Springer Show*, bellowing out defiantly like *South Park* bad boy Eric Cartman, "Whatever! I can do what I want." Ruth, by his own admission, was the personification of incorrigibility.

Before he mellowed with age, Ruth resented authority and being told what to do. He got into verbal altercations or fisticuffs with teammates, opponents, managers, umpires, the commissioner of baseball, and even spectators. Somewhat contradictorily, Ruth grew up to be a man capable of tenderness and generosity while also flashing displays of recalcitrance and defiance. In 1914, at the early age of 19, he left Baltimore and soon find himself a star in Boston and later New York. The journey from being an "orphan," to a rube or a "babe" during his short stint in the minor leagues, to being the brightest luminary in the nation took place with whirlwind speed.

With the Boston Red Sox, he quickly showcased his excellence as a pitcher, but soon gained fame as the game's first legitimate slugger and ultimately its greatest longball artist. Even Ruth, not an introspective person, recognized how fortuitous he was in that during an era in baseball that stressed defense and pitching, he earned a living on the mound. Then when offense held sway, Ruth was, as he said, given the opportunity "to 'take my cut' with the rest of the sluggers."[1]

Ruth is so legendary people have attributed accomplishments to him that he simply did not do. When asked to name one notable Ruthian feat, Baltimore All-Star second baseman Brian Roberts replied, "Didn't he win 300 games?" When told no, Roberts insisted, "200? Or something [remarkable]?" Such is the stuff of the Babe—he won fewer than 100 games (94), but did so in just 148 starts, good for a staggering .671 won-loss percentage.

As a rule, things came so easy for the charismatic and multitalented Ruth. Not at all coincidentally, his teams made it to the World Series in almost exactly half the seasons he donned a uniform. However, off the field, there were times his life took on elements of a soap opera. He took a wife, Helen, at the age of 19 but quickly grew restless, unaccustomed to domestic restraints. Guilty of numerous peccadilloes, he couldn't, for example, remain faithful. His first child, raised by Helen and Babe, was a product of an affair, and in a few short years, for all practical purposes, the sham of a marriage was over. As a Catholic, Ruth rejected thoughts of divorce, but after a fire took Helen's life, he soon married Claire, a woman he had been seeing for some time. His life was often fraught with conflict as he also butted heads with team owners and managers and even obstinately challenged baseball's commissioner.

Nevertheless, many historians consider Ruth to be a baseball messiah, crediting him with saving baseball from ruin when the sordid details of the fixing of the 1919 World Series by eight members of the Chicago White Sox came to light. Ruth's heroic deeds helped baseball spruce up its tarnished image. Ruth's bat belted out a message: Put the scandal behind us, and instead behold the magic of the home run. Ruth's solo fireworks display of a dazzling 54 home runs in 1920 revolutionized the game and stunned fans loved it, pouring into ballparks across the land.

The same year that saw Charles Augustus Lindbergh make his solo flight across the Atlantic Ocean, 1927, found Ruth making history as well, giving flight to a record 60 home runs. By 1932, the already enormous legend of Ruth was further embellished when he supposedly called his World Series shot, predicting not only that he would hit a home run, but also indicating where he would place the ensuing pitch. With his typical flamboyant flair, he put the final touch on his lifelong tale with a dramatic outburst of three home runs at the end of his career in May 1935. Mike Gibbons, the executive director of the Babe Ruth Museum, stated, "He was so extraordinary, so different. Everywhere he went, he [evoked], 'Wow! What the heck is that?!' So this guy was a superhero, a superman for his game and for his age, and that's why he has endured."[2]

Introduction

Few people attain the iconic status that Ruth did. In the 1970s, a story circulating on college campuses said that in the entire twentieth century only three American figures were instantly recognizable around virtually the entire world. One of those figures—Mickey Mouse—wasn't even human; the others were Muhhamad Ali and Babe Ruth.

Gibbons said he has "wondered if Ruth's celebrity would last and we're asked that question all the time."

> "Will Babe Ruth's importance to the game always be there?" And I think that the answer has to be yes. He is the standard, that's pretty well established. There are a few who challenge it, but, to me, he is the game of baseball and he is that because he was the greatest player. People say, "How can you make that statement with so many other greats out there?" And there's a pretty simple answer: There is no other player who comes close to having achieved what he did; he's the guy.
>
> He set all those records and he saved the game of baseball, the Called Shot, all that stuff, but in addition to all that, it's his off-the-field legacy that's so important. He was important to the Roaring Twenties and to the spirit and dynamics of America in that era. He has transcended into pop culture now—he's a cultural icon, not just a sports icon, and despite all the negatives about his behavior et cetera, he was the guy.[3]

A product of his times while also being a trendsetter, Ruth's fame truly was global even in the early days of the century. It follows, then, that the fashionable crowd courted Ruth; they just *had* to meet him. As Yankee pitcher Waite Hoyt put it, Ruth "penetrated the inner recesses of the social world. Even the Four Hundred of New York became curious. They wanted to know what made the big fellow tick."[4] Even the most sophisticated and refined took delight in Ruth's bawdiness and even his sometimes coarse ways. Hoyt further stated that to the guileless Ruth, "People were people. Everybody was a 'good fellow.'"[5] Yet Ruth felt most comfortable, most relaxed with the common man (and child).

Long-time Orioles coach Elrod Hendricks noted, "Ruth, seems to be everything that I've read, and from what I've seen about him, he had fun. And that's the way the game's supposed to be played. When Babe Ruth played, he did not complicate it, he had fun."[6] And, oh, the enjoyment he had; Ruth's broad smile was as big as his turbo-charged swing and as contagious as a pandemic influenza. Two lines from Shakespeare's *Julius Caesar* apply to the saga of Ruth, a man celebrated in life and in death. "When beggars die, there are no comets seen; The heavens themselves blaze forth the death of princes." Ruth, a true king of baseball, was mourned by millions.

Meanwhile, Ruth's departure from the baseball scene left fans mulling the loss much as Mark Antony lamented the death of mighty Caesar: "Here was a Caesar! When comes such another?" The resilient pastime of baseball always manages to survive and even thrive, but clearly the death of Ruth marked the demise of an era, but not of a legend that glows even now, decades after he passed away. Ruth lives.

NOTES

1. Babe Ruth, *Babe Ruth's Own Book of Baseball* (New York: G. P. Putnam's Son's, 1928), 25.

2. Mike Gibbons, from interview with author, September 7, 2005.

3. Mike Gibbons from interview with author, September 7, 2005.

4. Waite Hoyt, *Babe Ruth As I Knew Him* (New York: Dell, 1948), 7.

5. Hoyt, *Babe Ruth As I Knew Him*, 8.

6. Elrod Hendricks, from interview with author, September 6, 2005.

FORMATIVE YEARS, 1895–1914

When he wrote about his youth in his autobiographies, Babe Ruth was very honest about his dishonesty, saying simply that "I was a bad kid."[1] and describing how he "snitched" fruit from shopkeepers.[2] He was also quite candid about his living conditions—"We were poor. Very poor."[3] However, according to results from an archeological dig that unearthed artifacts from a home Ruth lived in, his family did not live in poverty. Greg Schwalenberg, the curator of the Babe Ruth Birthplace and Museum, stated, "They dug down into the privy which was where [household] things were thrown, and they found items from the era from broken wine bottles to glasses to pottery which they pieced back together. They had some fine dinnerware. Just from what they've found, the Ruths weren't poor. They were working class people who made a living. They were, I would guess, lower-middle class."[4] Perhaps Ruth didn't live in squalor, but his existence was as remote from a "Leave It to Beaver" lifestyle as a listless bunt dribbling in front of home plate is to a majestic home run soaring over the outfield wall.

Much of what is known of Ruth's youth comes from his own recollections. Some of Ruth's writings must be discounted due to his poor memory, his indifference to detail, and his occasional tendency to embellish. Also, some data regarding Ruth is hazy, and some accounts of events from his life are contradictory, but that's not all that unusual when dealing with legends from yesteryear. Roger Kahn wrote, "The greater the hero, the more prevalent the fictions."[5] That certainly is the case with such magical tales from Ruth's career as his Called Shot.

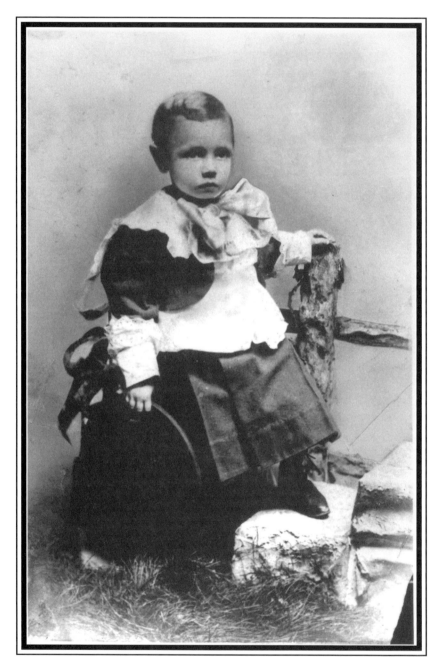

Babe Ruth as a child. *National Baseball Hall of Fame Library, Cooperstown, N.Y.*

George Herman Ruth Jr., was born in the brawling city of Baltimore, in a row house at 216 Emory Street that was owned by his maternal grandfather. Located only two blocks from the Baltimore Orioles' Camden Yards, that building now houses the Babe Ruth Birthplace and Museum. Ruth was born on February 6, 1895, a day the temperature plunged below zero and the headline of a local newspaper shuddered "TASTE OF THE ARCTIC." Grover Cleveland was the president of the United States and a nickel got you a schooner of beer—although it would be a few years before Ruth would first gulp down a beer or two, or three. Ruth's birth took place a mere thirty-four years after the Sixth Massachusetts Volunteer Militia Regiment was attacked by an angry mob in Baltimore, resulting in sixteen deaths and the first bloodshed of the Civil War. In the world of baseball, what would come to be known as the "modern era" was still five years away.

Ruth's parents were George Sr.—later known as "Big George"—and Catherine "Kate" Schamberger. While the couple then lived with George's father, Kate went to her father's home to give birth to her babe, doing so "to escape the lusty atmosphere of the apartment she and her husband lived in overtop the Ruth family saloon a few blocks away." George Sr., also worked with his father, who made lightning rods.[6]

The Ruths had been married on June 25, 1894, "and Babe came along about 7½ months later—a somewhat scandalous occurrence in those Victorian times." Although George Sr., was a Protestant, Katie, then only 20 years old, three years younger than her husband, was Catholic and Babe was baptized as a Catholic. In fact, author Paul F. Harris Sr., stated that Ruth, the son of "a rough and ready guy," was "actually baptized twice in the Catholic church, which was very unusual. On March 1st, his mother took him to St. Peter's church in the neighborhood. I don't think his father knew about it; then when he went to St. Mary's they didn't know about it so they baptized him again."[7]

Little George, as he was called, was the first of eight children, and he spent his first several years in a home on Frederick Avenue with his parents and paternal grandparents, who were most likely from Pennsylvania Dutch stock, and thus probably spoke German. However, only he and Mary Margaret, born in 1900 and called "Mamie," survived infancy. Mike Gibbons, of the Babe Ruth Museum, said, "Six died in childbirth and early infancy; it took a lot out of Kate."[8]

Ruth spent his earliest, tempestuous days on the streets around the city's waterfront, streets that were as raucous and bustling as they were dingy. From 1906 to 1912, he lived one story above the saloon his father ran at 406 West Conway Street, now the location of shallow centerfield at Camden Yards. Ruth's "pigtown" south-side neighborhood was one he called "rough and tough, but I liked it."[9]

Reports say Ruth smoked and chewed tobacco when he was 7 years old and sipped, or, given his Falstaffian ways, chugged beer since the age of eight. Later, said Ruth's charming and articulate granddaughter Linda Ruth Tosetti, Babe would "smoke, drink a martini, and chew tobacco at the same time. My mother said he did horrendous things to himself."[10] After dropping Mamie off at school, Babe would frequently "hook," or skip school, hiding from his parents. Mamie, though, said that her brother George was more mischievous than outright bad, but pointed out that if anyone dared him to do anything at all, "you might as well consider it done."[11]

In the meantime, Babe's parents were run ragged, operating their saloon seemingly around the clock—Ruth often claimed they toiled 20 hours per day. Schwalenberg observed, "That was common [then]. People who owned a business were there [from its opening] till it's closed—that's their livelihood. If the bar closed at 2:00 and opens again at 6:00, that wasn't much time to get your rest."[12] Ruth's daughter Julia said Babe's father "could not look after him at all because he was busy tending bar and Daddy was doing nothing but getting into trouble."[13]

Times were not happy for the family; Ruth was once quoted as saying he felt his mother hated him and he seldom even spoke of his father at all. All indications show his father was, at best, an indifferent parent, more concerned with his business than his children.

On August 11, 1912, the frail Katie died of exhaustion and pulmonary disease. She was only 38 years old. Meanwhile, Ruth's father seldom if ever visited Babe once he sent him away on a bleak Friday the 13th in June 1902, to an "orphanage," which was, in truth, St. Mary's Industrial School for Boys, a facility that housed about 800 boys and was made up of six stone buildings about four miles from the heart of Baltimore.

Later used exclusively as a reform school, it was not an orphanage, but was one of 29 institutions in Baltimore designed to supervise boys who, for various reasons, needed parental attention and care. For those services, the Ruths supposedly paid a monthly fee of $15. Schwalenberg believes Ruth's "parents did well sending him to St. Mary's. It was a school [where] they always learned a trade; I think close to 99 percent of kids that left there went right to a job." Ruth's parents "realized that they worked hard. The father was the bartender, the mother was the cook. One of their bars, which had all the docks and all the workers [nearby], opened up at 6:00 in the morning for breakfast and wouldn't close till late at night. You had two of them working full time; they realized they couldn't take care of Babe."[14]

A St. Mary's acquaintance of Ruth's said that Babe once commented that he was "too big and ugly for anyone to come to see me."[15] However, Julia said

Mamie and Kate "went to see Daddy maybe once or twice, and Mamie said, 'I just about cried every time because he was so sad and so lonesome.' She really just didn't know him that well because they grew up apart."[16] Clearly, the time spent time on rearing Little George had been tantamount to nothing. Even later, Big George reportedly only attended one game his son played.

Babe's first stay at St. Mary's lasted a little over a month before he was permitted to go home. He returned the following November for another month and didn't go back again until 1904, for four years this time. Then he was home until 1910 when he reentered St. Mary's for another year and then was "paroled" for a year. By that time, though, he had pretty much come to regard the brothers of St. Mary's as both his mother and father. His final tenure lasted from 1912 until he became a professional baseball player.[17] Julia wrote that the Ruths would pull him out of St. Mary's when they needed help around the bar, but he always returned to St. Mary's.[18]

Author Harry Rothgerber stated that Ruth "exhibited a severe pattern of irresponsible, antisocial and erratic behavior as a child and adolescent. Today, he would no doubt be labeled an 'at-risk' child in a multiple-problem family." Even Ruth conceded that when St. Mary's officials labeled him an incorrigible, they were correct.[19]

Still, Gibbons said the impression he got from speaking with Mamie was that it was Katie's idea to ship Babe out; Ruth's father "didn't want to do it. Her speculation was Babe was a handful and Mom wanted him out because she couldn't keep up with him."[20] Tosetti said her family believes he suffered from Attention Deficit Hyperactivity Disorder (ADHD), a common children's disorder characterized by impulsiveness, hyperactivity, and inattention.[21] That certainly could explain his parents' frustrations and their sending him to St. Mary's.

It is clear that Ruth's salvation at St. Mary's came in the bulky form of Brother Matthias of the Xaverian Order (Brothers of St. Francis Xavier), a Catholic order that focused on helping underprivileged boys. Incidentally, the school accepted non-Catholics, including a Jewish boy named Asa Yolson, who later changed his name to Al Jolson.

Matthias' love of baseball was instrumental in altering Ruth's young life. Matthias, a man Ruth respected and viewed as the father figure he so desperately lacked, helped teach the game to Ruth, who was a very eager pupil. Fortunately, Matthias didn't tamper with Ruth's left-handed hitting and throwing even though a St. Mary's teacher did convert him to writing right-handed. As Julia Ruth Stevens commented,

> Daddy had a God-given gift, he really did, and Brother Matthias
> encouraged it and helped him along, but I think he always was so

thankful to God for having given him that gift because he said himself he probably would have wound up in jail if he hadn't been at St. Mary's because he had started off on the wrong track. Who knows what might have happened? I think he was being helped by God all the way, along with Brother Matthias and the fact that his father put him there; it was just one of those things that was meant to be.[22]

Ruth, who normally loathed authority, said that he so admired the muscular Matthias, who stood around 6 feet 6 inches and about 250 pounds, that he emulated his pigeon-toed gait as well as his swing-for-the-fences approach to the game. When he was 15, Ruth even expressed a copycat desire to become a priest (quite the contrast to the occupation and lifestyle he would later embrace). Matthias gently talked him out of that aspiration.[23]

Ruth wrote of being "bug-eyed" as he'd observe Matthias lift the ball over the center field fence at St. Mary's, a shot he said had to travel "at least 350 feet." Ruth had begun his lifelong love affair with the longball.[24] He came to love Matthias for all his care and guidance. As Ruth's second wife Claire once wrote, "When Babe Ruth was 23, the world loved him. When he was 13, only Brother Matthias loved him."[25] Ruth once told of how he received 20,000 pieces of fan mail in 1927, but just one during his rookie season—from Matthias telling how proud he was of George. Clearly, the Xaverian brothers played a huge role in Ruth's development. In return, Ruth never forgot his roots and donated both his time and money to the brothers throughout his lifetime.

Ruth credited Matthias with teaching him how to field as well as converting him to becoming a pitcher, because Ruth had fancied himself to be a deft, albeit left-handed catcher. One report said Ruth was "adept at playing any position," enjoyed catching, but loved pitching since there "he could be the center of attraction, and he was never averse to that."[26]

One day when Ruth disparaged several of his peers who were taking their licks on the mound, Matthias goaded Ruth, saying, in effect, "If you think their plight is so funny, you try it." Ruth recounted that even though he had never been a pitcher, "as I took the position, I felt a strange relationship between myself and that pitcher's mound." He not only did well, but that first appearance on the hill ultimately lead to his ticket to professional ball just several years later.[27] At around age 15, Ruth wrote inside the cover of a hymnal, "World's Worse [sic] Singer, World's Best Pitcher."

Ruth also recognized Brother Gilbert as being an influential coach. Still, Ruth had an uncommon natural ability and, by the age of eight, he was playing on the 12-year-old team; when he reached 12, he was elevated to the 16-year-old squad. In later years, he often recalled, "I think I could hit the first time I picked up a bat."[28]

The impact of baseball aside, life at St. Mary's was more than merely playing ball. Brother John Joseph Sterne, who attended St. Mary's a few years after Ruth, wrote of a typical day at the facility. After an 8:00 P.M. bedtime, the new day began with a 6:00 A.M. wake-up followed by daily Mass. Then came a spartan breakfast, usually oatmeal or hominy—a huge contrast to the lavish meals Ruth would later consume. It hardly seems like a stretch to imagine the grown up Ruth vowing never to eat so meagerly again. Interestingly, and fittingly for Ruth, the boys enjoyed three hot dogs on Sunday morning; Julia said they only got meat once a week.[29] Sterne stated the students would even wager or barter their hot dogs or "credits" which they earned; they had no money: "I'm sure that Babe would have been involved in this 'action.'"[30]

After breakfast, it was on to the classroom until a penitentiary-like lunch of soup and bread, which was also their typical supper, was served. Julia recalled Babe saying, " 'I never, ever felt full, but I was never really *hungry*.' They managed to keep the kids filled, but never satisfied, in other words. All those things had a tremendous effect on him."[31]

Next came a short recess before the children trudged back to the classroom or, for some of the older students, into training sessions to learn trades. By the middle of the afternoon, it was time for several hours of recreation, and, as Sterne remembered, "the most popular game was always baseball."[32]

An early example of reports that don't entirely jibe concerning the Ruth legend revolve around when he was signed to a pro contract in 1914. Ruth, who had trained to become a shirtmaker and tailor, recounted his entry into pro ball by saying Brother Gilbert had made a promise to Jack Dunn, a friend of his who owned a minor league team called the Baltimore Orioles of the International League, to send him a prospect in 1914 from St. Mary's. Dunn asked for pitcher Ford Meadows, but Gilbert balked and convinced Dunn that Ruth would make a suitable substitute. He invited Dunn to take a look at a tall and trim Ruth, then just barely 19 years old.[33] Dunn, whose office was near the facility, dropped by and was wowed by what he saw that mid-February afternoon on a frozen yard of the school.

The most likely version of Ruth being "discovered," though, states a special contest was set up in 1913 to showcase Ruth versus Mount St. Joseph College and their highly touted local standout pitcher, Bill Morrisette. Ruth prevailed, firing a one-hit shutout while mowing down either 14 or 22 batters on strikes.[34] The arranged game was played, but not specifically for the sake of Dunn; exactly where he first heard of Ruth is in question. Robert W. Creamer stated Dunn may have discovered Ruth through Brother Gilbert, but added that during this period Gilbert was not at St. Mary's.[35]

At any rate, Dunn did offer Ruth a contract for $600, a sum that Ruth said "seemed to me to be all the wealth in the world."[36] In a way it was. In that era, a person could have dined at a fine New York restaurant then stayed overnight in a luxurious hotel for less than $5, which was equivalent to a day's wages at Henry Ford's automobile factory. Of course, nowadays, $600 is merely 30 days' worth of per diem money for a single-A minor leaguer.

Five days after signing the prospect Ruth, Dunn came by again, and on February 27, 1914, "claimed" Ruth, whisking him off to a new world. Ruth later wrote that because he was not of legal age at the time, Dunn took out papers to become his guardian. Ruth was still two years shy of legally being able to leave the institution on his own as an adult.

Gilbert's memoirs list Ruth's farewell to St. Mary's as having taken place on March 2, when Brother Paul, the superintendent for the school and his former guardian, took Ruth on a farewell trek through the dining rooms. Gilbert's account has Ruth sobbing, "I hate to say good-bye to the fellahs," and almost refusing to make his rounds.[37] Eventually, after Babe's promises to make good, and a touching, "You'll make it, George," from Matthias, Ruth made his exit.

NOTES

1. Babe Ruth and Bob Considine, *The Babe Ruth Story* (New York: Signet, 1992), 1.

2. Babe Ruth, *Babe Ruth's Own Book of Baseball* (New York: G. P. Putnam's Son's, 1928), 3.

3. Ibid., 4.

4. Greg Schwalenberg, from interview with author, September 7, 2005.

5. Roger Kahn, *Beyond the Boys of Summer: The Very Best of Roger Kahn* (New York: McGraw-Hill, 2005), 64.

6. From a Babe Ruth Museum display.

7. Paul F. Harris Sr., from telephone interview with author, 2005.

8. Mike Gibbons, from interview with author, September 7, 2005.

9. Brother Gilbert, *Young Babe Ruth: His Early Life and Baseball Career from the Memoirs of a Xaverian Brother*, ed. Harry Rothberger (Jefferson, NC: McFarland and Company, 1992), 1.

10. Linda Ruth Tosetti, from telephone interview with author, September 23, 2005.

11. Source unknown. From author's research files.

12. Greg Schwalenberg, from interview with author, September 7, 2005.

13. Julia Ruth Stevens, from interviews with author, November 2005.

14. Greg Schwalenberg, from interview with author, September 7, 2005.

15. Brother Gilbert, *Young Babe Ruth: His Early Life and Baseball Career from the Memoirs of a Xaverian Brother*, ed. Harry Rothberger (Jefferson, NC: McFarland and Company, 1992), 1.

16. Julia Ruth Stevens, from interviews with author, November 2005.

17. Mrs. Babe Ruth with Bill Slocum, *The Babe and I* (Englewood Cliffs, NJ: Prentice-Hall, 1959), 42.

18. Julia Ruth Stevens, *Major League Dad: A Daughter's Cherished Memories* (Chicago: Triumph Books, 2001), 46.

19. Gilbert, *Young Babe Ruth*, 1.

20. Mike Gibbons, from interview with author, September 7, 2005.

21. Linda Ruth Tosetti, from telephone interview with author, September 23, 2005.

22. Julia Ruth Stevens, from interviews with author, November 2005.

23. Ruth, with Slocum, *The Babe and I*, 45.

24. Ruth and Considine, *The Babe Ruth Story*, 5.

25. Ruth with Slocum, *The Babe and I*, 44.

26. Paul F. Harris Sr., *Babe Ruth: The Dark Side* (Glen Burnie, MD: Paul F. Harris, 1998), 43.

27. Ruth and Considine, *The Babe Ruth Story*, 7.

28. Ruth, with Slocum, *The Babe and I*, 45.

29. Julia Ruth Stevens, from interviews with author, November 2005.

30. Gilbert, *Young Babe Ruth*, ix.

31. Julia Ruth Stevens, from interviews with author, November 2005.

32. Gilbert, *Young Babe Ruth*, ix.

33. Ruth and Considine, *The Babe Ruth Story*, 9, 11.

34. Lawrence S. Ritter, *The Babe: A Life in Pictures* (New York: Ticknor and Fields, 1988), 12.

35. Robert W. Creamer, *Babe: The Legend Comes to Life* (New York: Penguin Books, 1974), 46, 50–51.

36. Ruth and Considine, *The Babe Ruth Story*, 10.

37. Gilbert, *Young Babe Ruth*, 40.

Ruth (far right) with his Red Sox teammates (from left) Ernie Shore, Dutch Leonard, and Rube Foster. *National Baseball Hall of Fame Library, Cooperstown, N.Y.*

A PERSONALITY STUDY

For a seemingly simple man, Ruth's personality was quite complex. A famous quote, supposedly a Jesuit maxim, states, "Give me a child for the first seven years, and you may do what you like with him afterwards." The obvious contention is that one's personality is established at an early age.

Without verbalizing it in scholarly terms, Ruth bought into this theory and saw himself as being "a victim of circumstances."[1] In many ways, Ruth truly was the product of poor parenting. Big George was "given" a child for seven years and exposed him to seedy surroundings. Borrowing a Ring Lardner line, the hot-tempered Big George subscribed to the simplistic "Shut up, he explained" school of parenting.

Mamie said her father whipped Babe unmercifully despite Kate's protestations, "but it didn't do any good in the long run."[2] Ruth once confessed of his childhood, "I honestly don't remember being aware of the difference between right and wrong."[3] The end product of such "rearing" was a rough and raw Babe Ruth who stated, "I liked the freedom of the street; like the gang of youngsters I played with and prowled with."[4]

The personification of incorrigibility, Ruth resented being told what to do. He got into verbal altercations or fisticuffs with teammates, opponents, managers, umpires, the commissioner of baseball, and even spectators. His thinking was short term and hedonistic and his goals were therefore often geared towards instant gratification. A man of peccadilloes, he did nothing in small measure as was evidenced by his girth. However, his appetite for not only food, but for tobacco (eventually he succumbed to throat cancer), alcohol, sex, and, for that matter, life in general, was gargantuan.

When Babe passed away on August 16, 1948, he managed to fulfill most of a line John Derek uttered in the movie *Knock On Any Door*—Ruth lived fast and died (relatively) young. During his 53 years, much of his thought process was adolescent-like; often he didn't give a first thought, let alone a second one, to the ramifications of his actions. Ruth's personality was paradoxical. He was capable of giving his time freely for others, but was also capable of fighting with authority figures for many years.

Ruth was, in many respects, animalistic, not only because of his strength— taking mighty cuts with bats 42 ounces and heavier was an unbelievable feat— but also because at times he could be crude (not unusual among many rugged ballplayers of his era). Behavior displaying both Ruth's naivete and coarseness was evident in his early years.

For instance, Ernie Shore, his 1915 roommate, once grew so irate with Ruth that he went to Red Sox manager Bill Carrigan, the man Ruth later insisted had been his best skipper ever, and demanded a new "roomie." Ruth later confessed he had been borrowing Shore's belongings with the abandon of a self-centered college freshman, including using Shore's toothbrush. Then, when Shore basically said, "Hey, you're using my brush," Ruth innocently replied, "That's all right, Ernie, I'm not particular."[5] Shore's version had Ruth using his shaving brush, not his toothbrush.

Bill Werber spent a short stint with the 1927 Yankees and realized Ruth was, at once, many things—"good natured, amoral, loving, loud, rough, vulgar, and kind and considerate of everyone, especially children." Stories of Ruth visiting children's hospitals to cheer up his legion of fans were not only true, but, according to Werber, Ruth made visits privately, without notifying the press, not needing or desiring the publicity.[6]

Linda Ruth Tosetti said an historian shared the following tale about his mother, who owned a store "in Philadelphia, on the way to Shibe Park":

> Because the train was so close to the park, all the players would carry their own luggage and they'd walk past her store. There was Lou [Gehrig], and he had his luggage and he'd carry some of the bats. The historian said, "And everybody carried something except your grandfather." And I'm going, "Oh, my God, I'm going to hear my first prima donna story." But he says, "Nope, your grandfather's job was to pick up two kids in his arm and take them to the ballpark. Every time, there was Babe. Everybody would go by and there was Babe with two kids."[7]

Schwalenberg recounted a story of the time "Ruth was up in Cooperstown for its opening in 1939. This guy who now owns the Cooperstown Motel told me that Ruth was with the group of other players [inductees] and here's a whole bunch of kids along a fence." Only Ruth made time for the kids. "This guy [the motel owner] was one of those kids. Ruth handed out quarters to them all. I asked the guy, 'Did you ask him for his autograph.' He says, 'No. It was just meeting him. Just the presence.' They weren't thinking about getting signatures. I said, 'What'd you do, keep the quarter?' He goes, 'Heck, no, we went to the ice cream store immediately and bought ice cream with it.' Today we would probably save the cigarette that somebody throws away or [treasure] a lock of hair from the Beatles or something like that."[8]

Even though Ruth loved cigars and gulped down gallons of alcohol, he refused offers to endorse tobacco and alcohol. Ruth felt that to promote those products was to let his young fans down. Thus, Ruth lived fully for himself, yet his love of children was both sincere and devout. His dedication in the autobiography *The Babe Ruth Story* is "to the kids of America." He selflessly and tirelessly signed autographs and gave away baseballs and equipment to children. For that matter, he also tried to please the media, endlessly feeding quotes and anecdotes to writers, making their jobs easier. As Ruth put it, he just wanted to make people happy.

Ruth himself was both child-like and sometimes childish. Writer Ernestine Miller commented, "Many people felt that Babe's love for kids was, on some level, a way for him to reclaim the childhood he never had."[9] Because Ruth never felt loved by his own parents, he wanted to make sure that the children he met would feel the love he so lavishly dished out.

Linda Ruth Tosetti, Babe's granddaughter, said, "He always had time for everybody he met. How'd he do it? Babe didn't have family per se. He had a father, but, really, he was abandoned. His family was his fans." They inspired him, she said, it was as if he was saying, "You liked that? Watch what I do now. They love me, they really like me; I am something. It was his esteem, his family, his career, and thus, he loved every part of it. He really loved people, kids, and what he did, and that's how he was able to do what he did. And that's why I think he burned himself out at 53."[10]

Tosetti's mother Dorothy told her that when holidays rolled around Babe "was gone a lot, he was busy at the hospitals and orphanages and the homes. The holidays were his busiest times." Those trips brightened lives but the misery and suffering he witnessed saddened Ruth who nevertheless lived up to his obligations. Tosetti said that at the time, Dorothy, not understanding his absences felt "the brunt of it. In her adult years she understood, but she still missed him a great deal."[11]

Dorothy said he gravitated towards children partly because he spoke their language, one "of innocence. Dad could truly be himself around kids and not have to worry about the repercussions of saying or doing something wrong."[12] In fact, when Ruth's second wife Claire first met him, she observed, "He's nice, but he's just a big kid."[13] Gibbons called Ruth "the Pied Piper of baseball for kids because he was 12 years old at heart. He was one of the gang. I think adults bored him." Writer Rodger H. Pippen put it differently, calling Ruth "the Peter Pan of baseball who never grew up."[14]

Dorothy also wrote that people believed Ruth was a simple guy, but he wasn't. She felt that "the public Babe Ruth was the antithesis of the private Babe Ruth." The public thought of the Babe as an "uninhibited individual: rejoicing after home runs, arguing with umpires, and weeping openly at the funerals of close friends."[15] However, at home, according to Dorothy, he kept his emotions under wraps and she attributes such stoicism to his never developing close bonds with his parents. She wrote that he never had the chance to "learn what primary relationships were all about."[16]

Claire called her husband "a very human fellow," and she knew first-hand of his faults and assets, as well as his worries and woes in life. She noted that Ruth became "a national baseball idol before he could vote. And he just wasn't equipped for it. Very few are. Everything had been so difficult. Now everything was so darned easy." She went on to call him a "robust man and he wanted all the things robust men should want. Only, unfortunately, in excess."[17]

Dorothy agreed that the Babe didn't miss out on very much. "He always lived life at breakneck speed, with no time to waste for red lights or slaps on the wrist. Sleep was no more than a rude interruption...."[18] The belief of Ruth descendants that he had ADHD makes sense of such an attitude toward life, as well as of Ruth's misbehavior. Tosetti elaborated, "Everybody says he was Peck's bad boy [breaking] curfew. People don't realize he had ADHD. That's why he got in so much trouble and he had ants in his pants and he could go on two hours sleep. My brother [Richie] had it, too, and the same personality as Babe, too—'What can I get into next?' It followed the lineage. Richie used to wake me up at 3:00 in the morning to play with him every night."[19]

A teammate of Ruth's said that when traveling by train the Babe would be awake at all hours, sometimes going down the aisle waking up and even knocking players out of their berths—sounding much like a plea to, "Come out and play."[20] Of course, said Tosetti, the ADHD diagnosis of the Babe is based on things his daughter Dorothy said as opposed to "an official document because it wasn't diagnosed [back] then, but when it turned out that Richie had it, Mother saw what happened first hand. And, as an adult, you keep the pattern, so Babe had it as a child, but as an adult, of course, he would have kept the pattern, but grown out of the rest. That's why he used to break curfew like he did...."[21]

Also, according to his granddaughter, Ruth had to

> . . . eat six times a day in order to fuel himself. When people say he died young, I just think he burnt himself out because my brother did the same thing—he would go and go and go. And then he was a year younger than my grandfather when he died, so you gotta' wonder. My mother always suspected that Babe had ADHD because of his actions and how he could go on so little sleep.
>
> And if my brother would drink, he wouldn't get drunk, his body would just literally burn it off. It was the same with Babe. That's when it dawned on my mother. I mean, do we have concrete proof Babe had it? Of course not, there was no such thing in his time, but from all the symptoms and all my mother's experience, going through it with my brother, Babe even had the "attention" part of [ADHD], too, but he mostly had the hyperactive part of it. My mother said he wouldn't sit still for a second. Even at home he really didn't sit, he'd listen to the game but he'd be putzing with something.[22]

Julia, however, disagrees. "He had a lot of gusto. From what I know of hyperactivity, I would not say that applied to him at all. It was just that whatever he did, he did with all of his energy and might, but he could relax and come home and have a couple of beers and eat a good dinner. We'd listen to the radio together." She stated he was "quiet and attentive to what was going on."[23]

Dorothy related that when her father left St. Mary's to embark on a career in baseball, "people remarked that it was as if a caged animal had been set loose. He was spontaneous and wanted to sample everything life had to offer. Babe was no saint, but then he never tried to be someone or something that he wasn't."[24]

Ruth was once asked if he had a hero, "someone you thought more of than anyone else." Before he could reply, Tony Lazzeri, standing within earshot, interjected, "Sure he has. Babe Ruth." Lazzeri also teased, "Gehrig thought Ruth was a big-mouth and Ruth thought Gehrig was cheap. They were both right."[25]

Some biographers have suggested that Ruth was a product of his times, arguing that the rollicking days and mores of 1920s America influenced him greatly. Ford Frick, for instance, opined, "He was the right man, in the right place, at the right time."[26] Certainly the fun-loving Ruth did fit right in with the zaniness of the 1920s, when a booming economy led to such mindless, frivolous antics as goldfish swallowing, flagpole sitting, and marathon dancing. Those were apt crazes because this was an era obsessed with breaking records, and that is yet another reason why Ruth, the ultimate record buster, was in the right time period.

If there was a *diem* that he could *carpe,* seize that day he would. The term "pleasure principle" could have been coined for Ruth, whose primary goal was frequently the satisfaction of his urges. Such a lifestyle fit in quite well with the

1920s, a time when society changed, in part due to its recent emergence from World War I and a virulent flu epidemic—an era when the nation "decided that life was meant to be lived 'one day at a time,' and at last emerged from its Victorian closet." Skirts grew shorter—to the delight of Ruth—and women became more visible and, with the recently acquired right to vote, more powerful than perhaps ever before.[27]

Still, it may be more accurate to argue that Ruth's personality was more swayed by parenting than place or time. After all, if psychiatrists are correct, Ruth's basic traits were formed and in place by around 1902, far removed from the Roaring Twenties. As for those who persist in the belief that he was in the ideal place, New York, it was likely that with his skill and personality he would have been a shining light on any era's stage. As Tosetti stated of the "right time, right place" concept, "It's more than that—it's how ahead of the times he was in some things. And people say, 'Oh, he was bigger because he went to New York. I say, 'You could've put him in Oshkosh, Wisconsin, playing for a team and it would have been a very famous team. A personality is a personality, and that's what he was. He never thought of himself as bigger than the game. Guess what, Babe is one that *is* bigger than the game."[28]

Hitting coach Gerald Perry said that few modern players can approach Ruth's larger-than-life personality. "You can't help but to think of Reggie [Jackson]; he was flamboyant and he backed it up. And, actually, I can tolerate a lot of trash talking when somebody can back it up."[29] Ruth backed up his good-natured boasts and did so with a charming grin.

Ruth knew himself well and saw the parallel between his style on the baseball field and his lifestyle. "I swing as hard as I can, and I try to swing right through the ball. I swing big with everything I've got. I hit big or I miss big. I like to live as big as I can."[30] At times his cut was so forceful, he'd nearly corkscrew himself into the dirt by home plate after missing a pitch. Julia chuckled, "He was always swinging for the fences. He said people didn't come to the ballpark to see him hit singles. He said, 'They came to see me hit home runs so I'm always trying.'"[31]

Even off the diamond, Ruth was obsessed with power and speed, so it wasn't surprising he bought big, fast cars—his favorites were Packards. One story of his days in Boston told of the time he took a girl for a ride late one night and managed to get his car wedged between two trolleys, which caused its front end to get flattened. Ruth had to pry himself out of the wreckage. Then, unconcerned, he left the disabled car "for the police to fret about."[32]

By 1919, the Red Sox hired a man to keep an eye on Ruth and keep him out of trouble. Ruth admitted that he "began working harder at having fun than I worked on the field," a charge that would be leveled against him many times.[33]

When scolded or punished he sometimes confided that he would feel pretty penitent, again, not unlike a small child. He'd get in trouble then soon be upset with himself for his infractions.

When asked what Ruth was like, New York sportswriter Lieb replied that he was a "pretty nice guy. He was certainly a rough character and certainly wasn't a cultured, cultivated man, and things happened to Babe Ruth I don't think could have happened to any other individual."[34]

Ruth and temptation had a sort of symbiotic relationship in that part of what made Ruth who he was came, as Paul Gallico put it, from the way "he succumbs to every temptation which comes his way." Gallico further commented, "Ruth is either planning to cut loose, is cutting loose, or is repenting the last time he cut loose. He is a news story on legs going about looking for a place to happen."[35] Ruth somehow extricated himself from messes, often by using his down to earth charm, his sincere apologies, or by shoveling out money.

He loved to take part in pranks, too. His sense of humor was hardly highbrow, but that's not unusual for ballplayers even nowadays. He loved, for example, to take items such as paper or cloth and, when a teammate wasn't watching, sneak it between the slices of bread of that player's sandwich.[36] Tosetti recalled, "He nailed Frank Crosetti's shoes to the floor and put eggs in the toes."[37]

Ruth was always game for anything. For instance, long before Larry Walker's antics versus the intimidating Randy Johnson in the 1997 All Star Game when, after Johnson's first pitch flew over his head, Walker flipped his batting helmet backward, laughed, and walked over to the other side of the plate for the next pitch, Ruth displayed his whimsical nature. On August 1, 1923, he faced Cleveland's Sherrod Smith and began his at bat by hitting righty. According to the Baseball Library Web site, "After taking a strike, he switches to left-handed and hits his 25th home run of the season."[38]

Meanwhile, Freudians would argue Ruth never progressed beyond the oral stage of development, citing symptoms of people with an oral fixation, which Ruth obviously displayed, including constant gum chewing, smoking, overeating, and drinking. It would be nearly impossible for a player of Ruth's mammoth talents to not have a sizeable ego as well. In 1934, after making a trip to Japan to play against some Japanese college teams and All-Stars, the Ruths decided to return to the United States via Europe because he had never trekked to that continent. Ruth found Paris to be a disappointment because, accustomed to being recognized and idolized by fans nearly everywhere, he complained that he wasn't noticed there, mumbling, "Nobody gave a damn."[39] It would seem that instead of seeing the sights, Ruth was more concerned about being seen.

The relationship between Ruth and Lou Gehrig had its ups and downs. Naturally, there was a sense of competition and some degree of jealousy between the two superstars. When things were going well between them, Ruth considered Gehrig to be his brother and Gehrig, in turn, looked up to Ruth. That being the case, sometimes there was a sort of figurative sibling rivalry between the two.

Gehrig first invited Ruth to a home cooked dinner which his mother, Christina, whipped up in 1926. Ruth accepted, relished her cooking—making Christina a surrogate mother to some extent—and the Ruth-Gehrig situation was fine early on. Ruth even showed his appreciation for the meals by buying Christina a chihuahua that she named "Jidge" after Ruth. He also bought her a parrot, then promptly taught it to swear. He once wrote that by around 1928 he often visited Gehrig's house and "Mom Gehrig would try to cook enough pig's knuckles for all of us." He called those times "one of the rare tastes of home life I had ever had."[40]

Gehrig's mother would also prepare a quart of pickled eels for Ruth, bringing them to Yankee double-headers. Between contests Ruth would consume the eels along with a quart of chocolate ice cream mixed in, and he was said to have loved it. A former teammate once quipped, "If you sawed the Babe in two, half the concessions of Yankee Stadium would roll out."

Dorothy, Ruth's daughter, also took to Mom Gehrig, seeing her as a source of the "motherly attention" she craved, much like what her own father may have been seeking somewhat with Christina and perhaps to some extent later with his second wife Claire.[41] At first Gehrig didn't resent the attention the Babe received. Gehrig commented that when he followed Ruth to the plate, the crowd, still agape from Ruth's performance, be it a dramatic homer or even a strikeout with a typical Ruthian flair, "wouldn't notice if I walked up to home plate on my hands, stood on my head, and held the bat between my toes."[42] Frank Ardolino wrote, "The friction between Ruth and Gehrig in their baseball careers developed primarily from their different personalities, their divergent public images, and from the influence of other people on their relationship." He felt the feud seemed both "inevitable and regrettable."[43]

Despite their shared German ancestry, their contrasts were sharp and numerous. Ruth, the extrovert, "indulged all of his appetites, earned fines, and caused physical collapse, Gehrig was the 'Iron Man,' a monument to clean living and steadiness" and averaged about ten hours sleep nightly. He was, as Joe McCarthy stated, a "perfect gentleman."[44] Gehrig spent much of his life as a shy child and was often basically a loner. Unlike the generous Ruth, Gehrig was quite frugal. As Claire Ruth wrote, her husband's tips were exorbitant, Gehrig's ten-cent tips "were just as silly."[45]

Lieb said of the Ruth-Gehrig falling out. "It really started between their wives." He continued, "Eleanor, Gehrig's wife, and Claire, Ruth's wife, had some misunderstanding or something. And then, of course, the feud spread to the husbands. I guess they didn't speak for a half-dozen years or so—until that last great performance they put on for Gehrig [the day of his 'luckiest man' speech]."[46]

A more specific version of the origin of the split has the domineering Mom Gehrig finding fault with Ruth's second wife, Claire. One time she commented that Claire was dressing Ruth's adopted daughter Dorothy like a tomboy but outfitted her natural daughter, Julia, "in the finest attire." Another time, Gehrig's mother was said to have told a wife of a Yankee player that Claire favored her own daughter over Dorothy. When this got back to Babe, he supposedly "told Lou to tell his mother to 'mind her own [expletive] business!' " Their friendship effectively died then and there.[47] "You couldn't say a word to Lou about his mother," recalled Julia. "Well, that's all right, I guess, for a son to defend his mother, but Daddy [in confronting Gehrig] just wanted to let Lou know his mother was sticking her nose in somebody else's business and it didn't belong there. And Lou was greatly offended by it, so that was the whole thing."[48]

It could be argued that when Ruth picked Hal Chase over Gehrig on his all-time team shortly before Ruth passed away, it indicated a need to downplay the importance of Gehrig. Ruth justified his selection of Chase due to his ability as a clutch hitter and for his slick fielding, but Gehrig's value on offense alone made it ludicrous to choose Chase. Gehrig hit .340 lifetime, with 493 homers, and 1,990 RBIs as contrasted to Chase's .291, 57 homers, and 941 runs driven in. It is probable that of all the "greatest" lists ever compiled, Ruth's is the only one with Chase at first base. Of course, in 1937, Gehrig picked Honus Wagner as the greatest player he had ever seen, calling him, in what may well have been a not-so-subtle dig at Ruth, "a marvelous player who went along doing a grand job without any thought of himself."[49]

Meanwhile, Tosetti stated that Dorothy did feel alienated living with Claire, "My mom was kinda' left out of a lot of stuff and she said, 'I spent a lot of time in my bedroom. I could tell you there was 300 and some odd flowers on my wallpaper.' " Tosetti conceded her mother, like Babe, could "be a real rebel. She'd get in trouble all the time."[50]

Aside from the Gehrig feud and a few dark periods, the Babe went through life eternally young. Perhaps that quality accounts for his informality, even when being introduced to people of regal status. One sweltering day he is said to have greeted President Calvin Coolidge with a grin and a booming, "Hot as hell, ain't it, Prez?" When introduced to the Queen of the Netherlands, his opening salutation was an ingenuous, "Hiya', Queenie."[51]

Ruth's attitude towards most things in life was quite casual. It's well documented that he rarely took the time to learn people's names. Instead, he'd call his contemporaries "keed" (as in "hiya, kid") and "Doc" or "Pop" was his greeting for older men, while "Mom" is what he used to address older women. John

Drebinger, a sportswriter for the *New York Times,* who was close to Ruth, proudly told fellow scribes, "I was the only writer the Babe ever called by his first name. He called me Joe."[52]

Like Jackie Gleason's larger-than-life character Ralph Kramden of "The Honeymooners," when Ruth obtained wealth, his generosity was unbound. One can hear Ruth in the words of Kramden, "It [money] came easy, and it went just as fast.... If anybody found out I had it, they could have it."[53] And, in the case of Ruth, everybody, even strangers knew he had it. He was, in short, an easy touch, and he didn't seem to mind at all.

Tosetti related what "Double Duty" Radcliffe, a Negro Leagues veteran, told her, "People used him. A lot of people took advantage of him; he knew what they were doing and he helped them anyway." So, they "thought he was a buffoon because they thought they were putting something over on him, but they weren't."[54] A typical gratuity for any minor service rendered was $10 while a special favor was rewarded with a munificent $100 tip.

For those nearer to him, Ruth would be lavish. He never forgot Brother Matthias from St. Mary's, once giving him a motorcycle and another time a Cadillac. When that car stalled on a train track and was struck by a freight train, Ruth nonchalantly bought him another one. Brother Gilbert singled out Ruth's kindness when he wrote, "Forgiving by nature, George Ruth was an emotional kid, with a deep and abiding sense of gratitude."[55]

Julia called her father "generous to a fault. Ballplayers who were down on their luck and out of baseball asked him for a loan." She called Babe "warm hearted" and "always there when you needed him. He'd do the best he could to help you in any kind of a situation and that did not just go for his family, that went for friends as well." Only later did Claire "little by little, in a very nice way manage to put a curb on his loaning $1,000 to this guy or $2,500 to another one, which, of course, he never got back—it was a gift, not a loan."[56]

> I think [said Ruth's daughter Julia] one of the reasons he was so generous was because he had had so little. Growing up at St. Mary's was a rough proposition. Once he got his hands on some money, he couldn't wait to spend it and on all these things that he'd never had or even seen before.
>
> "He would have given me anything in the world that I asked for, but Mother wouldn't let him. She said, 'She doesn't need it.' 'But I want it.' It didn't make any difference, she was determined that I not be spoiled.
>
> "I know that some of the celebrities' kids resent their father being monopolized; I never did. I just thought it was wonderful: they can like him, but he's my dad and *I* live with him and see him everyday.[57]

Ruth had a sense of acceptance, too. Radcliffe told Tosetti, "Me and your granddaddy, we were good friends. He was all for the Negro Leagues and the owners used to try to shut him up. He'd come to my games whenever he could." Tosetti added, "Babe was definitely not prejudiced. My mother said he kinda' liked everybody."[58]

By the time Ruth was around 18, he stood at 6 feet 2 inches, weighed in at 198 pounds, and was as muscular as he was popular at St. Mary's. For the record, Ruth's size placed him "a good four inches taller and 25 pounds heavier than the average major leaguer of that era."[59]

The younger children of St. Mary's looked up to Ruth then and young children everywhere continued this admiration. Years later, Ruth was known to sign autographs with Job-like patience because he knew that the bigger kids would shove the smaller ones to the rear of clusters of autograph seekers. So, by sticking around endlessly, he guaranteed even his tiny fans would get a souvenir. Tosetti said, "That is very true because at St. Mary's he used to take care of the little kids because the big kids would bully them and he would buy them all kinds of candy."[60]

Dorothy wrote that Babe's friends "weren't the affluent and influential; they were cabdrivers, paperboys, doormen, and small businessmen" and added that he was different than most of the celebrities because he was so approachable. That, she contended, made him "the hero of the common man."[61] Julia said, "I can remember when we used to leave Yankee Stadium and we'd get to Lennox Avenue and, I think, 145th Street. There was a cop there; as soon as he saw Daddy's car he'd stop all the traffic and say, 'Come along, Babe.' And Daddy would say, 'Hiya, keed, nice to see you,' and go on by."[62]

Browns infielder Jimmy Austin called Ruth friendly, generous, and always ready with a "wise-crack." He said Ruth "always had a twinkle in his eye, and when he'd hit a homer against us he'd never trot past third without giving me a wink." Austin added, "The big fellow wasn't perfect. Everybody knows that. But that guy had a heart. He really did. A heart as big as a watermelon, and made out of pure gold."[63]

Julia stated that as great as her father was, Babe wasn't pompous. "He wasn't smug or self-satisfied. He was quite aware that he was the greatest, but he never made a great show of it. He was always so gracious when people complimented him on what he had done. He'd say, 'Well, I was just lucky the Lord was good to me.' And I liked that."[64]

Ruth was also renowned for his innocent impetuosity, which led him into trouble at times. He once wrote that he met his first wife, Helen Woodford, on the first day he spent in Boston, seeing her working breakfast tables at Landers' Coffee Shop. "She used to wait on me in the mornings, and one day I said to her, 'How about you and me getting married, hon?' " Perhaps Helen was equally impulsive, as she "thought it over for a few minutes and said yes."[65] Legally, the marriage lasted fifteen years, but in truth, the newlyweds enjoyed happiness for only the first couple of their years together.

All-in-all, though, as Gilbert wrote, "Ruth's life was without guile." He further contended that when it came to the Bambino, "There was no pretense about him."[66] None—even among members of high society, this man from humble beginnings grew comfortable yet with no affectation. As grandson Tom Stevens commented, "Socially, he had to learn social graces—he was on a perpetual learning curve. This man came from nothing and made the acquaintance of kings and queens, and presidents. This guy was the embodiment of the American dream."[67]

Standout baseball historian Lawrence S. Ritter wrote that the young Ruth had "no self-discipline and not much education." In other words, he was just like many other young players back then. What separated Ruth, wrote Ritter, was his ability to deposit baseball great distances from home plate and his propensity for downing as many as six hot dogs and six soda pops in a sitting. After stuffing the dogs in, he'd "give a few belches, and before you knew it be ready for more."[68]

The same was true of his lust for life. It was not at all unusual for him to carouse all night, only to return to his hotel at dawn. He'd play a day game—there were no night games back then—go out and "party," and come back the next day ready to do it again. He was a living bacchanalian version of the movie *Groundhog Day*. Columnist Bob Considine wrote that the Babe "thought every night was New Year's Eve,"[69] and sportswriter Jimmy Cannon called Ruth "a parade all by himself."[70]

When Ruth's first roommate with the Yankees, Ping Bodie, an outfielder with them from 1918 to 1923, was asked what Ruth was like, Bodie countered he didn't know. "Why not," demanded the reporter? "I thought you roomed with him." Bodie replied, "I don't room with Babe. I room with his suitcase."[71]

Ruth had charisma long before the word became fashionable. However, not everyone loved the Babe. Ritter wrote that there were those who didn't care for him, "especially in his early years with the Boston Red Sox. Teammates Tris Speaker and Smoky Joe Wood thought he was a self-centered slob...." Some veterans even sawed Ruth's bats in half once.

Ruth could be "a thoughtless roughneck," but was also a kind man who was well aware of his obligations to his team and to the public that idolized him. He also matured somewhat as he grew older, gaining some degree of self-discipline as he mellowed.[72]

Interestingly, despite some carping, almost all retrospective looks at Ruth were favorable. Former major leaguer Buddy Hassett was quoted as saying Ruth was "just a fine human being. Naturally, he didn't have the greatest education in the world, but I thought he handled himself very well, as far as the public went. . . ." Hassett felt Ruth "didn't try to put on airs," and insightfully added, "He was just the Babe all his life." Truly, a marvelous summation.[73]

NOTES

1. Ruth and Considine, *The Babe Ruth Story*, 2.

2. Ken Burns, *Ken Burns Baseball* (Alexandria, VA: PBS Home Video, 2000).

3. Gilbert, *Young Babe Ruth*, 4.

4. Ruth, *Babe Ruth's Own Book of Baseball*, 5.

5. Ruth and Considine, *The Babe Ruth Story*, 31.

6. Bill Werber and C. Paul Rogers III, *Memories of a Ballplayer: Bill Werber and Baseball in the 1930s* (Cleveland: SABR, 2001), 11.

7. Linda Ruth Tosetti, from telephone interview with author, September 23, 2005.

8. Greg Schwalenberg, from interview with author, September 7, 2005.

9. Ernestine Gichner Miller, *The Babe Book: Baseball's Greatest Legend Remembered* (Kansas City: Andrew McNeel Publishing, 2000), 150.

10. Linda Ruth Tosetti, from telephone interview with author, September 23, 2005.

11. Ibid.

12. Dorothy Ruth Pirone and Chris Martens, *My Dad, the Babe: Growing Up with an American Hero* (Boston: Quinlan Press, 1988), 94.

13. Ruth, with Slocum, *The Babe and I*, 14.

14. Babe Ruth Museum display.

15. Pirone and Martens, *My Dad, the Babe*, 207.

16. Ibid.

17. Ruth, with Slocum, *The Babe and I*, 48, 59.

18. Pirone and Martens, *My Dad, the Babe*, 7.

19. Linda Ruth Tosetti, from telephone interview with author, September 23, 2005.

20. Widely quoted.

21. Linda Ruth Tosetti, from telephone interview with author, September 23, 2005.

22. Ibid.

23. Julia Ruth Stevens, from interviews with author, November 2005.

24. Gilbert, *Young Babe Ruth*, 91.

25. Creamer, *Babe*, 316.

26. Widely quoted.

27. Pirone and Martens, *My Dad, the Babe*, 1–2.

28. Linda Ruth Tosetti, from telephone interview with author, September 23, 2005.

29. Gerald Perry, interview with author, March 4, 2005.

30. Widely quoted.

31. Julia Ruth Stevens, from interviews with author, November 2005.

32. Robert Smith, *Babe Ruth's America* (New York: Thomas Y. Crowell Co., 1974), 10.

33. Ruth and Considine, *The Babe Ruth Story*, 67.

34. Ernie Harwell, *The Babe Signed My Shoe: Baseball as It Was—And Always Will Be* (South Bend, IN: Diamond Communications, Inc., 1994), 121.

35. Jonathan Eig, *Luckiest Man: The Life and Death of Lou Gehrig* (New York: Simon and Schuster, 2005), 101.

36. Smith, *Babe Ruth's America*, 13.

37. Linda Ruth Tosetti, from telephone interview with author, September 23, 2005.

38. From www.baseballLibrary.com.

39. Ruth and Considine, *The Babe Ruth Story*, 204.

40. Ibid., 166–167.

41. Pirone and Martens, *My Dad, the Babe*, 107.

42. Widely quoted.

43. Frank Ardolino, "Lou vs. Babe in Life and in *Pride of the Yankees*." *The Baseball Research Journal*, May 2003, 16.

44. Ardolino, "Lou vs. Babe in Life and in *Pride of the Yankees*," 16.

45. Ruth, with Slocum, *The Babe and I*, 156.

46. Harwell, *The Babe Signed My Shoe*, 122.

47. Ardolino, "Lou vs. Babe in Life and in *Pride of the Yankees*," 16.

48. Julia Ruth Stevens, from interviews with author, November 2005.

49. Eig, *Luckiest Man*, 223.

50. Linda Ruth Tosetti, from telephone interview with author, September 23, 2005.

51. Widely quoted.

52. Leonard Koppett, *The Rise and Fall of the Press Box* (Toronto: Sports Media Publishing, 2003), 48.

53. "Funny Money," *The Honeymooners* DVD, CBS Broadcasting, Inc., 2003.

54. Linda Ruth Tosetti, from telephone interview with author, September 23, 2005.

55. Gilbert, *Young Babe Ruth*, 71.

56. Julia Ruth Stevens, from interviews with author, November 2005.

57. Ibid.

58. Linda Ruth Tosetti, from telephone interview with author, September 23, 2005.

59. Ritter, *The Babe*, 34.

60. Linda Ruth Tosetti, from telephone interview with author, September 23, 2005.

61. Pirone and Martens, *My Dad, the Babe*, 68.

62. Julia Ruth Stevens, from interviews with author, November 2005.

63. Lawrence S. Ritter, *The Glory of Their Times: The Story of the Early Days of Baseball Told by the Men Who Played It* (New York: Macmillan Publishing Co. Inc., 1966), 82.

64. Julia Ruth Stevens, from interviews with author, November 2005.

65. Ruth and Considine, *The Babe Ruth Story*, 34–35.

66. Gilbert, *Young Babe Ruth*, 737, 188.

67. Tom Stevens, interview with author, November 5, 2005.

68. Ruth and Considine, *The Babe Ruth Story*, x.

69. Stevens, with Martens, *Major League Dad*, 101.

70. Ken Burns, *Baseball: A Film by Ken Burns* (Washington, DC: WETA-TV, Florentine Films, 1994).

71. Widely quoted.

72. Ritter, *The Babe*, 4–5.

73. Brent Kelley, *In the Shadow of the Babe: Interviews with Baseball Players who Played With or Against Babe Ruth* (Jefferson, NC: McFarland and Company, 1995), 180–181.

Ruth pitching for the Boston Red Sox. *National Baseball Hall of Fame Library, Cooperstown, N.Y.*

George Ruth becomes "The Babe," 1914–1919

Ruth set out into the world in March 1914. His first stop was Fayetteville, North Carolina, where his Baltimore Orioles trained. He was armed with just his talent and five dollars in his pocket; not much, but it represented more cash than he had ever had before.

Ruth was not unlike a hick at first, fascinated, for instance, by machinery. He was highly impressed when he boarded a train for the first time, en route to his training grounds. He once paid an elevator operator to allow him to man the controls and was nearly decapitated when he proved less than dextrous at the switch. He would trek to the train depot just to gawk when the mighty engines, symbols of sheer power, arrived and departed.

Young Babe was equally naive on his first trip when a veteran pulled a traditional prank on him. In that era, next to each Pullman upper berth was a sort of small hammock, stretching from one end of the sleeping berth to the other, for players to put their clothes. Catcher Ben Egan instructed Ruth to place his pitching arm in the hammock to rest it. He kept his arm in this awkward position to "act like a pro." In reality, his gullible ways resulted in a stiff arm the next morning.[1] Incidentally, Egan actually took good care of his "ward," and later praised Ruth: "It would be pleasant to say that I developed Ruth as a pitcher, but that would be hogwash. Ruth knew how to pitch the first day I saw him."[2]

Ruth's arsenal of pitches included a good fastball, which he could mix in with his change-up, and a curve, which he threw, unlike many pitchers of the day, with his thumb doubled under the ball, tucked near his ring and pinkie fingers (with his other two fingers placed on top of the ball on the seams). He was further aided by sharp control.[3]

When the nouveau-riche Ruth got his first paycheck, he truly acted like a babe as he trotted out and purchased, of all things, a bicycle, his first possession. Once, while riding the bike on the wrong side of the street, he waved to his minor league teammates. Paying attention to them and not to the road, he had to swerve at the last second to avoid a collision with a truck barreling down on him. One version of this story has team coach Scout Steinmann commenting that if Dunn's babe, referring to Orioles owner Jack Dunn, wasn't under a tighter leash he would "not be a Rube Waddell in the rough, he'll be a Babe Ruth in the cemetery." A writer overheard the comment and supposedly used the "Babe" nickname for the first time the next day, March 19, 1914, in the *Baltimore American*.[4] According to Mike Gibbons of the Ruth Museum, the idea of Ruth being Dunn's babe "all stems from the guardian issue—[Ruth was] Dunn's 'baby' to 'Babe.' "[5]

The exact origin of Ruth's nickname remains cloudy. For example, in one of his autobiographies, Ruth wrote that Steinmann observed, "Well, here's Jack's newest Babe now" the first day Ruth showed up at the clubhouse.[6] However, in another autobiography, Ruth told several slightly varying versions of his nickname's derivation. First, in that time period, generic, derisive nicknames such as "Rube" (e.g., pitchers Rube Foster, an Oklahoman, and Rube Waddell from a small town in Pennsylvania) and "Babe" (e.g., Tipton, Indiana's Babe Adams, already in his sixth year in the majors) were not uncommon for raw rookies. The moniker was often bestowed on innocent young players.

In addition, Dunn was proficient at discovering young talent, or "baby-faced kids." At any rate, Ruth wrote that the day he arrived, escorted by Dunn, onto the playing field with his new teammates, one older player yelled out, "Look at Dunnie and his new babe." Ruth also claims a veteran once took pity on him, saying, "You're just a babe in the woods." According to this rendition, "After that they called me Babe."[7] So, by about the end of the second week of spring training, George Ruth was "Babe." Gibbons said researchers at the Ruth Museum discovered "the first reference in print of 'Babe Ruth' and it occurs in mid-May of 1914."[8]

Furthermore, he soon showed everyone what this babe could do. After several days of rain and soggy grounds, forcing indoor workouts at an armory, scrimmages began. Interestingly, the media, which would later cover Ruth with paparazzi intensity, barely mentioned him in the spring of 1914. One Baltimore newspaper casually called attention to a pitcher in training camp by the name of "Frank" Ruth.

That quickly changed when, in his second pro at-bat during an intra squad contest on March 7, he launched a ball that catapulted over the right-field fence before it plopped into a cornfield. Ruth gave birth to a home run in his very first pro game, albeit a practice contest. This time the *Baltimore Sun* led their account of the game with the exploits of Ruth: "George Ruth, a pitcher Jack Dunn picked off the lots of Baltimore, is credited by Fayetteville fans with making the longest hit ever seen in their park." The article went on to say the former deepest drive there came off the bat of Jim Thorpe, and the box score of the game revealed Ruth played shortstop for his "Buzzards" squad, which topped the "Sparrows" by a 15-9 margin.

Because this took place in the dead-ball era, a period when the major league's home-run leaders typically managed 10–20 homers and fences were normally shy of 300 feet, this was a noteworthy shot. Years later, residents of Fayetteville placed a plaque on the spot where Ruth's monstrous homer was said to have landed, approximately 428 feet from home plate. Such homers led Dorothy to later comment that Babe's blows flew so high and deep, some "were literally hit clean out of sight." She said that as a result, the foul lines, which ended on the field level, had to be extended up to ballpark's roofs.[9]

On March 18, Ruth pitched in an exhibition game versus the Phillies, his first contest against a big league team. Displaying the confidence that he would exude throughout his career, he worked $2\frac{2}{3}$ innings out of the bullpen, blanking the Phils and earning a win. He whiffed in his only at-bat. Soon after, on March 25, just three weeks after he departed St. Mary's, Ruth scattered 13 hits to defeat the defending world champion Philadelphia Athletics, 6-2.

Brother Gilbert, taken with Ruth's ability to ignore the reputation of the opposing, established hitters, commented that Babe's coolness was refreshing. He was "no more concerned than the horse on the weather vane. . . ." Gilbert added that Ruth could not be intimidated, partially because he had never before heard of the big leaguers he was facing (and retiring). "[T]hey were nothing more or less than a team of North Carolina Sand-lotters draped in fancy equipment."[10]

Baltimore had been a major-league city once, but in 1903 their franchise moved to New York where they were dubbed the Highlanders, later to become the Yankees. Meanwhile, the citizens of Baltimore had to be content to be relegated to minor-league status when they were given a team in the Eastern League. Dunn managed that Orioles squad in 1907, and two years later he also took on ownership of the club.

A new league was formed in 1914, known as the Federal League; it claimed to be the third major league in organized baseball and one of 50 professional leagues then operating. Baltimore fans bought into the "big league" claim and shunned the Orioles in favor of the new league's Baltimore Terrapins franchise. Accordingly, the Orioles at times played for as few as fifteen spectators. The Terrapins played their contests in a new park right across the way from Orioles

Park. Thus, thousands of fans streamed by the minor league park and poured into the Terrapins' park.[11]

On April 22, in his official pro debut, Ruth started the second game of the regular season, and, in front of a sparse crowd, twirled a shutout over Buffalo and added two singles. Significantly, the second man he faced that day was Joe McCarthy who later would play a huge part in the Ruth saga. The next day, as a pinch hitter, Ruth banged out a triple—the hitting handwriting was on the wall already. By early May, Dunn, fearing Ruth might be tempted to jump to the Federal League, while also rewarding Ruth's fine work, upped his salary to $1,200 and would boost it to $1,800 the next month.

Around the middle of the 1914 season, Dunn, hemorrhaging money and unable to meet his second payroll obligation to his players, had to borrow cash. Despite Ruth's headline-grabbing exploits, the Orioles still weren't, as the old baseball cliché goes, drawing flies. Already in debt to Athletics owner Connie Mack, Dunn was too embarrassed to approach him for more money. Instead, he turned to Joe Lannin, the Red Sox owner, with a plea for a loan that was quickly granted.

The pecuniary problems continued for Dunn, and it reached a point where he had to jettison some of his talent. He gave Mack the first crack at buying Ruth's contract, but Mack's team, like Dunn's, was bleeding money. Dunn then felt Lannin deserved the next chance and, on July 8, dumped Egan along with pitchers Ernie Shore and Ruth to the Red Sox. Years later, Ruth wrote that his price was reported to him as $2,900 while Egan went for $3,500 and Shore, who would later author a perfect game, was peddled for $2,100. However, other sources show the total money exchanged for the three players to be between $25,000 and $30,000.[12] Dunn's Orioles stood 47-22 when Ruth, with a 14-6 slate, was sold off.

When Ruth first came up to the Red Sox, a teammate, outfielder Harry Hooper, noted that the Babe "had a slim waist, huge biceps, no self-discipline, and not much education—not so very different from a lot of other nineteen-year-old would-be players. Except for two things: he could eat more than anyone else, and he could hit a baseball further."[13]

The crude youngster, already a skirt chaser, was, wrote Robert Smith, "not really fit company for proper Boston boys," but most teammates took to him right away and found him to be good natured and a lot of fun, although his Red Sox teammates didn't use Babe for a nickname. There he became "Jidge," a Bostonian version of George.[14]

On July 11, 1914, Ruth made his debut with the Red Sox with his initial plate appearance, versus veteran southpaw Willie Mitchell; it resulted in the first of 1,330 strikeouts. Ruth went on to capture a 4-3 decision over Cleveland.

Doing so, he won the first major league game he ever saw, earning the win when, with the score knotted at 3-3 in the seventh inning, Duffy Lewis became the first man to pinch hit for Ruth, lacing a single to drive home the winning tally. Trivia lovers memorized the fact that the first batter to face Ruth was Jack Graney, who was also, in 1916 as part of a short-lived experiment, the first man ever to bat while wearing a numeral on his jersey. A commonly held belief is that only one man ever batted for Ruth. In reality, during the days he plied his trade as a pitcher at least three other men hit for Babe: Forrest Cady and Delos Gainor in 1915 and Olaf Henriksen in 1916.[15]

Five days later, Ruth absorbed his first big league loss, lasting less than four innings against Detroit. Ruth didn't work many innings; by August 17, his manager, Bill Carrigan, used him in a meaningless exhibition game in Manchester, New Hampshire, versus a local team. The Sox brass then decided to send him back to the minors, this time to the Providence Grays of the International League. There he went 8-3 to finish with an overall mark of 23-8 in that league.[16]

One version has Ruth being demoted to the Sox farm team in Providence on August 20 for him to get some seasoning; Brother Gilbert said that for seven weeks with Boston, Ruth sat the bench "gathering rust," benefiting neither the team nor himself. Another version states he was in the minors to help the Grays win the International League pennant. Either way, Ruth hooked up with Grays manager "Wild Bill" Donovan, a former big-league pitcher who imparted myriad insights to him.[17]

It was as a Gray that Ruth belted his only minor league home run. On September 5, 1914, Ruth engineered a one-hitter, supplying firepower with a three-run shot off Maple Leafs pitcher Ellis Johnson in Toronto's Hanlan Park. Baseball historian William Young said the ball "went into Toronto harbor, and as far as anybody knows is still there."[18] Additionally, in an exhibition contest versus the Cubs, Ruth pitched and won, belting a homer into Narragansett Bay, and, when he hit versus a lefty Chicago pitcher, batted righty and grounded out.[19] Ruth's mound work and explosive hitting helped Providence capture the pennant, coincidentally over Baltimore. The Red Sox then retrieved Ruth from his Providence exile in late September.

It may have been a meaningless, sloppy—the Yankees committed five errors—season-winding-down game in Boston back on October 2, 1914, but history was made when Ruth rapped out his first hit. It came in the seventh inning when Leonard "King" Cole, a former 20-game winner who was in his final season, fed a fastball to an always-hungry Ruth, who stroked it to the right-field corner for a double. The *New York Times* described Ruth as "Boston's rangy left-hander, who recently helped the Providence Grays to the International League championship."[20]

On October 17, during the off-season, Ruth took Helen Woodford as his bride. The courtship lasted less than four months and was followed by an elopement, with the wedding held in St. Paul's Catholic Church in Ellicott City, Maryland. Sources list Helen as being between 15 and 18 years of age at the time. Ruth and Helen spent that winter in an apartment above his father's saloon. Babe and his father are said to have patched up their relationship a bit over that period of time. Yet the next time he saw his father after the winter of 1914 was after the 1915 World Series.

Helen's state of happiness didn't last long. She was said to have been plagued by "loneliness, Babe's affairs, alcohol, pills, unwanted publicity, depression, 'nervous breakdowns,' frequent hospitalizations and physical ailments complicated by all of Ruth's jubilant pleasures."[21] Dorothy wrote that her mother was crushed by rumors of Babe's infidelities and that he would simply ignore her when she'd confront him. That indifference, according to Dorothy, is what hurt Helen the most and was a critical factor in her frequent breakdowns.[22]

Helen remained content to stay at home on their eighty-acre "Home Plate Farm" near Sudbury, Massachusetts, not far from Boston. Babe purchased the farm in 1916, viewing it as a retreat. Unlike his wife, Babe soon grew restless at home. Theirs was a marriage that was doomed from the start and was, for all intents and purposes, over by around the middle of 1925. If this had been a modern marriage, a divorce would have been inevitable, but due to religious convictions, neither Helen nor her wayward husband made a move in that legal direction.

On the playing field, though, Ruth continued to prosper. His theory on pitching encompassed the basics, with nothing fancy thrown in. He felt the keys to his craft were his fine control, mixing pitches up and changing speeds, a combination that has succeeded from the dawn of the game. Ruth's fastball probably was in the neighborhood of 90 miles per hour and he was therefore discussed "in the same breath with Walter Johnson," who was regarded as the fastest hurler around.[23]

Ruth's curve was said to have been outstanding, and he said that while it was true his fastball had "little hop," he did own "a natural sailer." He believed the ball moved away from right-handed hitters because he held the ball quite "loosely" even on his fastballs. He contrasted his grip to the tight one most fastball pitchers of the day seemed to favor. He said the movement on his ball once caused Ty Cobb to accuse him of doctoring the ball after being whiffed on six pitches from Babe.[24] Incidentally, Ruth felt that while he may not have "owned" Cobb, he did believe men such as "Shoeless" Joe Jackson gave him far more difficulty than the "Georgia Peach."[25]

According to one of Ruth's autobiographies, part of his success stemmed from his study of the game. However, it is also interesting to note the contrast between what passed for scouting in his time period versus the sophisticated computerized printouts and reports today's players scrutinize. For example, Ruth once wrote that his contemporaries would pore through box scores from out-of-town newspapers to discover what players from upcoming opponents had been doing. If a batter took an 0 for 3 against a "slow ball pitcher," one of Ruth's teammates might report that hitter "is having a tough time with slow balls these days," and they would pitch him accordingly.[26] (This type of thinking is nearly as archaic as the intercom system in *The Flintstones*. Who knows, the batter in question might have shattered three "slow balls" for wicked line drives, only to be robbed of hits. If so, he might be salivating for more slow offerings and pitching him that way could be folly.)

At the start of the 1915 season, Ruth was working on the Boston contract he had signed for 1914, which ran through the 1916 season and paid him $3,500 yearly. There was, of course, no way for him to imagine the money his skills would later bring him.

It didn't take Ruth long to make his first splash of 1915. On May 6, in a game Ruth pitched, he ripped his first big league homer, one of 3 hits that day and one of 15 homers he collected as a pitcher (counting a pinch-hit blow). It came at the Polo Grounds against his future team, the Yankees, off pitcher Jack Warhop. Like Cole who served up Ruth's first big-league safety, Warhop was in his final year in the majors. However, with the help of four Boston errors, the Yanks defeated Ruth in a heartbreaking 13-inning, 4-3 decision. Still, the *Boston Post* lauded Ruth, describing the homer he pulled to right field as traveling "so far into the stands that the ushers never made any attempt to recover it."[27] An estimated 5,000–8,000 fans witnessed history that day, yet were oblivious to the importance of the home run.

It took nearly a month for him to notch his second big league clout. It occurred on June 2, once more against the Yankees and Warhop at the Polo Grounds, in the final game of an exhausting twenty-nine-day road trip. Ruth surrendered five hits and earned the win. The Baseball Library Web site reported that, "After his second inning drive, the Babe is given two intentional walks. Ruth ends up kicking the bench and breaking his toe, sidelining him for two weeks."[28]

On August 14, a classic match-up took place although the fans then had no way of knowing what they had witnessed was the first of eight battles from 1915 to 1918 between Ruth and Johnson as mound rivals. Ruth won the duel by a 4-3 margin, the first of his six head-to-head wins—three of them were to be 1-0 classics—versus "The Big Train." Ruth even came up with two hits against the fire-balling Johnson.

Ruth's final home-run total in 1915 may have been just 4 puny homers, but he wasn't that far off the league leader who hit only 7. The Sox entered the 1915

World Series boasting of five pitchers with 15-plus wins: Rube Foster and Shore led the way with 19 and Ruth followed with 18, while Smoky Joe Wood and Dutch Leonard chipped in with 15 apiece. Ruth had the fourth best won-loss percentage and the second fewest hits per innings in the league. Despite his stats and his hunger for a chance to play in the Series, Ruth's only appearance came as a pinch hitter for Shore in Game 1; he harmlessly grounded out. The Sox used only three pitchers in dispatching Philadelphia in five games.

Ruth's salary was so low that his Series split of the winners' pool, $3,780, was more than his pay for the entire season; it was his first scrumptious taste of postseason lucre and he loved it.[29] Having earned over $7,000 for the year, Ruth felt flush. This was a time when one could buy a satisfying lunch in a hotel for 35 cents, rent a decent apartment for about $25 per month, or purchase a spanking new automobile for around $800.[30]

Ruth and Helen spent the off-season in Baltimore in their three-story row house on South Eutaw Street, which also housed a bar for his father. He purchased the bar for Big George even though, as Julia stated, "his father had practically abandoned him. He never felt any ill-feeling towards him."[31] A few times Babe helped tend bar with his father and there exists a picture of Babe behind the bar, helping him during the Christmas season. The resemblance between the two is uncanny, leading Tosetti, to say, "Talk about spitting out a mini-me, huh?"[32]

Given Ruth's ways with exotic women, it seems fitting that a strip club, called The Goddess, now sits on the site of what was Ruth's Café, just a handful of Baltimore chops from Camden Yards. Inside The Goddess, the picture of the Ruths tending bar is proudly displayed. There was some talk of changing the club's name to "Babe's," but, Tosetti observed, "That doesn't sound like something that would be kosher, not exactly something we'd want to foster. I wouldn't like to see 'Babe' on [a strip club], though Babe probably wouldn't care, he would've been in a front row seat."[33]

During the 1916 season, an oddity took place on July 11 when Boston swept the Chicago White Sox with Ruth starting both ends of their double-header. He retired the first hitter then left the first game after just one-third of an inning of work, but he came back to go the distance in the second game of the twin bill. According to the Baseball Library, the reason Ruth departed the first game so quickly was he had merely taken to the hill to give the Red Sox' real starter, Foster, additional time to warm up.

On August 15, Ruth knocked off Washington ace Walter Johnson in a 1-0 masterpiece that ran 13 strenuous innings. After the sixth inning, Ruth gave up one infield hit and nothing more. He enjoyed uncommon success against "The Big Train," winning four confrontations with Johnson in 1916 alone. As the dog days of the season wound down, Ruth won his 20th game of the year, topping Red Farber. A crowd of 40,000, reportedly the largest one ever in Chicago, witnessed Ruth's milestone victory.

The season came to an end on the next to last day of September when Ruth chalked up his 23rd win on his ninth shutout—the most shutouts in American League play by a southpaw until Yankee Ron Guidry tied him in 1978. He posted a microscopic league-leading ERA of 1.75 while logging 323⅔ innings. Additionally, he surrendered no regular-season homers (while hitting three himself), finished third in strikeouts, and also led the league in starts and hits allowed per nine innings. His miserly ways concerning serving up homers continued over his entire career. Only four men bettered Ruth's pace of giving up one homer for every 122 innings worked, about one homer every 13 games. As a batter he hit one out about every three games.[34]

The Red Sox took on the Brooklyn franchise, then nicknamed the Robins, in the 1916 Fall Classic. Boston survived a four-run, ninth inning rally to take the opening game, which ended up a 6-5 nailbiter. The sun was beaming down on a throng of 41,373 on October 9 for Game 2, which was housed not in Fenway, but in Braves Field to accommodate the crowd. However, by the time this fourteen-inning marathon contest ended, the longest ever by innings in Series play (tied in 2005), the day had grown so gloomy, play could not have continued much longer. Somehow, the game was completed in a brisk two hours and thirty-two minutes, some three hours and nine minutes shorter than the 2005 Series ordeal.

Ruth outdueled Sherry Smith to win a gut-wrenching 2-1 decision, with both men going the distance. Ruth wound up with a six-hitter, spending, according to the *Boston Traveler*, 148 pitches in the process. The single run he surrendered came on the only homer he dished up all year, a tainted inside-the-parker by Hy Myers that eluded Tilly Walker in center. Ruth felt Myers should have been held to a single, probably reasoning that the great glove Tris Speaker, who had normally handled center-field duties for the Sox from 1909 through 1915 but had moved on to Cleveland for 1916, would have prevented the home run.

Realizing he was in the midst of a battle royal, Ruth bore down and, after the eighth inning, was nearly untouchable, allowing only two Robins to reach base—one via a walk and the other on an error. His stretch of 13⅓ whitewashed innings after the homer marked the start of his record for scoreless Series innings pitched. Further, his fourteen-inning stint is another record, one that probably will never be erased. Today's pitchers labor to go six, seven, or eight innings and a complete game is as rare now as a phone booth sighting; working fourteen innings is unfathomable.

Just a few months after the conclusion of the Series, won by the Sox in five, Boston owner Joe Lannin sold the team to Harry Frazee, a New York theatrical producer. Not too long after that, Frazee, short of funds needed for unpaid notes on the Lannin debt, began a clearance sale, offering key players to the Yankees like so much second-hand goods. The only difference was that the players he unloaded were far from being damaged material. The Yankees owners since 1915, Colonel Jacob (or Jake) Ruppert—a wealthy brewery owner who, ironically, later wouldn't be too happy with Ruth's propensity for suds—and prosperous engineer Colonel T. L. "Cap" Huston, also known by his first name Tillinghast or Til for short, drooled over their additions.

On President Woodrow Wilson's request, the U.S. Congress declared war on Germany just five days before the 1917 season began. It was a period of rampant patriotism in the country. On Memorial Day 2005, 103-year-old Lloyd Brown, one of an estimated 30 surviving veterans of this war, told the Associated Press, "Everybody was patriotic; everybody wanted to join. Those who joined were local heroes, well received on the public streets."[35] Perhaps so, but Ruth was not about to enlist, yet he still remained much more than just a local hero.

The history of baseball could have been altered if Ruth had been drafted, but as a married man, he was given a deferment. While not all the country's draft boards ruled that a married man with no children would sit out the war, Ruth was able to continue his baseball career. He did join a unit of the National Guard, and pronounced that "despite his ancestry, there was not a pro-German corpuscle in his veins."[36]

As the war continued, the cost of living increased in the United States. Sugar, for instance, cost eight cents per pound, a jump of over 100 percent from what had previously been the norm in the Boston vicinity.[37]

On May 7, 1917, Ruth held the Senators to two singles, again frustrating Johnson, 1-0. The only run of the game came on a Ruth sacrifice fly. Ruth would not lose to Johnson until October 3, 1917. Cobb was known, of course, for his feral play, but Ruth could play a rough game, too. It was reported that on May 11, Cobb laid down a bunt single to open the ninth inning. When the next batter grounded out to third, Cobb, in his typical gambling, rollicking style, rounded the bag at second and steamed towards the unattended third-base bag. Ruth got there ahead of him, covering the bag and pile driving a tag so hard Cobb was said to have been laid out for several minutes before he recovered.[38]

About two weeks later, Ruth got involved in an even rougher event. Ruth said that when he faced Washington on June 23, 1917, he began fuming directly after umpire Brick Owens called the game's first pitch a ball, and became livid after Owens called four straight pitches for balls. "When he called the fourth one on me," said Ruth, who felt three pitches were strikes, "I just went crazy."[39]

It was another case of too much testosterone as Ruth stormed off the mound, squawking about the walk, which prompted Owens to set off his own salvo, issuing a warning that he'd thumb Ruth if he didn't shut up. Ruth threatened that if the umpire tossed him from the game he would punch him squarely on his jaw. Owens did indeed eject him and Ruth, in street parlance, promptly jacked his jaw. A policeman had to escort Ruth off the field before Shore came in to retire twenty-seven straight Senators, the leadoff walk erased when the man was caught stealing. Shore was credited with the fourth perfect game in the annals of the game—the only one involving a relief pitcher. Ruth related that American League President Ban Johnson fined him a mere $100 to go with an indefinite suspension that ultimately ran ten days.[40] Suspensions, which sapped playing time from Ruth, hurt, but the fine, probably not.

Things weren't as gloomy on August 31, when Ruth, who only homered twice all year, once more became a 20-game winner, topping the A's, 5-3. Overall, he went 24-13 with a nearly invisible 2.01 ERA for the second-place Red Sox.

By now, Ruth was well aware that hitters studied pitchers' tendencies to improve at the plate. He confessed, though, that earlier he had been guilty of tipping off, or "telegraphing," his curve ball. Ruth wrote that when he threw a curve, he would stick his tongue outside the corner of his mouth, a dead give away." Unlike the version reported in the hokey movie *The Babe Ruth Story*, featuring an unlikely William Bendix as the Babe, Ruth said he didn't learn of this tell-tale tongue until his pitching days were over. Other versions have Carrigan or Hooper straightening him out before his habit haunted him. Now, in the movie, it was his future wife Claire who set him straight, and did so the first time they met, an egregious error because Ruth was not a pitcher when he knew Claire.[41]

Due to the devastating influenza epidemic and the continuance of World War I, baseball drew only 3,000,000 fans in 1918. Thanks to legalized Sunday games, the radio broadcasting of some games, and Ruth's impact, that figure would soar to around 9,000,000 per season in the 1920s.[42]

Ruth's .299 batting average as a pitcher entering the 1918 season could not be ignored. In 1917, his last spent exclusively as a pitcher, he hit .325 over 123 at-bats. If he had sustained that for enough trips to the plate to qualify for the league lead, he would have wound up behind only superstars Cobb, George Sisler, and Speaker.

By 1918, Ruth frequently began playing at first base and in the outfield, specifically center. BoSox manager Ed Barrow who had once declared, "I would be the laughingstock of the league if I took the best pitcher in the league and made him an outfielder," realized he could no longer keep Ruth's bat out of the line-up. When the switch was made, Barrow, not totally convinced of the advisability of the change, cautioned, "the first time he has a slump he will be down on his knees begging to pitch."[43]

On May 4, during his fifth mound start, Ruth hoisted a ball way over the Polo Grounds roof, good for his first homer of the year. Then, on May 6, exactly three years after his first big league four-bagger, he was penciled into the line-up at a defensive spot other than pitcher—he manned first base—and in an offensive slot other than ninth; he promptly homered. Ruth wrote that from that day on he was in the starting line-up any time the other team threw a righty against Boston.[44]

The next day, he was moved into the cleanup position in the order and stung a ball for a home run in his third straight game. A few days later, after he took his turn on the hill, he played the outfield for the first time in the majors. When he went hitless, a newspaper story commented, "He didn't hit a thing, not even an umpire."[45]

In all, the Babe wound up playing 72 games in the field that year and rewarded Barrow by slugging 11 homers. This was also the first year he out-homered an entire team, as the rest of the Red Sox registered only four; Ruth also out-slugged five other teams. Barrow took credit for changing Ruth from a hurler into a regular in the outfield, thus altering the history of baseball.[46] In truth, it was Hooper who had to convince Barrow of the wisdom of moving Ruth from the mound. Barrow, the former president of the International League, was best skilled at running the front office. So he often left managerial matters, such as the monumental move of Ruth to the outfield, to his team captain, Hooper.

Ritter wrote that once Ruth grew comfortable with his new position, "Ruth's booming bat more than justified the switch. In city after city he rocketed his patented sky-high home runs spectacular distances. The ball was still as dead as a mushy cantaloupe, but you couldn't prove it by the Babe."[47] In true Ruthian fashion, he racked up homers in his first two starts as an outfielder.

Because the Babe was getting his share of time on the diamond and not on the bench when he wasn't pitching, his pinch-hit appearances fell off from highs of 10 and 19 in 1915 and 1916 to just 3 in 1918. He still worked in 20 games as a pitcher because his evolution to becoming a full-time player had not yet come to fruition.

Even around this late phase of his mound career, coinciding with his emerging slugger stage, Ruth still seems to have seen himself as a pitcher more than a power hitter. At least that is what writer Alan Schwarz unearthed from a 1918 *Baseball Magazine* article with Ruth's byline. The piece was called "Why a Pitcher Should Hit," and seldom mentioned home runs, although Ruth did write: "I believe I could qualify as a true .300 hitter." In fact, back then homers were regarded the way triples are today, "freak hits that were too rare to be fully appreciated."[48]

During a July 2 contest at Washington, Barrow reamed Ruth in the dugout for being guilty of making a "bum play," and fined him $500 on the spot. Babe bolted from the ballpark and hopped a train for Baltimore. After jumping the team, he looked into playing for a team associated with the Chester, Pennsylvania, shipyards. However, the turmoil was smoothed over and Ruth finally rejoined the Red Sox for the nightcap of an Independence Day double-header.[49]

Due to the war, the 1918 season was the shortest season ever played due to a decree by Secretary of War Newton D. Baker. The baseball season was forced to end on Labor Day as part of the standing "work or fight" order issued that spring by General Alvin T. Crowder, army Provost Marshall, in charge of manpower in the United States. The order required all men of draft age to either enter the military or to take a position in industries essential to the war effort. Then, on July 19, a ruling by Baker came down declaring that playing baseball was not an essential job. A week later, baseball was told it would have to cut around 30 games from its schedule.

This season was also one of the most chaotic years ever with many teams losing players and managers either via the draft or enlistment. It became "a season of scrambling for players and make-shift teams."[50] Thirty-one-year-old second baseman Jack Barry, who also managed the Sox in 1917, joined the Navy. Gone to the military, too, was their left fielder, Duffy Lewis, pitchers Herb Pennock and Leonard, as well as Dick Hoblitzell, their first baseman. Boston had only shortstop Everett Scott, catcher Sam Agnew, and Hooper as returning starters. Furthermore, Hooper was the only remaining member of the 1912 World Series team. It was clearly a new cast of characters that took the field in 1918.

Despite their problems, the Sox played at a won-loss percentage that neared .600, led by Ruth's team high .300 average—with more than half of his hits going for extra bases—and his .650 won-loss percentage, going 13-7 with a 2.22 ERA and 18 complete games in 19 starts. Ruth even pitched the pennant-clinching game on August 31. He also led the league for the first time in homers, tying Tilly Walker's 11 home runs. From 1900 until Ruth entered the majors, the home run derby had been won with 10 or fewer homers 18 times; Ruth would soon drastically change that. It also helped Boston's cause that the defending world champion White Sox were hit harder than the Red Sox by the draft and by having to work on draft-deferred jobs; Boston edged Cleveland for the 1918 American League pennant.

Baseball somehow endured the tribulations of the war and the World Series was granted a governmental reprieve, with the Red Sox squaring off against the Cubs in early September. To avoid unnecessary travel, a gesture that would help out with the war effort was made and the first three games were played in Chicago, the next three were scheduled for Boston, and the seventh game was to have been held in the Windy City.

The opening game of the Series was moved to Comiskey Park to house the anticipated mob of Cubs fans, but a mere 19,274 showed up despite the lowering of admission prices that year. Overall, big league attendance, due to the war, was off some 2,000,000 fans and the Sox drew less than 250,000.[51]

On September 5, 1918, Ruth was dazzling, winning Game 1. Fans who treated themselves to tickets for the most expensive seats in the house at $3.30 a pop witnessed Ruth holding their Cubbies to six hits, all singles. Hippo Vaughn dropped a tough one when he surrendered a solo tally in the fourth that held up.

Boston took two of the first three contests, then hopped a train. On their trip back to Boston, Ruth was "roughhousing" with teammate Walt Kinney. When Babe took a swing at him and missed, he struck the knuckles of his punching—that is to say, pitching—hand, on a steel wall. That resulted in his middle finger swelling badly and that, said Ruth, effected his grip on the ball the next day.

Nevertheless, he took his turn, was penciled into the *sixth* slot in the batting order where he tripled and drove home two runs, and blanked the Cubs to run his record streak to $29\frac{2}{3}$ consecutive scoreless innings in World Series play, topping Christy Mathewson's 28 straight shutout frames. The string was snapped in the eighth inning when the Cubs tied things up at 2-2.[52]

The Sox scraped for a run in the bottom of the eighth, but Ruth failed to nail the game down in the ninth. He was lifted in favor of Joe Bush after facing two hitters, but instead of departing the game, Ruth, who earned his third and final Series victory that day, plodded out to left field while Bush wrapped things up. All three of Ruth's Series victories were in pitchers' duels: 2-1, 1-0, and 3-2.

Just before the fifth game of the Series, the players from both teams threatened to go on strike. They met with baseball officials to gripe about the low players' share they would get due to meager attendance (the total receipts wound up at just under $180,000, the lowest sum since 1910) and the government-imposed freeze on the cost of Series tickets. On top of that, this was the first season that part of the players' pool of money was to be divvied up among players from every other big league team that finished in second, third, or fourth place, hence known as "finishing in the money."

When no agreement could be reached and game time rolled around, the disgruntled players refused to budge from their clubhouses. They were finally convinced to take the field—by then, an hour after the scheduled start.[53] The players, in a goodwill move, had agreed to donate a slice of their winnings for war charities, and, while they did not come off looking villainous after the aborted strike, they went home with the puniest Series shares in the history of the event. Winners pocketed $890—$1,102.51 before the charity deductions, or less than one-third of what Boston players earned in their 1915 World Series stint—while the Cubs earned only $535 each. The next year the losing share per player was over $3,200.[54]

Ultimately, the Sox won it in six games and did so by winning their four contests by a combined minuscule score of 8 to 4, capturing 1-0, 2-1, 3-2, and 2 1 decisions. By winning the World Series, the Red Sox had won it all in 1912, 1915, 1916, and 1918—four titles over a seven-year span. They would not win another championship until 2004.

It was clear that Ruth had become one of the game's best pitchers. He led the AL in ERA and shutouts in 1916, then notched his single season best of 24 victories in 1917. From 1915 to 1918, he had averaged 19½ victories per season. Ritter felt that the best two pitchers in the majors from this era were Johnson and Grover Cleveland Alexander, but Ruth, the best of all southpaws, was right there among the elite.[55]

Lifetime, Ruth managed to hit .304 as a pitcher with highs of .344 and .325. In 1915 and 1917 no pitcher hit for a higher average than Ruth. Additionally, he led or tied all pitchers in homers three times and remains the last World Series starting pitcher to be penciled into a line-up spot other than the number nine hole—in the fourth game of the 1918 Fall Classic he hit in the sixth slot.

One side note to the season, which may have had ramifications many years later, took place when Ruth came down with a sore throat, which the team trainer worked on. According to Ruth, the trainer put large amounts of silver nitrate deep into Ruth's throat, causing Ruth to strangle and suffer several spasms. He blamed the unskilled treatment of the trainer for the huskiness of his voice.

Then, on August 25, Babe's father died. Big George was living with his second wife, Martha Sipes Ruth, and her sister, whose husband, Oliver Beefelt, just out of jail on bail, entered Ruth's bar that night. The two women had a brother named Benjamin Sipes who also dropped by. When Benjamin learned of his sister's mistreatment at the hands of Beefelt, Benjamin confronted him in the bar beneath the Ruth living quarters. Big George broke the altercation up, but when Benjamin left the bar, Ruth followed and a fight ensued; George Ruth fell and smacked his head on the street resulting in a brain hemorrhage. He was rushed to a hospital where he died of a skull fracture.[56] And so, at the age of 23, Babe Ruth, mistakenly thought by many to have been an orphan from his days at St. Mary's, actually became one.

The world returned to peacetime in 1919, but Ruth blistered a ball with the force of a mortar shell. After a spring holdout—his first—Ruth eventually wound up with a three-year pact paying him $10,000 each season. Ruth started the season off scalding a ball in a spring training contest at the old Tampa, Florida, racetrack field. It "never rose more than 30 feet off the ground," but it traveled over a fence and rolled to its stop about 600 feet from the plate, 480 feet further than the distance of the Wright brothers' first flight.[57] Two baseball writers used a tape measure to determine the ball's distance, meaning this may well have been the first ever "tape-measure homer," predating Yankee P.R. man Red Patterson who is given credit for coining that phrase after chronicling the distance of a famous Mickey Mantle blow.

Not long after this, Ruth complained to Barrow that doing double duty was too tiring. He pointed out, "I'll win more games playing every day in the outfield than I will pitching every fourth day."[58] He did still pitch on occasion, going 9-5 that year, but the end of his mound days was imminent. By the end of July he was through with his regular pitching chores. Later with the Yankees, he would pitch sporadically, making only five more appearances, winning all five.

Aside from 1914, Ruth the pitcher hit as many or more home runs than he surrendered every season, and in all he gave up only 10. One of the most dramatic games to feature his arm and his bat came on May 20, 1919, when he won a 6-4 decision against St. Louis. Four of the Red Sox runs came on one swing—Ruth's first grand slam.

In 1919, a large part of St. Mary's was destroyed by a fire and Ruth, loyal to his roots, and famous enough to do something about the disaster, pitched in an exhibition game in Baltimore. The following year he continued to raise additional monies to help rebuild the school.

Back on the field, Ruth hit 29 home runs to become the new season record holder; he was helped in large part by an unprecedented spree in which he scorched 7 homers over a 12-game period. The first noteworthy record to fall was the league best for homers in a season, 16, held by Socks Seybold set in 1902. That record tumbled on August 14.

Actually, some of the old home run records were so sketchy, they weren't widely known, so Ruth first "broke" the major league standard set by Gavvy Cravath who peppered 24 with the Phillies in 1915. Then, a researcher with the skill of an archeologist, dug up an obscure pre-1900 record, Buck Freeman's 25 homers from 1899.

After Ruth surpassed that total, yet another "oldie" was discovered, that of Chicago's Ned Williamson who had 27 homers in 1884. The argument that his was a valid record, though, seemed a bit suspect because Williamson played in an era in which batters could actually dictate to the pitcher where the ball should be thrown, calling for either a high or low pitch (imagine a player today knowing basically where each upcoming delivery would be served up). Failure to place the ball where the batter wanted it resulted in a "ball" being called. Not only that, it took six balls to earn a walk and it wasn't until 1887 that the strike zone took on the shape of what Ruth and thousands of modern day players grew up with—the area between the top of the shoulder and the bottom of the knee.[59]

Finally, Williamson played in Lake Front Park, a ballpark with ludicrous dimensions: a mere 186 feet to left, 190 feet to right, and dead center that was just 300 feet away. When he set his home-run record, three other White Sox topped 20 home runs, meaning all four "sluggers"—the same quartet who, just one year earlier, had combined for just five homers—had exceeded the former highest season record. How? Normally a ground rule stated balls lofted over Lakefront Park fences were doubles, but in 1884 that rule was lifted and the team amassed 142 homers, up from 13 the previous year and more than four times the former season record by a club.[60]

Tainted records from the dark ages of baseball included, Ruth made people forget all of the old records. On September 20, 1919, he tied Williamson when he golfed number 27, a game-winning blast, off Lefty Williams of the White Sox. He wasted little time eclipsing the record when he torched a ball, driving it over the roof at the Polo Grounds four days later. Then, on September 27, he closed out his marvelous season of power when he connected for his 29th homer, taking Washington's Rip Jordan over the fence for his sole homer in Washington, D.C., that year. Thus, that salvo made him the first man to stroke one or more home runs in every ballpark in his league over a single season.

He was changing the very fabric and strategy of the game. Fans loved the longball. On the other hand, old schoolers such as John McGraw, who, as a player in 1899, generated a run by stealing second, third, then home in an inning—one of just 40 men to accomplish this ultimate "small ball" act—resented Ruth's "innovation." Ruth's brand of baseball was a huge departure from the style of baseball played by Cobb, Cap Anson, and certainly "Wee" Willie Keeler of "Hit 'em where they ain't" fame, who preceded Ruth.

Baseball broadcaster John Kennelly told HBO that McGraw was the best in the business at playing "inside baseball." Kennelly said, "He perfected the Baltimore chop, bunt, move the runner along, work for one run at a time. Then this guy [Ruth] came along and broke up ball games with one swing. He [McGraw] hated him. For 30 years he worked for one run, and Babe wrecked the whole afternoon with one swing."[61]

Likewise, Ty Cobb hated Ruth's style and was jealous of the fan adulation Ruth sapped from him. McGraw's bitterness was evident as far back as Ruth's pre-outfield days when the Giants manager groused, "If he plays every day, the big bum will hit into a hundred double plays a season."[62]

The 1919 season ended for the fifth-place Red Sox, winners of only 66 games, with their worst record since 1907 when they won only 59 times and wound up in next-to-last place. Despite Ruth's first 100-RBI season, 1919 was quite a tumble from Boston's championship season of just one year earlier. The season also concluded with those in the know saddened and shocked by the throwing of the World Series by the Chicago White Sox, forever after known as the infamous "Black Sox." While the news didn't break to the general public right away, dark days were ahead.

NOTES

1. Ruth and Considine, *The Babe Ruth Story*, 11.
2. Lee Allen, *Cooperstown Corner* (Cleveland: SABR, 1990), 11.
3. Ruth, *Babe Ruth's Own Book of Baseball*, 80, 89.
4. Gilbert, *Young Babe Ruth*, 72.
5. Mike Gibbons, from interview with author, September 7, 2005.
6. Ruth, *Babe Ruth's Own Book of Baseball*, 7.
7. Ruth and Considine, *The Babe Ruth Story*, 11.
8. Mike Gibbons, from interview with author, September 7, 2005.
9. Gilbert, *Young Babe Ruth*, 55.
10. Ibid., 85–87.
11. Ritter, *The Babe*, 32.
12. Ruth and Considine, *The Babe Ruth Story*, 21.
13. Ritter, *The Glory of Their Times*, 136–137.
14. Smith, *Babe Ruth's America*, 1.
15. Herbert Simmons, "They Pinch-Hit for the Greats," *Baseball Digest*, February 1962, 5–10.
16. Creamer, *Babe*, 99.
17. Gilbert, *Young Babe Ruth*, 118.
18. William Young, from interview with author, March 4, 2005.
19. Creamer, *Babe*, 99.
20. Mike Vaccaro, *Emperors and Idiots* (New York: Doubleday, 2005), 47.
21. Gilbert, *Young Babe Ruth*, 121.
22. Pirone and Martens, *My Dad, the Babe*, 36.
23. Ritter, *The Babe*, 30.
24. Ruth, *Babe Ruth's Own Book of Baseball*, 89–90.
25. Ibid., 150.
26. Ibid., 46.
27. Vaccaro, *Emperors and Idiots*, 48.
28. From baseballlibrary.com.
29. Ruth and Considine, *The Babe Ruth Story*, 44–45.
30. Smith, *Babe Ruth's America*, 8.
31. Julia Ruth Stevens, from interviews with author, November 2005.
32. Linda Ruth Tosetti, from telephone interview with author, September 23, 2005.
33. Ibid.
34. John Thorn and John Holway, *The Pitcher* (New York: Prentice Hall Press, 1987), 53–54.
35. Associated Press.

36. Smith, *Babe Ruth's America*, 28, 41.

37. Ibid., 47.

38. From www.baseballlibrary.com.

39. Ruth and Considine, *The Babe Ruth Story*, 45.

40. Ibid., 44–45.

41. Ruth, *Babe Ruth's Own Book of Baseball*, 59.

42. Jeanine Bucek, ed. director, *Baseball Encyclopedia* 10th Edition (New York: Macmillan, 1996), 6–7.

43. George Vass, "Remarkable One-Season Performances," *Baseball Digest*, September 2005, 22.

44. Ruth and Considine, *The Babe Ruth Story*, 52F.

45. Creamer, *Babe*, 154.

46. Gilbert, *Young Babe Ruth*, 136.

47. Ritter, *The Babe*, 60.

48. Alan Schwarz, *The Numbers Game: Baseball's Lifelong Fascination with Statistics* (New York: St. Martin's Press, 2004), 45.

49. Creamer, *Babe*, 162.

50. David S. Neft, Richard M. Cohen, and Michael L. Neft, *The Sports Encyclopedia: Baseball* 23rd Edition (New York: St. Martin's Griffin, 2003), 84.

51. Henry D. Fetter, *Taking on the Yankees: Winning and Losing in the Business of Baseball, 1903–2003* (New York: W. W. Norton and Company, 2003), 41.

52. Ruth and Considine, *The Babe Ruth Story*, 57–58.

53. Ibid., 56–57.

54. Craig Carter, ed., *Official World Series Records* (St. Louis: The Sporting News Publishing Company, 1979), 52.

55. Ritter, *The Babe*, 34.

56. Creamer, *Babe*, 169–170; Harris, *Babe Ruth: The Dark Side*, 22–23.

57. Ruth and Considine, *The Babe Ruth Story*, 62–63.

58. Creamer, *Babe*, 187.

59. Smith, *Babe Ruth's America*, 68.

60. Leonard Koppett, *Koppett's Concise History of Major League Baseball* (Philadelphia: Temple University Press, 1998), 49.

61. HBO Productions, *Babe Ruth: The Life Behind the Legend* (New York: HBO Home Video, 1998).

62. Widely quoted.

A Babe in the City That Doesn't Sleep, 1920–1924

As the 1920s began, the city of New York was electric; it was the Mecca of the country and, of course, of baseball, which, in turn, was truly the national pastime. There were more than twenty daily newspapers in the city, and purchasing a copy set a person back less than a nickel—even when Ruth died in 1948, the *Daily News* cost only five cents. In addition, for much of Ruth's career, a Polo Grounds bleacher seat cost around 55 cents while a closer view of Ruth could be purchased for the $2.20 price of a box seat. After all, this was an era when a yearly salary of about $4,000 was sufficient for a person to dwell "in a big frame house, own an automobile, raise a family and live comfortably."[1] It was an era when women were finally permitted to vote in a national election but booze and, in baseball, pitches involving doctoring a ball were banned.

Joe Dugan, a teammate of Ruth, once commented that Ruth was "born to play in New York. That swing, that ambition, that appetite? There was just no way a small town like Boston could contain him. What town could? Maybe Chicago. Maybe. No, the Babe was built for Broadway, for the big time. There was only one place for him."[2] For many reasons, Ruth was indeed a perfect fit for the "City That Never Sleeps." On the day after Christmas in 1919, the transaction sending the wonderful gift of Ruth to the Yankees was finalized, although it was not officially announced until January 5, 1920. The Yankees did this to give manager Miller Huggins a chance to meet with Ruth, to seek his promise that he'd behave himself.[3]

The Yankees purchased Ruth from Boston owner Harry Frazee for the eye-popping price of $100,000 in cash, twice the previous record high paid for a player. Twenty-five percent of that loot was paid on the spot, along with three promissory notes for $25,000 each, and a loan of $300,000 also followed, allowing Frazee to continue to operate in Fenway Park.

Frazee had to put his park up as security for the loan, but he was, at that point, quite desperate. That is, according to most sources. However, Mike Vaccaro's *Emperors and Idiots* states Frazee was far from being "on the brink of financial ruin as he's long been portrayed. The fact is, the Red Sox turned a profit in 1919, cashing in mightily on Ruth's pursuit of history. This also happened to be when Frazee was at the peak of his business interests."[4] Moreover, legend has it that Frazee was in a rush to peddle Ruth because he needed cash immediately to back his musical, *No No Nanette*, which did go on to earn him millions of dollars. The truth of the matter is that play didn't even begin its run on Broadway until 1925, long after Ruth had been sold to the Yanks.

In any event, according to writer Henry D. Fetter, Frazee had become disgusted with Ruth who, after the 1919 season, demanded a pay hike that would double his salary to $20,000. Furthermore, "Frazee and Barrow convinced themselves that Ruth, especially given the frustration, insubordination, and failure that had characterized the 1919 season, posed a discipline and morale problem that threatened the future prospects of the team."[5] They doubted Ruth's ability to continue his awesome power hitting; after all, they reasoned, they were still in a dead ball era. Perhaps rationalizing, they also factored in the poor start that Ruth got off to in 1919 as they considered why the team had failed so badly that year. With many such facets taken into consideration, the decision was finally made to dump their star in what has been called "a one-of-a-kind deal."

Noteworthy, too, is the fact that at the time of the transaction the opinion of sportswriters in Boston was mixed. Some felt Ruth was "an overly demanding prima donna, selfishly pursuing his own agenda at the expense of the team."[6] The headlines in the January 6, 1920, *Boston Globe* stated that Frazee "DISPOSES OF MIGHTY SLUGGER" adding "RUTH TERMED A HANDICAP AND NOT AN ASSET BY THE RED SOX PRESIDENT," while listing the sale price at $125,000.

Those words were similar to others issued by Frazee to the media: "Ruth had become impossible and the Boston club could no longer put up with his eccentricities. I think the Yankees are taking a gamble. While Ruth is without question the greatest hitter the game has ever seen, he is likewise one of the most inconsiderate men that ever wore a baseball uniform." Frazee implied that Ruth hugged "the limelight to himself," and alluded to Ruth's growing girth and failure to stay in shape. He even mentioned Ruth's "floating cartilage in his knee which may make him a cripple at any time," sounding almost as if he was trying to convince himself that he had make a shrewd move.[7]

Claire Ruth later wrote that while Barrow felt Ruth hurt the team's morale, "players' morales are never hurt by the presence of a [big] winner who helps them win pennants."[8] Modern managers such as Terry Francona contend that many transgressions of superstars can be tolerated. "If the person's performing well, they'll give him some leeway as far as the rules go. That isn't necessarily real popular among people—you'd like to have your superstar guys come out and do everything just like everybody else, but if a guy's going out there and he's hitting .350 and 50 home runs, you want to have that guy happy."[9]

The Ruth transaction had been foreshadowed as early as one week after the 1919 season ended and Frazee informed the press that, "The Red Sox are not, and never will be, a one-man team."[10] After the transaction was consummated, the austere Yankess owner, Jacob Ruppert, revealed that he had "offered $100,000 for Ruth some time ago" and was turned down. He had remained doggedly determined, he indicated, to bring a pennant winner to New York and felt Ruth could push them over the top.[11]

Incredibly, on June 10, 2005, the five-page contract that sent Ruth to the Yankees was purchased at a Sotheby's auction for just $4,000 shy of $1,000,000, and a bit short of what was reportedly the most expensive item of Ruth memorabilia—his 46-ounce Louisville Slugger, which he used to rip the first homer ever at Yankee Stadium. That treasure went for $1,265,000 in late 2004.

Frazee owned the Red Sox from 1917 to 1923, but is most remembered as the man who "moved Babe Ruth from supporting cast to the lead role, on Broadway instead of in Fenway...." His Sox were on the skids—from 1919 to 1923 they would finish in fifth place or lower every year.[12]

They were in for even worse times after Frazee departed, leaving many bad trades in his wake. For instance, after ending up in seventh place in 1924, Boston wound up in the AL basement from 1925 to 1932. Overall, Frazee dealt a plethora of players to the Yankees, including pitchers Sam Jones, George Pipgras, Carl Mays, and Joe Bush; infielders Everett Scott and Dugan; and catcher Wally Schang, as well as three future Hall of Famers—Waite Hoyt, Pennock, and Ruth.

Meanwhile, the prosperous Yankees appeared in three World Series during the waning years of Frazee's tenure in Boston. Fans felt betrayed and labeled the stripping of the team as the rape of the Red Sox. Frazee also took home more booty when he sold the franchise for $1,500,000, a profit of about $1,100,000 on a seven-year investment.

No matter, his machinations seemed short sighted in that he "had the hottest show-biz ticket of the Roaring Twenties in his vest pocket, the ultimate drawing card of the century, maybe the top box-office smash of all time—and in his infinite wisdom he practically gave him away."[13]

Years later a writer created the concept of "The Curse of the Bambino," stating Boston's World Series drought was due to the unloading of Ruth. That concept ignores additional factors such as the staid Red Sox team becoming the last team to break the color barrier—and even when they did break it, they did so by signing not a player of the caliber of a Jackie Robinson or a Larry Doby, but the obscure Pumpsie Green, a lifetime .246 hitter. Francona, the manager who snapped the curse in 2004, stated, "I just didn't care much about it. I don't think our players cared that much—it was probably more of a media thing."[14] Maybe so, but as the Baseball Library's Web site states, "the sale initiated the enduring rivalry between the two teams and shifted the balance of league power from Boston to New York."[15]

Boston had won the first modern World Series in 1903 and went on to play in four of the next 14 Series, winning each time. Then, especially significant after Ruth's departure, in 85 opportunities to return to the Series from 1919 to 2004 (a players' strike cancelled the 1994 Series), Boston lost every bid for a pennant save four. On those four occasions, the Sox lost the World Series, each time in demoralizing seven-game sets. The Ruth-less Red Sox became the league's punching bag, stumbling through 14 straight losing years.

Conversely, the Yankees had never won the pennant before Ruth joined them and suffered through some abysmal years (e.g., 196 combined losses in 1912 and 1913) but went on to win the AL flag in three of Ruth's first four seasons in New York, and six over his first nine Yankee years. In fact, with Ruth aboard, the Yankees took the AL flag seven times over the next 13 seasons, winning four championships during the period. More amazingly, the Yankees also won 26 world championships and 14 pennants before the Red Sox won another one in 2004.

Another fallacy to the curse is clear: Boston's demise wasn't just due to Ruth's departure. Frazee had run a Boston clearance sale, jettisoning a truckload of stars. Harry Hooper bitterly stated that the "Yankees dynasty of the 1920s was three-quarters the Red Sox of a few years before."[16] Obviously then, the sale of Ruth alone did not ruin the Red Sox and buoy the Yanks.

Interestingly, Ed Barrow, who had managed the Red Sox and Ruth in 1918 and 1919, would become even more important to the Babe Ruth saga in New York where he took on the role of general manager in 1920. Typically, Ruth would battle him, seeing him as a rigid disciplinarian and yet another authority figure in his life. Many Yankees privately called Barrow "Simon Legree." However, even Barrow conceded that Ruth was a steal despite the then-exorbitant price the Yankees had to pay.

Ruth paid instant dividends at the box office. Prior to his arrival, the Yanks had only twice drawn more than 500,000 fans and had pulled in fewer than

300,000 three times in the eight years before Babe. In 1920 alone, their attendance shot up to 1,289,422, making them the first team to reach the million figure, with over one third more spectators than the former big league attendance record set by the 1908 Giants.[17] Additionally, their 1921 attendance was more than double their draw of 619,164 from one year earlier in the pre-Babe days.

Ruth loved Boston, but he quickly grew to love New York too. Strutting around in silk shirts, each one said to be more expensive than what he formerly had paid for a suit, Ruth was quite the sight. He puffed away on imported cigars, a dozen or so daily, and tooled around town in a new maroon Packard, a car that packed as much power in its 12 cylinders as Ruth's mighty bat. He was said to have purchased a roadster for $10,000 only to crash it into a tree about a month later "while speeding from Washington to Philadelphia in the dark."[18]

For their living quarters in New York, Babe and Helen took a suite at the Ansonia Hotel on bustling Broadway and 73rd Street—a far cry from a Baltimore row house, which typically cost $1,500 when Ruth was born. Ruth's daughter Julia recalled that, "Daddy wanted to go to all the parties. Helen was a little girl, just not up to it. She said, 'I don't like it here. I want to go back home.' He said, 'Well, I do like it here.' So she went back [to their farm] and he stayed in New York."[19]

While Fenway Park, called "death to left-handed power hitters," kept Ruth's power dormant to some extent, the Polo Grounds embraced Ruth. In 1919, only 9 of his 29 homers came at Fenway; in 1920, his homer surge at home in the Polo Grounds more than tripled.[20] Virtually every baseball expert agrees that, along with the game's first commissioner, Kenesaw Mountain Landis, hired in November 1920 to clean up baseball's "act," Ruth saved the game after the ignominy of the 1919 Black Sox Scandal permeated the nation and its primary pastime.

In Dorothy's book, *My Dad, the Babe*, Eliot Asinof, author of the definitive book on the scandal, *Eight Men Out*, is quoted as saying fans of the era had become cynical after the World Series was discovered to have been rigged. Ruth's emergence changed that thinking as fans felt instead, "Even though everything may have been fixed, you couldn't 'fix' Babe Ruth." Asinof also diminished Landis' role in patching up the game, comparing him to an axe-wielding executioner whose role was merely to lop off "a few heads."[21]

Some felt the unofficial date for the start of the salvation of baseball was May 1, 1920, when Ruth teed off for his first four-bagger in a Yankee uniform. The ball whistled off his bat, soaring majestically over the Polo Grounds roof. However, this version of the "salvation" came in retrospect only. Actually, the grand jury indictment of eight players accused of throwing the fixed Series didn't break until monstrously large, bold headlines appeared on September 28,

1920 (although a Philadelphia newspaper broke the story a day earlier), shouting out the treachery of the White Sox conspirators who were immediately suspended from further play.[22] So another way of looking at the issue is that even *before* 1920, Ruth had insured the game's popularity because "he had already injected such excitement into the baseball scene that not even such a major disgrace could change it."[23]

On January 16, 1920, at the stroke of midnight, just eleven days after the sale of Ruth to the Yankees was announced, the United States went dry and the age of Prohibition began. The laws banning alcohol lasted until 1933. Of course, Ruth and a legion of other Americans were far from parched. A story has it that Ruth attended a party in New Orleans in 1923 where beer was flowing freely even though the gathering was thrown by that city's police chief.[24] Ruth's daughter Dorothy recalled bootleggers smuggling liquor by the cases "wrapped in burlap bags and old newspapers" to Ruth's apartment in New York.[25]

Ruth had filled out to tip the scales at 220 pounds, up over 25 pounds from his 1917 weight of 194, and he continued to fuel himself with gargantuan amounts of food and drink. However, he stated that he felt 220 was his ideal playing weight and those pounds certainly did back his swings up with a great deal of heft.

By now, Ruth had elbowed Ty Cobb out as the top attraction in baseball. A *New York Times* item from May 1920 stated that Ruth had "stolen all of Cobb's thunder." Worse for Cobb, when Ruth visited the Tigers, H. G. Salsinger, a writer for the *Detroit Free Press*, stated, "He got the applause, the shrieking adoration of the multitude, in Cobb's own city. . . . He [Cobb] saw before him a new king acclaimed."[26]

Some experts feel the offensive explosion that began in 1920 came about because it was then that baseball banned pitchers from throwing doctored baseballs (e.g., the spitball, shine ball, and emery ball). Actually, there was a grandfather clause that allowed each team to declare two of their pitchers as a sort of designated spitball thrower—in all, 17 big league pitchers were selected. Only these men were granted carte blanche to continue to throw spitters for the rest of their careers, and the last legal one was thrown in 1934 by Burleigh Grimes.

The ball itself was juiced as baseball realized that fans wanted to see the home run, and if that helped them develop a form of selective amnesia about the corruption and gambling surrounding the game, then so be it. Back in the midseason of 1910, when the game was under attack for being "a dull duel between pitchers," the National League had introduced a new ball possessing a cork center that was so large, twine had to be wrapped around it tighter than was the case for previously used balls, having centers made exclusively of rubber. This lively ball was more difficult to grip effectively on curve balls and, in general, led to more home runs being tagged.

The rabbit ball, put into play in 1920, bounded off bats like never before due to "the use of Australian wool, unavailable during World War I, and the tighter winding made possible by new machinery." As a matter of fact, an official of the Reach Company, which produced the balls used in AL play, later stated "that the winding would be periodically tightened or loosened as requested."[27]

On August 16, 1920, an event occurred that would also have huge ramifications for sluggers. Ray Chapman was struck in the head by a pitch from Carl Mays and died the following morning in major league baseball's only death directly related to on-the-field play. This tragedy led to a change in policy concerning use of the new baseballs. Prior to 1921, it was not at all unusual for a single ball to be used throughout an entire game, although two or three was more typical. The ball that leveled Chapman was "dingy brown from overuse, and Chapman barely even saw it."[28] After that, "off-season rule makers . . . instructed umpires to replace dirty balls with new white ones that hitters could pick up better."[29] For the first time, batters could request the ump to put a new, clean ball in play and foul balls were no longer returned from the fans to the field for continued use. The result was that by 1924 the NL put 54,030 balls in play compared to just 22,095 in 1919.[30]

With the dead ball era ended, the two major leagues, which had hit a collective .270 or better only three times from 1901 to 1919, began a hitting spree. From 1920 through 1932, the NL hit .270 or better every season and the AL hit that high each and every year until 1941. Home run totals escalated like a runaway national debt. From 1919 to 1921, the home-run output doubled and "by 1930, they had nearly doubled again." Baseball had entered an era when "the ball was, comparatively, a grenade, and every man in the lineup could hurt you. . . ."[31] And a big man like Ruth, could *really* hurt a pitcher.

Ruth, who began the year hitting cleanup, was moved to the three hole by Huggins to get him more good pitches to look at. He tattooed a remarkable 54 longballs while his nearest rival, George Sisler, could manage only 19, or "seven more than any AL player not named Ruth since 1903. All hitters went deep more often; over two seasons home run frequencies more than doubled."[32]

By July 19, 1920, Ruth had shattered his own home run record set the previous season, becoming the first player ever to compile 30. When the smoke cleared, he had annihilated the former high, with his 54 nearly doubling his 1919 output, and representing exactly twice as many homers as the dubious record once set by Ned Williamson. The Bambino out-homered 14 of the 16 teams in baseball—every team except the Yankees who powered 61 without Ruth's help and the Phillies with 64; and he more than tripled the Pirates' power output that year. Alone he accounted for nearly 15 percent of AL home runs, owning about one of every seven homers pounded out in his league.

It's little wonder he received special treatment in the Yankees clubhouse. He requested to have his own phone installed in the locker room and the team quickly acquiesced. It took an oversized wire basket to contain all the fan mail he received. Ruth was above wading through the mounds of paper; quite often his teammates performed that task. Their motivation was simple—they sought letters from females who begged to meet the Babe. At times a teammate would pick out a promising letter, phone the girl to set up a date, and then show up at the rendezvous point to scout the girl. If he liked what he saw, he'd sidle up next to her. If he didn't, he'd slip away, leaving the impression that Ruth had stood her up.[33] One story has Ruth impatiently shredding a batch of unopened mail to rid himself of the heap. A teammate, Doc Wood, jigsaw-puzzled some mail together and produced more than $6,000 in endorsements and royalty checks.[34]

Amidst all this, the highly entertaining Yankees of 1920 fell just shy—three games—of winning their first pennant. While Ruth's pitching days were basically over, there was one story Ruth relished relating. He was ahead 1-0 against Chicago with two outs and two White Sox on base in the ninth when Chick Gandil, who had a trick knee, stepped to the plate. He laced a ball to deep center, chasing the winning run home, but Gandil never got out of the box. He was hitting himself on his bad knee to pop it back into place. Meanwhile, the ball was retrieved and relayed in to first base where Gandil was declared out. Thus, neither run counted—it was as if Gandil had merely grounded out rather than starched what should have been a double—and Ruth chalked up a shutout.

By 1921, Ruth's fame "penetrated the inner recesses of the social world. Even the Four Hundred of New York became curious. They wanted to know what made the big fellow tick."[35] In October, *Popular Science Monthly* featured the article "Why Babe Ruth Is Greatest Home Run Hitter" with results from laboratory tests at Columbia that had examined his uncanny skills. To test his coordination, he was given a stylus and instructed to tap it for one minute, rotating the instrument into three holes placed on a triangular board. The average person managed 82 taps; Ruth rapid-fired the stylus 132 times. To study the quickness of his brain, eyes, and muscles, he was told to press a telegraph key when a light was flashed. The results revealed he was 10 percent quicker than the norm. That, scientists concluded, was how he could follow the path of a ball and connect for such terrific power. In another test, a row of eight letters was exposed to Ruth for 1/50,000th of a second. Here the average person identified four-and-a-half letters; Ruth nailed six. The article stated that "a pitcher must throw a ball 20/1,000ths of a second faster to 'fool' Babe than to 'fool' the average person."[36]

At the end of the 1920 season, Barrow had departed Boston and joined Ruth with the Yankees, becoming their general manager, a position then known as the business manger. Along with Ruppert and Miller Huggins, these three men formed a "management triumvirate . . . that would carry the Yankees to the top and keep them there."[37] Ruppert, a former congressman from New York City, was a wealthy beer baron with an aristocratic air who had purchased the Yankees for $460,000 with partner Huston. Huston was "gregarious, loquacious, and well loved by his newspaper and baseball cronies."[38] As experts saw it, the pieces were in place for the 1921 season.

Now, Ted Williams' best batting average was his .406 in 1941, but his most splendid hitting may well have come in 1957 when he hit .388 and was a handful of hits shy of attaining .400 despite finishing that season a year from his 40th birthday. Likewise, most fans spout that 1927 was Ruth's greatest season, and while it was in terms of home runs, 1921 was his finest all around season.

As early as the pre-season prior to the 1921 campaign, F. C. Lane wrote in *Baseball Magazine* of "a race between Babe Ruth and the [home run] record." Ruth was already being called the "Home Run King" by the media and, as would be the case for years to come, had only one person's power records to smash—his own. As Lane put it, "the Ruth of 1921 will race against the Ruth of 1920." Ruth quickly won. To use a horse racing metaphor, he won by 20 lengths, hitting his 30th homer ridiculously early, on July 19.[39]

Special treatment for Ruth continued. Often he did not travel with the team, instead motoring through eastern road trips in his limo-like car. He earned $30,000 in 1921, while hardly petty cash then, an absurd bargain by today's measures. And for that sum he gave the Yankees what is arguably the greatest return for their money ever. He scored 177 times while driving in 171 runs, still seventh best ever, and hit .378 with a slugging percentage, just .001 lower than his record-setting mark from the previous year. The most startling statistic of all, though, was his new record of 59 home runs.

He was scorching hot from spring training on. Like a prototype for Barry Bonds, Ruth was offered few juicy pitches; he stated that he worked hard for about half of his homers, off pitches he "had to reach for." Unlike Bonds—who racked up walks at an astonishing rate in the early 2000s by refusing to chase junk—Ruth said that if a pitch was in the vicinity of the strike zone, he took his hacks.[40]

When Ruth clobbered a ball on June 6, 1921, against Cleveland's Jim Bagby, it stood as the 120th of his career, breaking the post-1900 career high of Gavvy Cravath. Roger Connor, a player from the "pre-modern" era, hit more than Cravath, with 136, but when the 26-year-old Ruth blazed by that total, the media seemed curiously blasé or oblivious. Schwarz reports that not a single word of this feat was printed in baseball's prestigious publication *The Sporting News*.[41] Ruth went on to pulverize his own record 577 times.

Records from the Connor era are sketchy, but one source says Ruth knocked off the old record on July 12, 1921, when he struck his 137th home run, but more recent accounts have Connor with 138. In any event, it was clear that by 1921 Ruth was a major force in baseball.

Off the diamond, Ruth continued to make news. On June 8, his love for fast cars, often borrowed from one of his romantic interests, led to his arrest. He reportedly was slapped with a $100 fine for speeding and held in a New York jail until 45 minutes after the first pitch of a Yankees contest. A uniform was rushed to Ruth and he suited up while still in his cell. Then a cooperative police force escorted him to the stadium in a scene straight out of a Hollywood screwball comedy. According to legend, he arrived with the Yankees trailing 3-2, but they dramatically came back to win it 4-3. Perhaps Ruth's presence helped them rally, but, in truth, he accomplished nothing at the plate that day.[42]

An event occurred in Pittsburgh on August 5, which would soon increase Ruth's popularity. KDKA radio station carried the first baseball game ever broadcast, an 8-5 Pirate win over their cross-state rivals, the Phillies. As far as baseball went, this marked the birth of the electronic media, and nobody, of course, could imagine what a powerful, robust adult this medium would become. By 1922, "New Yorkers who could afford a sixty-dollar Westinghouse radio were able to tune in to a regional broadcast of the World Series."[43] Soon radio's growth spurt was enormous; by the close of the decade approximately 33 percent of the country's families owned radios. By the early 1930s, every big league team was airing their games.

It was on September 15, 1921, that Ruth crashed through his own record for home runs in a season and added four more as he tuned up for the World Series against the cross-town (more accurately, "cross-river") Giants. After the Yankees had mathematically clinched the pennant, their final warm up for the World Series against the Giants came when they faced the Athletics. A story from broadcaster Ernie Harwell relates how Ruth, indirectly, cost Waite Hoyt his 20th win that year.

Hoyt had worked the first seven innings of that contest and was in line for the win, nursing a 7-0 lead. It was then that Huggins informed Hoyt that, with the "game in the bag," he was going to insert Ruth as the pitcher to mop things up, because the spectators "want to see Babe Ruth pitch. He hasn't pitched all year and it would be a treat for them." Ruth's rustiness showed and he soon blew the lead. Then, when he homered in the ninth, Ruth got the win that Hoyt truly deserved.[44]

By the conclusion of the 1921 season, Ruth had accumulated 32 homers at his home ballpark, which still looms as the all-time record for left-handed hitters. He crushed 35 homers more than his nearest rival. In addition, his .542

on-base percentage ranked number one until 1941 when Ted Williams bettered it. Add to that the fact that nobody's ever had more extra-base hits than Ruth's 119. Single-handedly, he produced just shy of one-third (30.5 percent) of all the runs the Yankees tallied. By way of comparison, the year Bonds amassed 73 homers, he accounted for just under 25 percent of the Giants' runs scored. What few fans today realize is that the younger, slimmer version of the Babe they envision was not slow; he even generated a career-high 16 triples in 1921 and compiled 10 career inside-the-park homers.[45]

Most of Ruth's teammates had no Series experience so, with four appearances in the autumn showcase, he represented something he was not normally associated with—stability. It was an unusual Series in that all the contests in this, the last of the best-of-nine championship clashes, had the same venue, the Polo Grounds. It was not a pleasant encounter for the Yanks who lost in eight games. Ruth, playing most of the games with an infected elbow, squeezed out just one home run while hitting .313, which seemingly sounds good but is almost 30 points below his career batting average. Worse, he struck out in exactly 50 percent of his 16 at-bats and was of no help to the Yankees over the last three games when the Yankees scored just six times and Ruth appeared in just one pinch-hit appearance, resulting in a harmless ground out. Giants manager McGraw gloated that they threw him mostly slow stuff, serving up only three fastballs, while also knocking him off the plate eleven times.

Often in Ruth's career, his defiant nature led to, and worsened, his woes. In 1922, he met his match in Commissioner Landis, possessor of a scowl and latent temper that rivaled Jack Nicholson's character in *The Shining*. Landis let it be known that he would enforce the National Baseball Commission rule of January 1911 stating no player from a World Series–winning team could take part in postseason exhibition games.

Ruth considered Landis to be an enemy, a "bad guy" he lumped together with authority figures such as Barrow, Huggins, and, later, Joe McCarthy.[46] Accustomed to pulling in extra cash for such appearances—he had doubled his regular salary through exhibitions in both 1919 and 1920—Babe contended the rule was unfair and had blithely set out on a tour following the 1921 Series. This marked the third time Ruth violated the rule; it would be the final time.

Yankee teammates Mays and Schang had decided not to go on the tour at all; for the others, it was an ill-fated trip, beginning in a soggy, cold, and wet Buffalo, New York, in front of a sparse crowd. Worse, some of the games scheduled to be played in big league ballparks were cancelled by the team owners of those parks who feared Landis' wrath. So, before half of the trip's games could be played, Ruth and company returned to New York.[47] Ruth contended that he began the barnstorming trek in part because he felt that he had to honor his obligation to the tour's promoter. His team had played in only three contests before, according to Ruth, Colonel Huston paid off the promoter, and the tour came to an end in Scranton, Pennsylvania.

That was not nearly enough to placate Landis, who was coming to the end of his first year as the commissioner. He lashed out and withheld the winning shares of the 1921 World Series ($3,362) and also slapped Ruth and teammates, Bob Meusel and Bill Piercy, with a stinging and lengthy suspension on October 16, 1921.[48]

The penalties were much stricter than Ruth expected. Like many modern pampered players, Ruth felt a sense of entitlement. Therefore, anything more severe than the baseball equivalent of having him scrawl sentences on a blackboard for punishment enraged him. Landis, who called Ruth's behavior "mutinous defiance," hurt Ruth's wallet and sat him in a corner from April 12 until May 20.[49]

The pain of the suspension without pay was exacerbated further when Ruth wound up losing the home run derby by a scant four homers. Disappointingly, he finished the year as only the third best slugger in his league, trailing St. Louis outfielder Ken Williams (39 HR) and Philadelphia's Tilly Walker who hammered 37 (oddly, a career high in his last full season, and at the age of 35) to Ruth's 35.

Had Ruth won the home-run title, he would have monopolized that title every year from 1918 until 1925 and every season save one from 1918 until 1932. Because he missed 39 days of the season due to the punishment, it's a safe assumption that he certainly would have had at least four additional homers— based on his home-run percentage that year, he probably would have tacked on about eight more homers.

New York fans flooded Landis' office with petitions asking him to reinstate Ruth, but the stern and stoical commissioner remained unmoved. So, for the 1922 season opener, Ruth watched the Yankees not from his outfield spot, but from, of all places, the box of President Warren G. Harding, who had earlier thrown out the ceremonial first pitch. Somehow, like a precocious yet charming child, even when Ruth was being admonished, he was still indulged (not unlike the incident with the police escort to Yankee Stadium after his speeding arrest). Babe even made some money during the suspension by allowing a ghost writer to pen a column of baseball commentary under his name.[50]

At this stage of his life, when Ruth got angry he didn't simply fly off the handle, he rocketed off with the propulsive force of Apollo 13. Suspensions and fines weren't exactly uncommon for Ruth who bucked the establishment. In the wake of his suspension for barnstorming, an event of May 25, 1922, resulted in, what seems in retrospect to be, a mere ruler slap to the knuckles, a penalty Ruth could pretty much laugh off.

When Ruth, carrying a lame .093 average into the game, attempted to stretch a single into a double, he was called out by umpire George Hildebrand, and went ballistic over the call. He wound up firing a fistful of dirt in the ump's face. Then, in a rage, he sallied into the stands after a heckler in what seems like an earlier shade of antics by modern players such as Albert Belle. After he chased the heckler up an aisle, police had to subdue Ruth. He began to make his way to the clubhouse but not before he spewed venom once more, posing on top of the Yankee dugout, challenging the home crowd to fight him "You're all yellow," he ranted while flailing away with his arms, boos cascading on him.

This, incidentally, was not the first time Ruth rampaged into the stands. Two years earlier, in Clearwater, Florida, during an exhibition game versus the Dodgers as both teams broke camp and headed north, "a heckler lured Ruth into the stands. Ruth and coach Charley O'Leary were confronted by a knife-wielding antagonist. Ruth and O'Leary retreated." The incident was kept relatively quiet because no action was taken by the police.[51]

Ruth later growled, "I didn't mean to hit the umpire with the dirt, but I did mean to hit that bastard in the stands."[52] Shockingly, the league felt that a suitable sentence was a one-day suspension and a $200 fine.[53] By comparison, the five-day suspension of Robbie Alomar for spitting on an umpire in 1996 seems like capital punishment.

It was speculated that Babe got off so easy because there was some sympathy for his having just come off serving hard time. Also, baseball officials knew the game and the owners' purses were more hale when Ruth was drawing crowds, not sitting on the sidelines. In particular, Senators' owner Clark Griffith, who was to play host to Ruth in the Yankees' next series, was strapped for cash. Realizing Ruth's first trip to town would prove lucrative, Griffith pleaded for Ban Johnson to lift his original indefinite suspension.

Johnson agreed after Ruth sat out one game, explaining, "Dust on umpires happens in the heat of the moment, but we cannot condone anyone going into the stands."[54] It's hard to imagine today's umpires' union being pleased with such a statement. Nevertheless, Johnson also stripped him of his captain's title, unequivocally stating that Ruth's "present mental temperament disqualifies him from the position."[55] Ruth's name listed along the names of other Yankees captains seems to be an incongruous fit, given his bad boy behavior. Consider, by contrast, captains such as Lou Gehrig, Thurman Munson, and Don Mattingly. Ruth's reign as captain was absurdly short, lasting less than a week, from May 20 until the 25. No other team captain had a tenure shorter than one full season.

As a side note, the comparison with Albert Belle goes further. According to Baseball Library's Web site, on June 11, 1927, Ruth had connected for two straight home runs, but on his next trip to the plate he was "set upon by

Cleveland catcher Luke Sewell who demands that the umpires inspect the Bambino's bat. The umps find nothing illegal, but the crowd of 30,000 cheer the Babe, who strikes out."[56]

On June 19, 1922, Ruth again made headlines when his tirade against umpire Bill Dinneen earned him an ejection and a three-day suspension. This was the same Dinneen who, in 1903, won three games, including the finale, when he whiffed Honus Wagner to nail down the first-ever World Series. When Ruth continued his diatribe against Dinneen the next day during batting practice and physically threatened the arbiter, Johnson upped the suspension to five days. Ruth's next tantrum came on August 30. After Tom Connolly rang him up on strikes, Ruth's language was so raw he was ejected from the game and earned another three-day "vacation." In all, he was suspended five times in the tumultuous 1922 season.

Sometimes in his autobiographies, Ruth didn't merely sugarcoat the truth, he, to borrow from a cereal commercial, shot it with sugar, through and through. In 1928, Ruth would write of his brushes with baseball's "law." He downplayed his transgressions, saying that like all young men, he had made some mistakes, then stated, "Once or twice I've been in bad with baseball authorities." *Once or twice* is clearly a gross understatement, but is typical of Ruth's propensity for playing with the truth on occasion. He also claimed that he had learned his lesson and that "those days are over," but that would not prove to be true.[57]

It's true, considering his temper and suspensions, that Ruth was flawed; he was, after all, human. Tot Pressnell, who played in the majors from 1938 to 1942, addressed the whole Ruth paradoxical package. "He was a gentleman but everybody knows that his morals were terrible and he drank a lot." He added that the stars of sports aren't, or can't be, told to change their ways. Noone, said Pressnell, was about to stop Ruth's drinking or, for that matter, his other bad habits.[58]

It should be noted that not all of Ruth's barnstorming was non-sanctioned, and by the end of the 1922 Series barnstorming rules were relaxed. As a rule, Babe's tours began in the East and wended their way to the West Coast. It was not at all unusual for Ruth to play in such small venues as Sharon, Pennsylvania, or cities that would not have a major league franchise for years, such as Minneapolis, Minnesota.

Bob Feller remembered seeing Ruth "in Des Moines, Iowa, when he and Lou Gehrig were playing exhibition games in 1928. It was the Larrupin' Lous versus the Bustin' Babes—they had their own uniforms."[59] It was a thrill for the young Feller and thousands upon thousands of other fans to see those heroes. Such opportunities meant a lot to spectators in remote areas across the country who might otherwise not have had the chance to see the Babe.

Feller observed the only autograph he ever sought and obtained in his entire lifetime was one "of Babe when I was nine."[60] Feller would, of course, go on to sign countless autographs himself—a joke among collectors states that the most rare baseball of all is one *without* Feller's signature on it. Of course, Ruth also was so generous with his signature, one imagines he suffered from chronic writer's cramp.

At any rate, Feller recalled that "Babe pitched for one inning and he and Gehrig led off each inning."

> They put on a hitting exhibition prior to the game, too. They auto-graphed a bushel basketful of balls and the money they got [five dollars per ball] went to the hospital where my mom took her nurse's training, the Mercy Hospital in Des Moines.
>
> I went out and got the five dollars by catching rodents, gophers, in alfalfa fields. They gave you a bounty, 10 cents a pair for the claws of these gophers. I bought the ball with my own money.[61]

Ruth was paid a lofty salary of $52,000 for 1922, more than three times what the second best paid Yankee, 36-year-old Frank "Home Run" Baker, earned at $16,000. Going into negotiations, Ruth had a mental scenario of earning $1,000 per week, and that's exactly what he eventually signed for. His five-year deal at that figure gave him over a quarter of a million dollars, which, for the time, was a mind-boggling sum.

It was also a hefty amount considering that baseball, according to a recent court decree, was not even engaged in a business. However, the clicking of the turnstiles belied that concept. With Ruth pulling in a slew of spectators, the 1921 Yanks nearly tied their record attendance from 1920, attracting 1,230,696—it would take until 1946 for them to eclipse their record high.

Yet Ruth's 1922 production was paltry by his criteria. Part of his plight, unlike his suspensions, was caused by a seldom-discussed factor: the obscure Hub Pruett of the Browns who first toed the rubber against the Yankees at the Polo Grounds under its classy Roman Coliseum facade. His gaze fell upon the looming figure of Ruth in the batter's box, seemingly just a Ruth check swing away from the inviting target of the right-field fence, 256¼ feet from home plate. Remarkably, instead of being intimidated, Pruett, standing only 5 feet 10 inches and weighing just 135 pounds, went right at Ruth.

Moreover, he'd soon learn that he had little to fear in future duels as well. Ruth was *his*; he "owned" Ruth. Throughout his career, Pruett would com-pletely baffle the Babe. Looking back on his first confrontation with Ruth on April 22, 1922, Pruett said, "It didn't bother me, facing Ruth for the first time.

All I knew was that he batted left-handed and I didn't have much trouble with left-handers. When I went out to the mound, I didn't know who he was. I struck him out on three pitches." For that matter, he whiffed the slugger three times that afternoon as St. Louis toppled the Yankees 7-1.

Indeed, it was no fluke; the 21-year-old rookie southpaw continued to dominate Babe—almost 20 percent of all his strikeouts that year came at Ruth's expense. During Ruth's first unlucky 13 tries versus Pruett, he tapped out to the pitcher, drew 2 walks, and fanned an abysmal 10 times. Of his 21 plate appearances in 1922, Ruth whiffed 13 times, a stupefying 62 percent of those futile trips to the plate. Pruett only lasted three years in the AL where he'd face Ruth 30 times in all. Ruth could muster only a paltry 4-of-21 (.190) against Pruett with just one homer. He struck out in precisely half of their battles, leading Pruett to say, "Seeing the Babe strike out was almost as exciting as seeing him hit a home run."[62]

Ruth's lone homer versus Pruett came when the pitcher did not go with his best pitch, his fadeaway—reporters called it "the pitch that Bamboozled Babe," but nowadays would be labeled a screwball. Pruett wanted to throw it for an out pitch to Ruth, but his catcher, Hank Severeid, shook Pruett off and, remembered Pruett ruefully, "called for the curve. I hung it and Ruth hit a line drive over the low right field wall [in St. Louis]. I don't think he ever hit my fadeaway." The press called it one of the most notable jinxes in baseball.

Pruett, who only went 29-48 scattered over seven seasons, spoke to Ruth only once in his life. As players they "passed each other without speaking. But every once in awhile Ruth did something that gave me a kick, he would wink at me," said Pruett. Many years later, about two months before Ruth's death in 1948, the two adversaries met at a baseball dinner. Pruett approached Ruth and said, "If it hadn't been for you, nobody would ever have heard of me." Ruth replied in a raspy cancer-stricken voice, "That's all right, kid, but I'm glad there weren't many more like you or no one would have heard of me."[63]

On September 23, 1922, the country discovered that Babe Ruth was a father. The *New York Daily News* plastered the headline "THE SECRET IS OUT! BABE RUTH HAS A BABY SIXTEEN MONTHS OLD!" on its front page. The papers also reported Babe and Helen couldn't get their story straight concerning their daughter, Dorothy. Helen said the child was born June 7, 1921, while Babe had the birth date as February 2.

Ruth shrugged off the revelation nonchalantly, but told reporters she weighed a scant two pounds at birth. Helen was grilled by reporters about the daughter having been adopted. When no record of Dorothy's birth could be located at the Bureau of Vital Statistics, the mystery grew deeper and darker. Helen indignantly insisted she was the real mother and that Dorothy, suffering from rickets, had been under the care of a nurse for the first 14 months of her life.[64]

Dorothy, however, later stated that she was the product of an affair between Babe and Juanita Jennings whose grandfather, Don Francisco Madero, had been the president of Mexico from 1911 until his assassination in 1913. Linda Ruth Tosetti, Ruth's granddaughter, said that her mother, Dorothy, incredibly, didn't learn the truth until 1980.

"She [Juanita] stated on her death bed that she was our grandmother and she had a baby with Babe—my mother Dorothy. When they called my mother adopted, from what we look like you'd say, 'Nah, can't be.' They even call me Babe Ruth in drag, but I've got a nicer nose." Tosetti also feels her mother favors Juanita in appearance, especially in stature, but shared Babe's "drop lid over her eye, one lid that drops more than the other—if you look at a picture of Babe you'll see it, a subtle thing."[65]

Tosetti asserted it's also untrue that Dorothy was the product of "an affair with the maid. My grandmother's probably rolling in her grave. She was a socialite from San Francisco, a flapper, and an 'ahead-of-her-time' kind of gal, so she was no maid."[66]

Juanita's affair with Babe took place in California during the summer of 1920. A few months later she contacted him again, informing him that she was carrying his child. Ruth told her to come to New York, that he'd take care of everything there. After Dorothy was born, she lived with Juanita before Babe convinced Juanita that he and Helen should raise the baby. He informed Juanita that if she agreed to part with the baby Ruth would continue to pay for an apartment he had set up for her. With that, he took the child to his wife. The Ruths legally adopted Dorothy and Helen had the child she always yearned for, alleviating some of the problems of her marriage.[67]

Tosetti recalled how little she knew about her grandfather when she was young.

> My mother grew up during the Lindbergh kidnapping so she kept us pretty much "tucked." So, until I was old enough to take care of myself, she kept us pretty hidden. If you went up to her and said, "Are you Babe Ruth's daughter?" she would have told you no. She was afraid somebody would get it into their head that we had money.
>
> I remember growing up, feeling strange when I was about 10 or 11, everybody talked about their grandfather and we talked about my father's father, but we never said anything about mom's. So I brought up, "What about your dad," and she said, "We don't talk about my dad."
>
> I said, "Why, was he a crook?" She goes, "No, he just played baseball for a living, no big deal. Now go play." I didn't think anymore about it until my teenage years.[68]

The 1922 World Series held little joy for Ruth. The first Series ever to be broadcast over the radio began on October 4 with Ruth going 1 for 4 in a 3-2 heartbreaking loss to the Giants who came up with a three-spot in the bottom of the eighth, then held on to win it. Just four days later it was over; the Giants won in a "sort-of" sweep. That is to say, they took four games to the Yankees zero, but with a 10-inning tie game, called due to darkness, thrown in. Ruth struggled with an anemic .118 average, rarely meeting the ball crisply, with just one single, a double, and a lone run driven in. McGraw delighted in Ruth's misery, boasting that he "had the big monkey's number—just pitch him low curves and slow stuff and he falls all over himself."[69]

After the season, on November 15, Jimmy Walker, then a New York state senator, gave a speech at the baseball writers' dinner. Walker reportedly began his oration with great shock value saying Ruth was "not only a great athlete; he is also a great fool." He continued to address and reprimand Ruth, pounding away, "Babe, are you going to once again let down those dirty-faced kids in the streets of America?"

He even compared Ruth to a Santa Claus figure who "took off his beard to reveal the features of a villain. The kids have seen their idol shattered and their dreams broken." Ruth, who saw himself as a role model, despite needing the cooperation of the media to hide some flaws from children, felt the chastisement sharply. He began to sob and vowed on the spot to change his ways.[70] "Tomorrow I'm going to my farm," he began. "I'm going to work my head off—and maybe part of my stomach."[71] He chopped wood, watched his diet, and dropped about 20 pounds.

The 1923 season dawned after Huston had sold his portion of the team to Ruppert, who then owned the team outright. Huston had offered sympathy and support to Ruth in the past, but now the slugger was left to fight his own battles against, for example, manager Huggins.[72] On Opening Day, though, such conflicts were in the distant future. Michael Gershman wrote of the thrilling unveiling of Yankee Stadium, the first big league setting to be called a "stadium," in their home opener of April 18, 1923, an event that had "all the pomp and circumstance befitting the new king of baseball stadiums. Before, the largest crowd to watch a baseball game had been the 47,373 at Game 2 of the 1916 World Series at Braves Field."[73]

The massive park dwarfed its rivals with its 58,000 seating capacity, but the attendance figure listed by the *New York Times* of 74,200 with another 25,000 turned away, was padded, even if the stadium was bulging at the seams with a standing-room-only crowd. The fans were rewarded with a 4-1 win over Ruth's former Red Sox team.

Earlier, McGraw's Giants, landlords of the Polo Grounds, had grown disgusted at being outdrawn by the Yankees, so they evicted them. The Giants believed that by banishing them, the Yanks would wind up exiled to an outer borough of the city. Instead, they situated their new facility in the Bronx, just across the Harlem River from the Polo Grounds, a mere subway hop away. Ruppert, realizing that Ruth could pack 'em in, had Yankee Stadium built on a grand scale—it was the first triple-decked park—and his team continued to outdraw the Giants. To further grind it in, the Yanks won the 1923 Series, taking three of their four victories at the Polo Grounds.

Credit was given to Fred Lieb of the *Evening Telegram* for dubbing the stadium, "The House that Ruth Built." It cost $2,500,000 and took 284 working days, about the same amount of time as the gestation period for humans, to build the stadium—Ruth's creation, so to speak. A great deal of the money that fans had pumped into the Yankees' coffers was subsequently spent to give life to the grand structure. Gershman quoted the *Times*, "In the third inning with two mates on the base lines, Babe Ruth smashed a savage home run into the right field bleachers, and that was the real baptism of Yankee Stadium." That section of the ballpark soon came to be known as Ruthville.[74] There was no way Ruth could even begin to guess the value of the ball he blasted that day. Some 75 years later, a buyer plunked down $126,500 to purchase that piece of memorabilia.

With his home run, Ruth sent the message that he was back, and wary pitchers soon began to walk him at an astounding clip. He did, in fact, wind up with 170 bases on balls, the most in the chronicles of the game to that point and for decades to come. Fans griped that they had paid to see their hero hit, not trot to first. According to Robert Smith, "A few sportswriters urged that the intentional walk be outlawed so fans would get their money's worth." Those words would be echoed decades later when Barry Bonds received a plethora of walks.[75]

Reporter John C. Tatpersall tracked Ruth's intentional walks, coming up with 80 on the year. St. Louis was the stingiest in that department and Ruth punished them to the tune of 10 homers over 20 games. Cleveland gave him a munificent 21 intentional passes and surrendered the fewest homers of any club that year, only four. Over one span, the Indians walked him on purpose six times over two days.

Prior to a team meeting when the Pirates had to face Ruth years later (in 1935), former Yankee teammate Waite Hoyt was asked how they should handle the aging Ruth. Hoyt calmly explained that "the best way to pitch to Ruth is to pitch behind him. He has no weaknesses except for deliberate walks. You have your choice—one base on four balls, or four bases on one ball." The pitchers weren't listening—Ruth jacked three homers that day.[76]

Of the 1923 season, Tatpersall wrote, "Time after time that season Ruth was intentionally passed if first base was open, or if any base was open, in order to pitch to [Wally] Pipp, considered a much safer risk."[77] However, on September 26, Lou Gehrig broke up that strategy with a "shadow of things to come" when he slugged a three-run double after Ruth had been pitched around.[78]

The original dimensions of Yankee Stadium featured a friendly distance of 294¾ feet to the right-field foul pole, a cozy target for Ruth, but a four-bagger to the deepest spot in left, in the area that became known as "Death Valley," had to travel around 500 feet from home plate.

Ruth won his only MVP Award, then called the League Trophy award, in 1923. There had been no official AL MVPs from 1915 to 1921 and from 1929 to 1930, and he was denied MVP consideration from 1924 to 1928 due to an ill-conceived rule stating a previous League Trophy winner could not win it again.

Ruth established a new league record when he reached base a total of 379 times, meaning he was on base 54.5 percent of all his trips to the plate, a record for years to come. He felt he had atoned for his lackluster 1922 output. The Yankees won the flag again thrusting them into their third consecutive Series clash with the Giants. Almost exactly half of the Yankees roster consisted of players plundered from Boston during the Frazee regime. The Giants fell in six despite the fact that McGraw's pitchers again worked Ruth carefully, walking him eight times. When he got a pitch to handle, though, he made good.

This time Babe truly felt he had earned his $6,160 winners' portion of the World Series pot. And it felt good to deprive McGraw of another title. The Sultan of Swat scored a team high eight times with three solo shots to go with his .368 average. Ruth would later look back upon this as his finest season of all.

In some ways the 1924 season was a mixed bag. Physically, Ruth began slipping back to his old ways, his promise to Jimmy Walker seemingly now forgotten. It was the time period when the Babe "began to nurture the beer belly that eventually became his trademark."[79] Ruth still enjoyed a fine season statistically. Just one year earlier he hit his career high of .393 but fell short of the batting title to Harry Heilman's .403, costing him a Triple Crown. Given a bit more speed, Ruth may have gained four infield hits, enough to make him a .400 hitter. In 1924, his average dipped, yet he won his only batting title when he attacked the ball to a .378 clip. Oddly enough, he led the league in average and strikeouts in the same year—only he and Jimmie Foxx ever did this.

In addition, he flirted once more with a Triple Crown, topping the AL in homers while finishing behind only Goose Goslin in RBIs, 129 to 121. As usual, Ruth led the league in a ton of offensive categories. However, despite Ruth's numbers, the dynastic Yanks faltered to second place. The Senators, a team that would later gain a reputation for being a perennial loser—"Washington: first in war, first in peace, and last in the American League"—managed to knock off the Yanks, finishing a scant, tantalizing two games ahead of them.

Ruth's behavior was far from stellar. One 1924 tale has manager Huggins telling Bob Connery, a scout, that he was about to fine and suspend Ruth, but the next day Babe drove two homers. Connery said, "You said you were going to fine and suspend him." Huggins mumbled, "Hell, no. How can I fine and suspend him the way he played today."[80] Interestingly, in 1924, when Connie Mack purchased Lefty Grove from the minor league Orioles of Jack Dunn, Ruth's first employer, he dished out $100,600, tossing in the penny ante extra $600 to break the former record of $100,000 the Yankees announced that they had forked over to obtain Ruth.[81]

NOTES

1. Creamer, *Babe*, 253–254.

2. Vaccaro, *Emperors and Idiots*, 46.

3. Creamer, *Babe*, 210.

4. Vaccaro, *Emperors and Idiots*, 61.

5. Fetter, *Taking on the Yankees*, 46.

6. Ibid., 53.

7. Vaccaro, *Emperors and Idiots*, 57.

8. Ruth, with Slocum, *The Babe and I*, 62.

9. Terry Francona, from interview with author, June 21, 2005.

10. Vaccaro, *Emperors and Idiots*, 54.

11. Ibid., 56.

12. From a Baseball Hall of Fame news release, January 5, 2005.

13. Ritter, *The Babe*, 62.

14. Terry Francona, from interview with author, June 21, 2005.

15. From www.baseballlibrary.com.

16. Burns, *Baseball.*

17. Elliot Kalb, *Who's Better, Who's Best in Baseball?: Mr. Stats Sets the Record Straight on the Top 75 Players of All Time* (New York: McGraw-Hill, 2005), 22.

18. Smith, *Babe Ruth's America*, 77, 82.

19. Julia Ruth Stevens, from interviews with author, November 2005.

20. Eric Enders, *Ballparks Then and Now* (San Diego: Thunder Bay Press, 2005), 25–26.

21. Pirone and Martens, *My Dad, the Babe*, 20.

22. Koppett, *Koppett's Concise History of Major League Baseball*, 140.

23. Jack Kavanagh and Norman Macht, *Uncle Robbie* (Cleveland: The Society for American Baseball Research, 1999), 118.

24. Ruth and Considine, *The Babe Ruth Story*, 120.

25. Pirone and Martens, *My Dad, the Babe*, 54–55.

26. Charles C. Alexander, *Our Game: An American Baseball History* (New York: Henry Holt and Company, Inc., 1991), 118.

27. Thorn and Holway, *The Pitcher*, 10.

28. Schwarz, *The Numbers Game*, 47–48.

29. Ibid.

30. Thorn and Holway, *The Pitcher*, 10.

31. Ibid., 11.

32. Schwarz, *The Numbers Game*, 47

33. Smith, *Babe Ruth's America*, 91.

34. Ruth, with Slocum, *The Babe and I*, 135.

35. Waite Hoyt, *Babe Ruth As I Knew Him* (New York: Dell, 1948), 7.

36. Hugh S. Fullerton, "Why Babe Ruth is the Greatest Home Run Hitter," *Popular Science Monthly*, October 21, 1921, 20–21, 110.

37. Fetter, *Taking on the Yankees*, 51.

38. Ruth, with Slocum, *The Babe and I*, 66.

39. Schwarz, *The Numbers Game*, 43, 49.

40. Ruth and Considine, *The Babe Ruth Story*, 90.

41. Schwarz, *The Numbers Game*, 49.

42. From www.baseballlibrary.com.

43. Eig, *Luckiest Man*, 51.

44. Harwell, *The Babe Signed My Shoe*, 98–99.

45. Vass, "Remarkable One-Season Performances," 22.

46. Ruth, with Slocum, *The Babe and I*, 60.

47. Smith, *Babe Ruth's America*, 116.

48. Ruth and Considine, *The Babe Ruth Story*, 97–98.

49. Ritter, *The Babe*, 96.

50. Smith, *Babe Ruth's America*, 120, 121.

51. Kavanagh and Macht, *Uncle Robbie*, 113.

52. From www.baseballalmanac.com.

53. From www.baseballlibrary.com.

54. Creamer, *Babe*, 259.

55. Pirone and Martens, *My Dad, the Babe*, 32.

56. From www.baseballlibrary.com.

57. Ruth, *Babe Ruth's Own Book of Baseball*, 16–17.

58. Kelley, *In the Shadow of the Babe*, 190.

59. Bob Feller, from telephone interview with author, 1999.

60. Ibid.

61. Ibid.

62. Wayne Stewart, *Pitching Secrets of the Pros: Big-League Hurlers Reveal the Tricks of Their Trade* (New York: McGraw-Hill, 2004), 151.

63. Ibid., 151–152.

64. Pirone and Martens, *My Dad, the Babe*, 22–25.

65. Linda Ruth Tosetti, from telephone interview with author, September 23, 2005.

66. Ibid.

67. Pirone and Martens, *My Dad, the Babe*, 194–196.

68. Linda Ruth Tosetti, from telephone interview with author, September 23, 2005.

69. Ritter, *The Babe*, 97.

70. Ibid., 99.

71. Creamer, *Babe*, 275.

72. Smith, *Babe Ruth's America*, 139, 140.

73. Michael Gershman, *Diamonds: The Evolution of the Ballpark* (Boston: Houghton Mifflin Company, 1993), 138.

74. Ibid.

75. Smith, *Babe Ruth's America*, 141.

76. Hoyt, *Babe Ruth as I Knew Him*, 33.

77. From Babe Ruth Museum archives.

78. From Babe Ruth Museum archives.

79. Ritter, *The Babe*, 101.

80. Creamer, *Babe*, 279.

81. Thorn and Holway, *The Pitcher*, 206.

Ruth in his early years with the New York Yankees. *National Baseball Hall of Fame Library, Cooperstown, N.Y.*

THE COLLAPSE AND REVIVAL
OF RUTH, 1925–1926

In 1925, the nation focused on evolution during the Scopes Monkey Trial, a controversial case featuring a battle between leviathan lawyers William Jennings Bryan and Clarence Darrow, who represented a Tennessee teacher named John T. Scopes. Scopes had dared to violate a new law that forbade any theory that refuted the Bible's concept of Devine Creation.

Ruth, oblivious to such social issues, found that 1925 was also a year, like 1922, of devolution—ironic in that statistics elsewhere were juiced and home-run output was firecracker hot, shooting up from 338 eight years earlier to 1,167. In the minors, future Yankee Tony Lazzeri became the first man to tee off for 60 homers in pro ball and he drove in a fantastic 222 runs.

Overall scoring had boomed as well, despite improvements to fielders' gloves, which helped errors decrease by almost 10 percent over that same eight-year span. A Columbia University scientist analyzed the baseball used in 1925, comparing and contrasting it to those used in 1914. He discovered the balls' design and composition were unchanged but the materials in the 1925 baseballs "were of a higher quality," and even the Spalding company conceded that, "but nothing more."[1]

Ruth, dwelling on his plight, recognized his professional collapse, but blamed "outside forces" for helping his fall. He confessed he wasn't strong enough to overcome many temptations. He seems to have recognized that he was surrounded by hangers-on, sycophants, and parasites, but he still tried, not merely to burn the candle at both ends, but to incinerate it.[2]

As Ruth went, so went the team, and the Yankees skidded badly that year, finishing next to last, ahead of only the Red Sox whose won-loss percentage was a dismal .309. The Yanks had stumbled a remote 28½ games behind the Senators, 16 below .500. The 1925 team was the last Yankee team to finish in the second division until 1965, and between 1918 and 1965, they'd finish lower than third in only 1925 and 1945. Not only that, except for the anomalous 1925 season, the Yanks outdrew the rival Giants every single year but one until the "G-men" moved to San Francisco.[3]

Ruth was no longer the trim boy who left St. Mary's bound for fame. One writer said that Ruth "looked like a beer keg on stilts."[4] When he reported to Hot Springs, Arkansas, to get into shape for the upcoming season, he made the scales cringe with his weight of around 250, said to be the highest weight of his playing days, well over his more suitable playing weight of around 215.[5]

Despite his expanding midriff and the first hint of sickness in the Florida camp, he got off to a fine start. In late March, the squad broke camp and headed north for additional tune-up games, playing, as usual, in southern ballparks with a segregated seating policy. Ruth homered twice in Birmingham and doubled and tripled in Nashville. Then, in Atlanta, troubles began when he felt ill "with the shaking chills," and had to call the hotel doctor in the middle of the night.[6]

In Claire's biography of Ruth, she stated his illness began earlier that day when he slid violently into first base, injuring his groin. She wrote that back then it was indelicate to speak of such injuries, so the team fabricated the story of "the big bellyache" to describe Ruth's situation.[7]

Ruth, running a temperature of about 102, was instructed to sit out the game in Chattanooga, but he said he had an obligation to his fans and insisted upon suiting up. Five innings and two home runs later, Ruth taxied back to his hotel. He also played in Knoxville, despite suffering from stomach cramps and a fever. There, after striking out against Brooklyn's Dazzy Vance, the Babe hit another home run.[8]

The team's next stop was on April 8 in Asheville, North Carolina. At the train station, Ruth keeled over shortly after disembarking the train. If teammate Steve O'Neal hadn't caught him, Ruth's head would have smacked on the marble floor of the train station and done considerable damage. As it was, he did strike his head on his train's washbasin en route to New York, knocking himself out.

Ruth eventually wound up in St. Vincent's, a New York hospital, suffering from what the media called "the stomach ache [or bellyache] heard 'round the world." His problem truly was heard near and far—one London newspaper proclaimed "BABE RUTH DEAD" in a two-column story with a subtitle of "Expires of Overeating."

On April 17, according to conflicting sources, he underwent surgery for the groin problem, and an ulcer or an intestinal abscess. The public was fed pablum, being told Ruth had eaten too many hot dogs and washed them down with too much soda pop resulting in acute indigestion. Ruth required bed rest and a seven-week stay in the hospital, a place he loathed. Even when he visited children in hospitals, displaying a cheerful front, he'd come home depressed by the sadness and sickness he'd witnessed.[9]

He didn't make his shaky return to the line-up until June 1, doing so some 20 to 30 pounds lighter than before his setback. As late as August, the defending batting champ couldn't crack the .250 level, meaning at that point he was living out a dreaded baseball cliche; he was struggling to hit his weight. So, once more, as was the case in 1922 when he played in only 110 games, Ruth's stats suffered. In all, he'd play just 98 games and produce only 12 doubles, his lowest total since way back in 1917. Furthermore, he'd never again hit less than 12 until his final season in which he played a mere 28 contests. His home run total was 25, his weakest output since 1918; he would only hit fewer than 25 again in his final two seasons. Likewise, his 66 RBIs was less than lackluster and represented the worst total since he had become a full-time outfielder. In short, this year, one of the few in which he dipped below .300 (at .290) was a miserable one for the Bambino.

Things were so bad that on August 9 Huggins pinch hit for Ruth, sending Bobby Veach, a good hitter, but a man who had all 64 of his career homers and 36 years on earth behind him, to the plate in place of the 30-year-old "Bam." According to *Baseball Digest*, this was the only time in Ruth's career, excluding his pitching days, that a pinch hitter stepped to the plate in his stead. However, other sources list Ben Paschal as having hit for Ruth on Opening Day in 1927.[10]

There is a tendency for boxing promoters to give grandiloquent titles to bouts such as the Muhammad Ali-generated moniker, "The Thriller in Manilla." A fitting name for the power struggle between Ruth and Huggins in 1925 could have been "The Clash for Clout: Ruth vs. The Mighty Mite." At 5 feet 6 inches, Huggins was a scrappy survivor of 13 big league seasons. Huggins, who held a law degree from the University of Cincinnati, was described as a man who displayed fine leadership qualities, but leading Ruth was never an easy chore. It was almost inevitable that Huggins would come to resent and battle Ruth. For one thing, Huggins lacked the "size, athletic grace, and a certain rough charm" that Ruth exuded. He also hated the fact that Ruth wasted some of his talent as if it were so much loose change.[11]

The team's losing ways in 1925 helped foster dissension and anti-Huggins grumbling on the squad. With Ruth out of the line-up and then struggling with the bat upon his return, it wasn't shocking that the beleaguered Yankees plunged to seventh place. Nor was it surprising that when Huggins made line-up alterations, veterans squawked, with Ruth, who once publicly called Huggins incompetent, being among the most vociferous.

One of the more unbelievable instances of defiance towards a manager supposedly took place on a road trip when Ruth and Huggins were standing on the back of an observation car. Fed up with Huggins, who had recently ripped Bob Meusel and Babe, Ruth later claimed that he hoisted his manager in the air and over the train's rail.[12] That Ruth could get away with such behavior seems positively staggering. Perhaps he didn't—teammate Bob Shawkey said the story probably stemmed from a time Ruth and Meusel were teasing Huggins on a train ride, and while they did bang on his locked compartment door, nobody held anybody off a moving train.[13]

Ben Chapman who played in the same outfield as Ruth did for several seasons once quipped, "I've heard people say the Yankees had one set of rules for Ruth and another set for everyone else. That's not true. There were no rules for Ruth." Even Dorothy wrote that her father tried his best to break existing team rules.[14]

There were limits, though, even for Ruth. On August 29, not too long after the alleged train incident, the culmination of the Ruth Rebellion came to pass. Confident he could continue to behave any way he chose, Ruth had stayed out all night two times running and went AWOL from his team's hotel, the Buckingham. (By this time period Ruth did stay in the same hotel as his teammates, but in an opulent suite.) He was said to have spent those nights at his favorite St. Louis brothel.

Huggins, finally thoroughly disgusted with Ruth's behavior, reportedly had been waiting for another infraction of the rules by Ruth to flex his muscles and this was it. In a way, Ruth had been set up. Huggins had asked Yankees owner Jacob Ruppert and Yankees executive Ed Barrow ahead of time if he had their blessings to confront and deal harshly with the Babe. When he was given approval to penalize Ruth in the way he saw fit, the stage was set.

In St. Louis, when Ruth showed up late at the park, well after batting practice was over, an apoplectic Huggins confronted him. He immediately ignored Ruth's knee-jerk apology, and exploded, telling his star not to bother suiting up. Continuing his tirade, Huggins informed Ruth that he was tired of his behavior and feeble excuses and then slapped him with a whopping $5,000 fine while notifying him he was suspended indefinitely. It was to be a suspension that cost Ruth a reported additional $26,000 in lost wages. To put the severity of the fine in today's terms, if Alex Rodriguez was smacked with a fine equivalent to Ruth's, he'd be out $2,471,153.85, based on his 2005 salary of $25.7 million. Former Yankee John Olerud pointed out that today a manager couldn't go as far as Huggins did "because I'm sure there would be grievances filed with the union."[15]

Ruth threatened physical violence and shouted that he would, in effect, run to Mama by going over Huggins' head to complain to team owner Ruppert. At that point, Huggins barked that he wanted Ruth to go ahead and "bust into Ruppert's office, carrying that .246 average and telling him I'm picking on you." Despite Ruth's protestations and vows never to play for Huggins again in a "it's him or me" scenario, the front office remained steadfast in their support of Huggins, saying they had hired detectives to follow Ruth and knew all about his indiscretions.[16]

Soon after, a chastened Ruth left a meeting with Ruppert and general manager Barrow, and faced the press, having been informed he would play again only when Huggins said so. Ruppert told the press that Ruth had changed his mind and, turning to Ruth, forced him to give the schoolboy reply to his question: "Haven't you, Ruth?" Shamefacedly, he surrendered; he had indeed decided to play ball with Ruppert and Huggins.

Ruth eventually issued an apology to his skipper, who initially refused to listen to Ruth's protestations. "I'm not impressed with his apologies and his promises to be good," said Huggins grimly. "I've heard them before, and I'm tired of them."[17] Huggins eventually accepted an apology, but mandated that Ruth serve up his *mea culpa* in front of the entire team. Even then, Huggins sat Ruth one additional day before he was permitted to return to the line-up after nine days of exile, on September 7. A seemingly contrite Ruth, promising to do better, returned to the line-up with a whimper, eking out a hit in a 5-1 loss to Boston. The next day found Ruth back in form when he smoked a ball for career homer number 300. As impressive a plateau as that was, Ruth still had 58 percent of his eventual lifetime total ahead of him; he was hardly washed up despite his woeful off-season.

Meusel wound up leading the team, and the league, in homers with 33 and RBI at 138. Ruth's mere 25 homers in this aberration of a season was still good for a second-place tie in the league. This was also the year that Ruth officially split from Helen who had long realized their marriage was a sham. On August 4, after living apart for seven months, Ruth agreed to a separation that called for him to award a gargantuan sum of $100,000 to her as well as the custody of their 4-year-old daughter, Dorothy. In 1926, Helen would sell their Sudbury, Massachusetts, farm, pack up her belongings, depart their two-story colonial residence, and bolt to Watertown, a suburb of Boston.[18]

A $50,000 paternity suit, later dropped, but one of several during filed against Ruth during his younger day, hadn't help matters. Helen was finally fed up with her husband who had been guilty of infidelity, and who had compounded his indiscretions by "the manner in which he sometimes flaunted his adulteries." Still, when the Yankees were on the road in Boston, Ruth would bring Helen and Dorothy to his hotel, trying to play some semblance of "house" with his family.[19]

Things changed quickly in 1926. On the diamond, Ruth rebounded, finding solace in the routine of his game; his batting average rose 82 points from his 1925 season-long slumber. Likewise, his power numbers, 47 homers with 145

RBI, were up to his par once more. For the third time in four years, he narrowly missed winning a Triple Crown. And, for the first time since 1923, the Yankees were Series bound. They had gone from seventh place to winning the pennant, a sterling 31½ game turnabout.

By now, Lou Gehrig, who first was called up to the team in 1923 and again briefly in 1924, was beginning to establish his relationship with Ruth. The veteran slugger felt Gehrig admired him and had therefore been shy at first about socializing with him. Ruth said he grew to love Gehrig as if he were a brother and that he gave him countless hitting tips.[20] Of course, this was a relationship that would change over time, with Gehrig's emergence as a power hitter, and with an explosive incident that would occur years later.

A touching side note to the season was the Johnny Sylvester incident. Sylvester was an 11-year-old boy bedridden and suffering from osteomyelitis of the skull (although some sources say he suffered from a back problem) caused by a fall from a horse. When Johnny didn't seem to be improving, a colleague of his father, a vice president of a New York bank, brought the matter to the attention of the Yankees, and then Ruth got involved. Baseball lore has Ruth visiting the boy, vowing to homer in the Series for him; Ruth makes good on his promise and Sylvester rallies, bestowing a faith healer-like aura on Ruth.

However, that story is full of holes. Chairman of the Essex Fells History Committee and author Charles A. Poekel Jr., stated that while the story of Sylvester "is one of the most popular stories in all of sports, the facts have never been truly presented correctly."[21] Contrary to many versions, Ruth did not visit Sylvester in a hospital, but in his room in his home located on Roseland Avenue in Essex Fells, New Jersey. The visit took place on October 11, *after* the Series, and after all the homers—with "the publicity coup assured."[22]

There Ruth presented his autographed baseball and another ball signed by the St. Louis Cardinals. Ruth's visit made the front page of the *New York Times* the following day and is "still talked about in Essex Falls," according to Poekel.[23] Additionally, Ruth had not make his promise in person, rather he telegraphed his promise to slug a homer for Johnny.

Facts, such as the dates and location of his trek, didn't get in Ruth's way as he related how he had promised to make a trip from New York to the Sylvester residence on October 1, the day before the Series was scheduled to begin. Some sources have the Series beginning the day of the visit to Sylvester and claim that Ruth drilled a home run that same day, but Ruth did not homer in Game 1 on October 2. He didn't connect until Game 4 in St. Louis on the October 6, and his homer in New York wasn't until the Series finale on October 10.

Because the ball he gave to Sylvester is inscribed "I'll knock a homer for Wednesday's game" as if the game had yet to take place, Ruth apparently was going along with the publicity stunt, making it sound as if he was signing the ball before the Series started. No doubt he chose to predict a homer on Wednesday because that was the day he had already hit three homers against the Cardinals. Greg Schwalenberg, curator of the Ruth Museum, said his understanding, though, was that Ruth "signed the ball and his prediction, and the ball was sent to Johnny's house before Wednesday's game."[24]

Ruth also later wrote that Johnny began to improve from the time of his visit on, with every homer giving the boy additional strength. The home runs, wrote Babe, "were 'his.'" Ruth said he kept in touch with the boy who grew up to serve on a Navy submarine in World War II. Years later, when Ruth was nearing death, Sylvester was one of just a few callers permitted to see the Babe.[25]

Author Paul Gallico described Ruth's entry into Sylvester's room dramatically, comparing Ruth to God entering the room attired "in a camel's hair polo coat and a flat, camel's hair cap, God with a flat nose and little piggy eyes, a big grin, and a fat black cigar sticking out of the side of it."[26]

One thing, said Ruth's daughter Julia, is for sure, "There were other days when he didn't hit home runs, but he always seemed to come through *just* at the most critical and dramatic moment."[27] At any rate, on October 6, Ruth, as hot as an incinerator, had become the first man to clobber three home runs in a World Series contest. He would match this feat two years later, but nobody else achieved such Series glamour until Reggie Jackson in 1977.

Ruth and his Yankees lit up Flint Rhem, a 20-game winner that season, and a parade of four other pitchers in a 10-5 win. Waite Hoyt went the distance, flirting with disaster, serving up 14 hits but stranding 10 Cardinals. Ruth's third blast of the day, the first time he'd ever hit more than two in any contest, was called the longest homer ever lashed in St. Louis. The bottle rocket of a shot not only left the park, flying over a 20-foot wall in center field, but it took on the shape of a parabola as majestic as that of the Gateway Arch, and finally rested only after shattering a window of an auto dealer across the street.

Ruth's overall stats for the Series were solid but not spectacular. He hit an even .300, but his homers were good only for five runs batted in, his lone RBIs of the Series. He did lead his team in runs and runs driven in, but the way the seventh game ended made the Fall Classic an ignominious one for Ruth. He reached base in the ninth inning on his eleventh free pass of the Series and decided to steal, dashing for second on the first pitch. The move failed. Aside from Ruth, no man has ever been caught stealing to end a World Series. Making matters worse, he represented the tying run, but threw that opportunity away when he was gunned out by Bob O'Farrell. Ruth later granted that his steal attempt was his own decision and was a rash one at that. Although sluggers Meusel and Gehrig were due to bat next, Ruth believed that the steal made sense because it was an unexpected move and would put the potential tying run in scoring position.[28] Nevertheless, the disappointing Series loss was to be the last time the Yankees departed postseason play as the loser until 1942 when the Cardinals would again defeat them.

In the off-season Ruth picked up additional loot, reportedly $8,333 per week, or $100,000 in all, more than stars such as W.C. Fields or Al Jolson ever commanded by appearing for 12 weeks on the prestigious Pantages vaudeville circuit.[29] Schwalenberg stated, "You see some of these great photographs of him in these old-time bathing suits on the stage. To think that Ruth would do that kind of stuff. But he was a natural for that; he loved it."[30] Although he was far from being a polished singer or dancer, he was a great performer and the ham in him permitted him to put on a quite a show.

NOTES

1. Alexander, *Our Game*, 137, 139.

2. Ruth and Considine, *The Babe Ruth Story*, 131.

3. Fetter, *Taking on the Yankees*, 87.

4. Quoted by Miller, *The Babe Book*, 48, from Stan Hochman, *Philadelphia Daily News*, August 1998.

5. Smith, *Babe Ruth's America*, 152.

6. Ibid.

7. Ruth, with Slocum, *The Babe and I*, 86–87.

8. Ibid.

9. Ibid., 116.

10. Simons, "They Pinch-Hit for the Greats," 8–9.

11. Eig, *Luckiest Man*, 43.

12. Ruth and Considine, *The Babe Ruth Story*, 136.

13. Creamer, *Babe*, 299–300.

14. Pirone and Martens, *My Dad, the Babe*, 203.

15. John Olerud, from interview with author, June 21, 2005.

16. Ruth and Considine, *The Babe Ruth Story*, 136–139.

17. Creamer, *Babe*, 299–300.

18. Pirone and Martens, *My Dad, the Babe*, 38.

19. Smith, *Babe Ruth's America*, 180–181.

20. Ruth and Considine, *The Babe Ruth Story*, 143.

21. Charles A. Poekel Jr., from telephone interview with author, 2005.

22. Eig, *Luckiest Man*, 80–81.

23. Charles A. Poekel Jr., from telephone interview with author, 2005.

24. Greg Schwalenberg, from interview with author, September 7, 2005.

25. Ruth and Considine, *The Babe Ruth Story*, 172–174.

26. Ritter, *The Babe*, 137–138.
27. Julia Ruth Stevens, from interviews with author, November 2005.
28. Ruth and Considine, *The Babe Ruth Story*, 149–150.
29. Eig, *Luckiest Man*, 81.
30. Greg Schwalenberg, from interview with author, September 7, 2005.

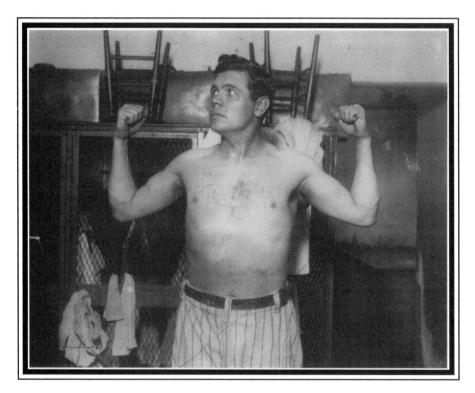

Ruth in a typical humorous pose in front of his Yankees locker. *National Baseball Hall of Fame Library, Cooperstown, N.Y.*

WHAT A RIDE, 1927–1932

If 1926 marked the revival of Ruth, then 1927 was, in many ways, the apex of the man. It was to be a wild ride indeed for the Yankees and Ruth. By now, Ruth's salary had reached an insanely high level. On March 3, 1927, Ruth signed a three-year contract at $70,000 per season. To put Ruth's salary in a better perspective, Robert W. Creamer sited the salaries of other Yankees of the famous 1927 squad. "After Ruth, at $70,000, the next highest paid player was Pennock, at $17,500. Meusel made $13,000, Dugan and Hoyt $12,000, [Earle] Combs $10,000 [one source has him at $19,500]. Gehrig made $8,000 [which was about the average per man after subtracting Ruth's hefty pay], Lazzeri $8,000, [Mark] Koenig $7,000. Wilcy Moore, who won 19 games, got $3,000."[1]

Plus, with his outside interests, it's safe to estimate his income at around a quarter of a million dollars. Even after his "agent," Christy Walsh, and the government got their shares of the pot—taxes were not a major factor back then with one report stating he owed a measly $1,500 income tax on his salary of $70,000 for a tax rate just a tad over 2 percent—Ruth lugged home somewhere around $180,000 at a time when many people in the country were struggling. It's been written that Ruth's lifetime baseball income was $1,076,474 with an additional $1,000,000 or so in auxiliary earnings.[2] However, *The Sporting News* of August 25, 1948, stated Ruth's total salaries were $925,900.

In May, Helen Ruth moved in with a man named Dr. Edward Kinder and had sent Dorothy away to a boarding school. The 7-year-old girl complained that her parents never visited her, ironically much the same way as Babe's parents had shuffled him off to St. Mary's and virtually forgotten him.[3] She also complained that her father seldom took her to Yankee Stadium, but would occasionally take her on a road trip. In short, she called him "a good father, given the circumstances. He never deliberately neglected me, and I know he loved me very much. He was just uncomfortable showing it."[4] Her assessment seems to point out yet another irony of Babe's personality: he loved children and lavished time and attention on them, yet seemed a bit frugal with the love he doled out to his own daughter. On the other hand, Dorothy's daughter, Linda Tosetti, paints a playful father portrait of Ruth: "He pulled a puppy out of his raccoon coat for my mother and he'd throw the coat on her—it used to make her collapse, it was so heavy and she was built so tiny."

Because 1927 was such a huge year for Ruth at the plate, a note on the bats he used is in order here. Bill Williams of the Hillerich and Bradsby Company, producers of the famous Louisville Slugger line of bats, stated that previously "players used much heavier bats. Babe Ruth used 40-ounce bats in 1927 when he hit 60 homers."[5] Another source disagrees, claiming Ruth actually used a 47-ounce hickory "stick" for the majority of his record-setting homers.[6]

He would insist on getting bats with small "pin knots" in the barrel, believing that "added distance" to his hits. When he took to using a 44-ouncer, it measured 36 inches in length. Even his original 1914 bats weighed in at a cumbersome 48 ounces and at times he took cuts with 50- and 52-ounce war clubs. It has also been written that he once (and one must imagine only once and probably only in practice) wielded a 56-ounce bat.[7]

In his 1928 autobiography, he stated that a few years earlier he had used a 54-ounce bat and that he was then swinging a 46-ounce war club "and each season when I have a new set of bats made, I have an additional ounce taken off."[8] Ruth clearly wielded a heavy bat and used his enormous strength to do so effectively.

Eventually, his bats dropped down in weight to the 36-ounce weapon for his final year in the majors. His favorite club, a black model, was the one he called "Black Betsy," a bat he claims lasted almost three years before breaking.[9] By way of contrast, Hank Aaron was comfortable with 31- and 32-ounce bats. According to Robert K. Adair, after Ruth only two men, Ernie Lombardi and the enormously strong Dick Allen, used bats over 40 ounces in the majors. Pictures of Ruth show him grasping his bat with part of his bottom hand wrapped under the bat's knob, a ploy several modern sluggers have used.

As a final note on bats, and as another point of contrast, Ruth once used a special bat he called "one of those trick things made out of four separate sections, pasted and fitted together," which he loved. However, when Yankee owner Jacob Ruppert learned they cost $6 each, a pittance by today's standards, he was floored. Incidentally, a few days after Ruth's initial success with the bat in a game in which he pounded out four hits, including a home run, a manager

pointed out Ruth was using an illegal bat and the umpires banned it.[10] Another source says it was league president Ban Johnson who ruled the bats illegal and had them confiscated.

Twenty-one years after the glorious ride of 1927, Ruth himself called the Murderers' Row squad the greatest team ever. It was to be a sensational year in many respects. Early into the 1927 baseball season, on May 21, Charles Lindbergh completed his nonstop, solo flight from New York to Paris in 33½ hours, a heroic feat that made him one of only a few others to vie for headlines with Ruth and Company that year.

The term "Murderers' Row" was first coined in baseball for the 1919 Yankees by cartoonist Robert Ripley who later gained fame for his "Believe it or Not" cartoons. The 1927 Yankee bats were much more lethal and famous than that of such 1919 stars as Frank Baker, Roger Peckinpaugh, and first baseman Wally Pipp, the man who lost his job to the iron man Gehrig when Pipp figuratively called in sick one day due to a headache.[11]

The Yankees did what pennant winners are supposed to do: they played .500 ball or better against other contenders while obliterating second division teams. They took 21 of 22 versus the hapless St. Louis Browns, for example. When the dust cleared, the Yanks had set league records with their celestial 110 wins and their .714 (coincidentally the same number as Ruth's final home run total) won-loss percentage, only 6 wins and .049 percentage points shy of the single season records set by the NL's Chicago Cubs of 1906, and, through 2005, still the third best percentage in AL play. The slugging Yanks became famous for their trademark late-inning power displays. Writers began to call these uncanny occurrences, "five-o'clock lightning."[12]

They not only led the league from wire-to-wire, a rarity; they clinched the flag by Labor Day with a commanding lead of 24 games when only 23 contests remained on the schedule, good then for yet another astonishing, yet obscure record.[13] When Ruth starched a new record 60 homers, he readily gave credit to Lou Gehrig, who hit 47, for giving him excellent protection in the line-up. Pitchers realized if they walked Ruth, they'd still have to face a dangerous Gehrig.

According to a story Dick Miller told to *The Sporting News*, Ruth ordained a change in the Yankees batting order. When Tony Lazzeri had been hitting behind Ruth, pitchers issued nearly 150 walks each year to the Bambino. Finally, when Joe McCarthy became the Yankees manager, Ruth walked over to him and said, "I'll tell you how to make out the lineup. I'm going to bat third and I want Gehrig behind me. You can fill in the other seven spots." Reportedly McCarthy replied, "That's fine with me, Babe."

It's a fine story, illustrative of Ruth's clout as a superstar, but it wasn't an accurate anecdote. McCarthy first managed the Yankees in 1931 and Gehrig clearly hit in the cleanup slot before then. For example, on September 10, 1925, Meusel went deep and was followed by Ruth then Gehrig for back-to-back-to-back shots. In the 1926 World Series, Meusel, not Gehrig, followed Ruth, but by the next Series, Gehrig was entrenched in the cleanup slot behind the Babe.

Clearly, the Iron Horse was the antithesis of the Babe. Gehrig was forever the steady, conservative homebody. It was therefore only natural that he'd look down on Ruth's philandering ways. He also resented Ruth's criticism of Huggins, a man Gehrig would call "that wonderful little fellow" in his famous farewell speech, a speech that praised everyone from fans to groundskeepers, but did not mention Ruth. Ruth and Gehrig were often bridge partners, and they were indeed a peculiar pair—Ruth made wild bids and couldn't relate at all to Gehrig's cautious play.[14]

Ruth, according to Waite Hoyt, who called the majority of the Yankees of 1927 a bevy of night owls, was the team's social director. He would rent out a hotel suite then "put on a red robe and a pair of Moroccan slippers, and hold court for anyone interested in a good time. He had plenty of company. There were always women in the Ruth suite, and they were not the sort who required seduction."[15]

At this point in the Ruth-Gehrig relationship, Babe was still on record as saying he liked and admired Gehrig, but he still couldn't help getting in a dig about Gehrig's college education, then unusual for baseball players. Actually, many of the players who did not attend college perceived those who did as "eggheads," and mocked them.

Even if there had been no professional jealousy between the two men, the media paid close attention to the race to win the home run derby in 1927. The newspapers ran a "home-run barometer" to record day-to-day updates on the two stars' statistics.[16] Gehrig led for part of the year; for instance, on July 5, he had 28 while Ruth had 25, and at the end of July Gehrig was ahead by one. On August 25, Ruth led by a narrow 40 to 39 margin. With 23 games left on the schedule both power hitters had 44 homers, and Gehrig was tied with him as late as September 6 before the Babe swiftly surpassed his teammate. By September 11, Ruth stood 10 homers shy of the 60 strata. In all, Ruth parked 17 that month—helping overcome his mere four homers in April—to easily outdistance Gehrig's final total of 47 round trippers.[17]

Those 17 home runs are still the highest total for any month by a lefty (tied with Barry Bonds) and his 32 homers hit on the road remains an AL high-water mark. Finally, he topped off his sizzling September with 43 RBIs, also still the league high for that month. Ruth had out-homered every major league team but four—the Yanks and three NL clubs.

The excitement Ruth stirred had neared its climax on September 29 when he slashed two home runs to tie his own record of 59 round trippers in a season, and his Yankees shellacked Washington 15-4. Then, he did it, notching number 60 with a game to spare. Ruth was the undisputed monarch of home runs. As an oddity, his 60th came in the same game in which Walter Johnson made his final appearance, pinch hitting in the ninth, flying out to Ruth.

Trailing Gehrig in third place for AL homers was yet another Yankee, Tony Lazzeri, who managed a relatively meager 18. In all, AL players produced 439 homers helped by a new big league record 158 by Yankees. Incredibly, Ruth and Gehrig accounted for nearly 25 percent of all AL round trippers.

Tom Zachary, the Washington Senators pitcher who surrendered the historic bomb to Babe, was quoted as saying, "After I served him four balls in the first inning, I said to myself, 'Well, Babe, if you want to hit any homers today, you'd better start swinging.' I had made up my mind I wasn't going to give him a good pitch all afternoon." Zachary contended he threw a high curve that was aimed like a beanball "straight at him" because he wanted to back Ruth off the plate. Instead Ruth's eyes lit up and he lunged for the ball. Said Zachary, "I don't see yet how he did it."[18]

Another account said the curve that Ruth scalded snapped off briskly "six inches inside the plate and low, and the big fellow altered his swing, which was half way completed, to meet the change in the path of the ball. When Ruth finally hit the ball, he hit it off his shoe tops and golfed it into the right field bleachers...."[19] How two writers can differ so much on the location of the pitch is typical of many discrepancies regarding Ruth's accomplishments.

One thing about this feat that remains unquestioned is Ruth's take on his record-setting showing. When he was in the clubhouse after the game, he bellowed, "Sixty, count 'em, sixty! Let's see some other son-of-a-bitch match that!" The quote, including the unintended inference that he, too, was a "son of a bitch," was typical of the Babe. He reveled in the moment and took delight in his remarkable feats. He stroked 41 of his homers that season off right-handed pitchers, and Ruth, in Old West gunslinger fashion, put notches in his bat after each homer until that famous bat split with 21 tally marks etched on it.

Just three years after Ruth's mutinous act, when he supposedly held Huggins off a moving train, he wrote that Huggins' job of managing in the 1927 World Series vividly revealed "that baseball men don't come any smarter than Miller Huggins." As evidence, he recalled how the skipper had orchestrated the Yankees workout the day before the Series opened. Many of the Pittsburgh Pirates, finished with their practice session, were dressed and sitting in the stands to observe the Yanks.

Ruth stated Huggins called over Pennock, who was about to throw batting practice, and ordered him to serve the ball up right over the plate so the Yankees line-up could show the Pirates "some real hitting."[20] As a result, Combs and

Koenig laced the ball and Ruth followed by pulverizing a pitch over the distant roof of Forbes Field's right field grandstand.

Legend has it Pirates such as Pie Traynor were agog. Ruth quotes him as saying, "Boy, did you ever see such hitting? They're even better than they're advertised!" Intimidated, the Pirate team "left the park that afternoon half licked before the series ever opened."[21] Ruth once added that one "could actually hear them gulp while they watched us."[22] The Yankees swept the Pirates.

As the 1928 season neared, Ruth predicted 61 home runs. "With Gehrig following me at the bat, most of the intentional pass stuff is eliminated, and as long as pitchers will pitch to me I see no reason why I shouldn't break my record." While he didn't fulfill his prophecy, by the end of June, Ruth's total of 30 had him on pace to shatter his own record.[23]

Certainly, Ruth was taken seriously when he spoke of the art of hitting. To listen to him was to believe he was an ardent student of baseball. Some find that hard to believe, as studying was hardly his forte, but he did share solid hitting tips. And while he stated he borrowed the batting approach of Joe Jackson, he advised young hitters to observe Ty Cobb and his stance, swing, and timing. Ruth felt that if he had adapted Cobb's approach, rather than his own lusty style, he would have added 100 points to his batting average.[24] As it was, Ruth did quite well (.342 lifetime, tenth best all-time) employing his "loose and easy" golf-type slight uppercut swing. He contrasted his style to that of Lou Gehrig, who Ruth felt hit "stiff-armed," with feet farther spread, and with a shorter stride.

Ruth also felt his cut, coming off a stance emphasizing his weight being evenly distributed, led to high flies as opposed to Gehrig's line drives. Sometimes, therefore, a well-hit smash by Gehrig might bound off the fence for a double whereas Ruth's towering blows would carry over the wall.[25] Ruth's self-analysis revealed he had, during his early years especially, a tendency to become overly anxious to take a healthy cut, often making him vulnerable to change-ups. Having discovered that flaw, he said he set out to work on that by taking hours of batting practice. Again, whether Ruth exaggerated his hours of study and toil or not is uncertain, but even if the word studious has never been applied to him, one could argue he did pay heed to the science of hitting.

In his 1928 autobiography, Ruth listed additional batting tips, from choking up (which he says he did on occasion) to breaking out of a slump (he would force himself to take the first pitch to combat his tendency to get over-anxious).[26] Some of the advice he gave was ironic, such as his insistence that young players must save their money—an apparent bit of "do as I say, not as I do" advice. Likewise, he told players that a primary lesson from his book was not to "fight with umpires. It's bad business!"[27]

Some of Ruth's peers did give him credit for putting thought into his game. Pitcher Elon "Chief" Hogsett spoke of Ruth's willingness to make adjustments as a hitter, saying he would move around in the box depending upon the situation. All hitters are different, of course, and men such as Rod Carew were famous for their adaptability while, early on, Tony Gwynn took the approach that to hit successfully was to "use a basic approach. Never change."[28] Hogsett remembered, "I'd catch Ruth kind of sneaking back away from the plate two or three inches laying for my sinker."[29]

By 1928, Ruth, now 33 years old, checked in at 230 pounds. Despite winning 101 contests, the Yankees had to scrape to win another pennant, eventually prevailing by 2½ games over Connie Mack's Athletics. It was the second time in the 1920s that the Yanks had won three consecutive pennants. The 1928 campaign was another fabulous season for Ruth. He broke his own fledgling home-run pace; by the 88th game of the year at the end of July he owned 41 home runs—still the best ever in AL play for that stretch of time. By season's end, he had walloped 54 homers and scored 163 times to go with his hardy 142 runs driven in. Through the 1928 season, 40-plus homers had been achieved in the annals of baseball on 10 occasions—a stellar seven times by Ruth. No wonder the Yanks had won the pennant six of the first nine years Ruth wore their uniform.

In the World Series versus St. Louis, Ruth went absolutely berserk with the bat, drilling three round trippers in Game 4 at Sportsman's Park on October 9. In the eighth inning, Ruth exacted some revenge against the Cards and pitcher Grover Alexander, who had stymied the Yanks in 1926, when he drove his third homer of the day. It was the second time he had done this in a Series contest; a record that still stands.

To be sure, the Series, a Yankees sweep, was a great one for Ruth as he hit .625. That figure stood as a record for the highest batting average in a Series until Cincinnati's Billy Hatcher hit .750 in 1990. Ruth further banged out 10 hits, which is still the most for a four-game set, as are his records from that World Series for scoring nine times while racking up 22 total bases.

In 1928, the Yankees first placed numbers on the backs of their uniforms. They became the first baseball team to start continuous use of the numbers to help fans recognize players and, for the most part, the players' corresponding positions in the batting order. That, of course, was why they announced in January that Ruth was to wear number 3 and cleanup hitter Gehrig number 4. By 1931, all the AL teams had numbers sewn on their jerseys; two years later the NL followed suit.

Only 11 days into 1929, Helen Woodford, the first Mrs. Babe Ruth, perished in her sleep from burns and suffocation due to a fire in her Watertown,

Massachusetts, residence. Firemen arrived to a house already filled with thick, billowy smoke; Helen's body eventually was found upstairs. Luckily, Dorothy, then 8 years of age, was at a boarding school at the time (she had complained of being lonely there, but that saved her life). Helen, only 31 years old, had been living with Dr. Kinder as his wife since 1927. Kinder was spared because he was at the Boston Garden watching a boxing match. His absence seemed suspicious to Helen's family who demanded a police investigation. Helen's mother insisted that her daughter "never died by accident; she was done to death." One of Helen's brothers, William, a former policeman, insisted the fire was set intentionally and that Helen "was drugged so she would not be able to escape."[30]

Eventually the fire was ruled accidental because Kinder had recently remodeled his house and defective wiring and the overloading of those wires caused the fire. Fuses of up to 30 amps were being used where 10-amp fuses should have been in use. A short-circuit took place and the fuses overheated the wires, thus starting the fire. New York editors pasted headlines such as: "BABE RUTH'S WIFE DIES IN FIRE AT SECRET LOVE-LIFE BUNGALOW." It wasn't until a second autopsy, precipitated by more pressure exerted by the Woodfords, was performed that a final ruling was issued and the matter laid to rest. The involvement of alcohol, drugs, and, more importantly, "foul play" was ruled out.[31]

After Helen's death, two nuns roused Dorothy from her sleep, informed her of the accident, and whisked her away from her boarding school, taking her to a New York hospital where she, once more, "was abandoned." Dorothy contended that her personality grew colder due to spending time in institutions "without any love or guidance." She was placed with a Miss Dooley, a hospital worker, where she'd stay for some time. Dorothy speculated that the cloak and dagger events came about as "an extra precaution, which my father took to ensure retaining custody of me. . . ."[32] Sure enough, five months later Babe finally claimed his daughter and informed her that his new love, Claire Hodgson, was soon to be her new mother. Those were trying times for Dorothy especially when Dooley, according to Linda Ruth Tosetti, Ruth's granddaughter, "was telling her that her name wasn't Dorothy Ruth any more. It must have been traumatic for a little girl; I'm surprised my mother was as stable as she was."[33]

At any rate, shortly after Helen's death, Ruth headed south to train, about a month before the full squad reported for spring training. He rained telephone calls on Claire, compiling a telephone bill of $1,600 by the time the exhibition season ended. Clearly he was hooked on Claire.[34] On April 17, 1929, at the Roman Catholic Church of St. Gregory the Great in Manhattan, the 34-year-old Ruth took a second wife. Claire was 28, and with her resume as a model, actress (including small parts in silent movies), and Ziegfeld Follies dancer, was believed by Ruth to possess the "culture, background, and good looks" that he lacked. They exchanged vows at an ungodly hour, around 5:45 A.M., to avoid the pandemonium of fans wanting to catch a glimpse of the couple. Even at that, he wound up signing autographs, posing for pictures, and, upon departing the church, being surrounded by somewhere between 2,000 and 6,000 fans.[35]

Six years earlier in Washington, D.C., Ruth had attended a stage show called *Dew Drop Inn*, and he was taken with an actress who had a small role. This was Claire Hodgson, a girl he first spoke to when she accepted an invitation from a friend of Ruth's to meet the slugger. She went to see him on his "stage" during a game the Senators hosted against the Yanks. When she was introduced to Ruth prior to the game, her reactions were, "He is famous, so it's nice to be able to say you've met him; he is pleasant, he has a growling voice, a pleasant-enough smile, and he's married." Still, she fell for Ruth and later said that she wasn't "breaking up a home. It was broken."[36] She also noted that his "banter was not up to a 29-year-old man's" and that he had a fat face and stomach, yet had "legs like a chorus girl's." She felt that he also was a person who was "very much in need of a sympathetic ear," which she readily provided.[37]

The next day Ruth sent her a note inviting her for dinner. When the evening was over, his parting line to Claire was, "So long, Keed." In return, her parting line to him, according to Claire's daughter Julia, was, " 'You know, Mr. Ruth, you drink too much.' He'd never met anyone like Mother before."[38] Julia's son Tom Stevens added, "Nobody had ever said that to him before. He did whatever he wanted, nobody ever [confronted him] so it made him pay attention to her. I don't know that it changed his drinking any—at that point, anyway."[39]

Their relationship clicked and he was destined to see her "off and on over the next five or six years." He told everyone that he and Claire were simply friends, but the newspapers of the day liberally sprinkled gossip of the romance on its pages and Dorothy later wrote that her father "spent more time at her apartment" than in his own lodgings. She also indicated Claire tagged along with Ruth when he visited his wife at their farm. Claire would check into a hotel while Ruth spent time with Helen. Interestingly, even earlier Claire had dated Ty Cobb and, at around the age of 15, married a widower named Frank Hodgson who, at 33, was more than double her age. They eventually separated and he died in 1922, freeing Claire, who then moved to New York.

Ruth was scheduled to play the season's opener in New York on the day of his wedding, but the game was rained out. However, the following day, in the grand style of the Babe, he presented her with a wedding gift of a home run in his first at-bat of the new season. With typical Ruthian flair, as he rounded third, he tipped his cap to Claire and blew a kiss her way. After the game, they returned to their first residence, an opulent 14-room, 5-bathroom Manhattan apartment at 345 West 88th just off Riverside Drive. Soon, Babe and Claire adopted each other's children. Twelve-year-old Julia became his daughter and Dorothy, then eight, became Claire's.

Unlike Ruth's first wife, Claire, being more worldly, "made sure she accompanied the Babe when the club went on the road." She did so despite the team's normal policy for wives not to travel with the club and despite other wives resenting her special privilege. Claire almost intuitively sensed when to be firm with her husband, while also realizing at times she'd have to squeeze her eyes very firmly shut to some of his dalliances.[40]

According to Claire, Yankees owner Jacob Ruppert wanted her to go along with her husband, as "a good influence." Julia said her mother "kept things calm and serene as much as she could."[41] Claire saw it as her wifely duty to institute some reforms, especially since, despite Ruth's massive monetary intake—several years he raked in $200,000, a 1927 barnstorming tour yielded close to $70,000, and another time he, perhaps the world's most famous cigar smoker, got $5,000 to endorse cigarettes—the cash flowing out was even larger. As Claire wrote, "in the spring of 1929 he was broke. And in debt." Claire added that there was always a drain on his money: "fast cars, faster women, slow horses, inspired performances by professional moochers...."[42] Tom Stevens said Claire, fortuitously, was "the turning point in his life."[43]

Claire dished money to Ruth upon his every request, but did so by writing small checks, typically $50. A trip to the barber shop, a purchase of an item or two such as cigars, and he was back, ready for another $50 check. She explained, "It was a tiring thing...but it served the purpose of cutting down on such habits as tipping a hundred dollars for a thirty-five cent ham sandwich."[44] However, Julia chuckled that she doubted Claire took over as completely as some sources have it, that she "would ever go that far because that would not have set well with Daddy. She would kind of put a curb on tips in a nice way."[45]

Claire also quickly banned hard liquor consumption during the baseball season. The Babe had to be content to guzzle beer until the long shadows and stinging chill of autumn appeared and the last baseball of the season had been struck.[46] She also established a curfew for guests visiting the Babe. Julia recalled, "If he wanted people in for, or after dinner, she'd make sure that they left within a reasonable time so he could get to bed and get the proper amount of sleep—she looked after him."[47] She understood his propensity for consuming massive meals around 11:00 P.M., but managed to have him cut his food intake down to a sandwich rather than, say, a thick steak.[48]

The couple's on-the-road arrangements included having a private compartment on the team train, as well as a hotel suite where they would eat their meals via room service to avoid the throngs of adoring fans who would cluster around Ruth at restaurants like so many pigeons near a park bench.[49] On game days, he was good about eating a light lunch, but he would cheat from time to time, sometimes scarfing down some ballpark hot dogs before or even during a game.

When it came to even the most remote chance of injuring himself, Claire pampered Ruth—she wouldn't permit him to open a window for fear he would strain a wrist or his back. He rarely even shaved himself or used a can opener and she read to him to spare his eyes.[50] Julia disagreed somewhat with this picture, stating Claire was not a mother figure to Babe. "Not really, and I'm sure that Mother didn't have that idea either. And, oh my goodness alive! Wouldn't she get mad if anybody said a word about Daddy not being this or not being that. Sparks would fly! She was so protective of him and she loved him so much."[51]

Dorothy, who never warmed up to her new mother, believed Claire did indeed love Babe, but she also felt Claire "was soon placing restrictions on Babe's extravagant lifestyle and treating him more like a naughty schoolboy than a baseball hero." She wrote that Claire even screened Babe's phone calls.[52]

In 1929, a rookie outfielder named Sammy Byrd got his call up to the Yankees. While he'd go on to play in only 744 major league games, he basically became a curious footnote in the history of baseball's greatest legend. Ruth had reached the age of 34 and his legs had lost some resiliency, so in the latter stages of many contests he would be replaced in the outfield by Byrd. He came to be known by the colorful, but rather awkward nickname of "Babe Ruth's Legs."

Byrd stayed with the Yankees through 1934, also Ruth's final season with the club. His obituary stated that he was considered to be "the best golfer in baseball because he had consistently beaten teammates who challenged him, including Ruth." Ruth was a good golfer, but he couldn't handle Bryd who left baseball and joined the world of pro golfing, winning 23 tournaments in the era of Byron Nelson, Sam Snead, and Ben Hogan.[53]

By around mid-May it was obvious that the Yanks were floundering. Huggins even flip-flopped Ruth and Gehrig in the batting order. Nothing worked. To paraphrase a line from *On the Waterfront*, they shoulda' been a contender, but it just wasn't their year. On August 11, Ruth reached the 500-homer plateau when he connected off Cleveland's right-hander Willis Hudlin, giving him six homers over his last seven contests. It took him only 5,801 at-bats to reach 500; in the annals of the game only four men were younger than Ruth's 34½ years of age when they joined the 500 home-run club.

This was one baseball Ruth wanted for a souvenir so he asked an usher to locate the ball. A young boy who had retrieved the ball was escorted to Ruth and surrendered the priceless piece of memorabilia for an autographed ball, the opportunity to sit in the Yankee dugout the next day, and $20.[54] Contrast that with the exorbitant demands modern fans have made when they were able to grab a historic ball.

It was a fine statistical year for Ruth, but the Yankees lost the flag and their leader, Miller Huggins during the dog days of the season. The powerhouse Philadelphia Athletics of Al Simmons, Lefty Grove, and Jimmie Foxx went on to win the pennant in a breeze. Huggins left the team September 20 with 11 games left on their schedule. On September 25, he died at the age of 50 from a rare skin disease known as erysipelas, an event Ruth ranked as one of the largest shocks he ever experienced.[55]

The Yankees appointed Art Fletcher as their interim manager, but when he turned down the job for the following season, Ruth, a 16-year veteran, decided to toss his baseball cap into the managerial ring for the first time. After gaining an audience from Ruppert and after presenting his case about how he could help both pitchers and hitters, Ruth was devastated to hear the now-famous Ruppert line, "How can you manage the Yankees, when you can't manage yourself?" Ruth's grandson Tom Stevens commented, "His wild ways haunted him."[56]

Ruth was persistent so Ruppert placated him by using the "Well, we'll see" approach mothers have used on children for years; then, after a few days, Ruppert named Bob Shawkey their new skipper. Not only did Ruppert not consider hiring Ruth, but he is said to have offered the job to three other men before finally hiring Shawkey.[57] Furthermore, while Shawkey had been a Yankees coach, he had no big league managerial experience, and after his one-year term of office as the Yanks manager, he would never again lead a major league squad. After the Yankees finished a remote 16 games out of first place, Shawkey had a huge task in front of them for his debut season. The Athletics, who won the World Championship in 1929, looked formidable.

The 1920s, often called the Golden Age of Baseball, featured a plethora of homers, more than ever before. Fans loved this brand of ball and for most of the decade the Yanks, a great draw both at home and on the road, reached at least the 2,000,000 mark in total attendance. They also netted a lofty profit of $3.5 million over the 1920s. Ruth, a one-man dynamo, provided much of the decade's electricity. For the record, to this day no man has tagged more home runs in a decade as the 467 Ruth registered in the 1920s.[58] Ruth torched almost exactly 10 percent of the 4,684 homers hit in his league for the entire decade—an astonishing one-man output.

Ruth's gigantic salary certainly made headlines as the torrid 1920s melted into the 1930s and the average American's income would erode to $1,000 per year. The shattering events of Black Thursday as the stock market plummeted on October 29, 1929 (a day in which a record 16,000,000 shares of stock were traded on the New York Stock Exchange), and the Great Depression which ultimately, but not immediately ensued, led to former businessmen being "reduced to selling apples on street corners" and worse.[59]

Actually, the market's decline began on Saturday, October 19, 1929, but the market, in a not uncommon situation that conformed to the investment cliche, "Even a dead cat will bounce if dropped from high enough," did rebound the next Tuesday. The cat was clearly D.O.A., though, and by the October 29 the panic and despair were evident. It's been written that hotels in midtown New York "learned to be wary of guests who sought rooms on upper floors." While suicides weren't rife, some did occur, yet such a degree of despair was not prevalent among, say, suburbanites.[60] Notwithstanding that, within three years a share of General Motors had lost 92 percent of the value it held before the 1929 crash. By then, "the average weekly wage of those who had jobs was $16.21."[61] It was the time of bread lines and bloodshed, and of lost dignity, a time in which myriad desperate people resorted to just about anything to survive.

Yet, amidst all the tribulations, Ruth, having signed a two-year pact for $160,000 on March 8, 1930, was pulling in the highest salary in the history of sports, and way ahead of the league average of around $7,000, albeit mere chump change by today's standards. When it was pointed out that he was earning $5,000 more per year than President Herbert Hoover, Ruth supposedly quipped, "I had a better year than he did." Yankees general manager Ed Barrow, perhaps in an effort to save face, tried to calm things down as he predicted (quite inaccurately, of course), "No one will ever be paid more than Ruth." Famed sportswriter Red Smith always claimed Ruth's allusion to Hoover had to be contrived and untrue because "Ruth was too uninformed about politics."[62]

However, one can imagine Ruth wished he had uttered the "better year" line in connection with the Commissioner of Baseball, old nemesis "Kennesaw Mountain" Landis, who was soon destined to experience a $15,000 chop in pay. Harry Rothberger wrote that the American public did not resent Ruth's enormous paychecks, instead they were fascinated with what he earned, amounts that "became the stuff of legends."[63]

Ruth had extra income still pouring in due to his endorsements, his appearances in show business, and his weekly articles, which were ghost-written by Ford Frick, who would later become baseball's commissioner. At first, baseball didn't suffer due to the economy, and attendance increased as idle Americans needed something to do. Vicarious thrills could also be found at the movies and the motion picture industry, featuring "talkies," also benefited. Night baseball games were sometimes played in the minors, and that boosted their cash intake. Nevertheless, private banks were collapsing and the future looked bleak.

Conversely, 1930 was a boom year in baseball. It proved to be a season as freakish as a carnival sideshow and as anomalous as an honest used-car salesman. Chuck Klein had 170 RBIs and finished 21 behind Hack Wilson. Actually, Klein was 20 behind Wilson, but MLB later altered Hack's official total to 191.

Collectively, the NL hit .303 and 26 men reached 300 total bases. It was also the year of the "Rabbit Ball." Realizing that fans idolized the longball, baseball officials juiced the ball liberally. "By all accounts, the baseball that was put in play didn't have the usual raised stitches." Instead, they were "almost recessed and the cover of the ball was wound so tight that the ball was difficult to grip." Naturally, the ball played havoc on pitchers, especially those trying to throw effective breaking balls.[64] Spectators didn't mind one bit; they filled 10.1 million seats, a record that, due to the Depression, would stand into the 1940s.

Ruth was on fire in June when he jacked 15 homers. He established a major league high for that month which stood until Sammy Sosa pounded 20 in 1998. Even at the age of 35, Ruth's multitalents held out. On September 28, he took to the hill again and worked a complete game victory at Fenway Park over his former team, the Boston Red Sox.

At season's end Ruth had 49 homers but a then-existing rule robbed him of 2 additional homers. Twice he belted balls that deflected off a loudspeaker horn in the stands and ricocheted back onto the field at Shibe Park—he was awarded doubles, not home runs. For the record, he never once hit a ball that bounced off the playing field and into the stands, a hit that was considered a home run prior to 1931 when such hits became "ground-rule doubles."

The Shawkey-led Yankees finished third in 1930. Ruth again tried to get the job of managing the Yankees after Shawkey was fired just days after the season's end, only to have Ruppert throw a litany of Ruth's transgressions in his face. Ruppert then hired Joe McCarthy, fresh from a five-year tenure with the Cubs, to run the team in 1931.

Clearly, Ruth resented McCarthy, considering him unworthy of the job as McCarthy had never made it to the majors, toiling only in the minors for 15 years. However, a realistic view of the situation justifies the hiring and subsequent retaining of McCarthy, a man who would go on to win .615 of the games he managed over 24 seasons. While it took Mack 50 years to produce eight pennants with the A's, and 31 seasons for McGraw to hoist 10 flags as the Giants skipper, McCarthy won eight pennants in 16 seasons for the Yankees—and nine overall. Only Casey Stengel with 10 had more. McCarthy also averaged over 90 wins per season for his 1931–1946 stint with the Yankees. More impressively, once his troops made it to the World Series, they usually won—seven times, more than any man ever who ran the same club for 15 or more seasons.

It seems ludicrous to think Ruth could have been more successful than McCarthy. When Gehrig gave his farewell speech in 1939, he paid tribute to McCarthy, labeling him "that outstanding leader, that smart student of psychology, the best manager in baseball today." The conservative McCarthy was as uncomfortable with Ruth as Ruth was with his new skipper. Aware of Ruth's track record with managers, McCarthy knew Ruth might try to rob him of his power or, at the very least, subvert his authority.

At home, Dorothy felt Claire's favoritism for Julia brought about a "no win situation." Dorothy wrote that while Julia attended ritzy private schools, she was relegated to public schools, and that while Julia shopped at only the finest stores, Dorothy had to be content to wear hand-me-down clothing. Dorothy insisted, however, that her father treated both girls equally.[65]

Tosetti noted that Babe "was her [Dorothy's] only ally" and said the atmosphere in the Ruth household "wasn't great. My mom was kinda' left out of a lot of stuff and she said, 'I spent a lot of time in my bedroom. I could tell you there was 300 and some odd flowers on my wallpaper.'"[66]

Ruth, always up for a diversion, was part of a publicity stunt on the day after a rain out canceled an April Fool's Day game in 1931. During the first inning of an exhibition contest in Chattanooga, the minor league Lookouts waited for Ruth's turn to bat before calling Jackie Mitchell, a talented 17-year-old female pitcher into her pro debut.

On a 1-2 delivery, after missing on two big cuts, Ruth was caught looking. Gehrig followed and whiffed, swinging at three straight sinkers; it had taken Mitchell seven pitches to dismiss the Yankees' mighty one-two punch. Lazzeri walked and that ended her stint. When Landis voided her contract a few days later, it ended her career in organized baseball. No one is uncertain if Ruth and Gehrig fanned on purpose or not, but the Yankees had been given pregame instructions not to hit the ball back through the box against her.[67]

On August 21, 1931, almost exactly two years after he cracked his 500th career homer, Ruth reached 600, doing so at a younger age and in far fewer at-bats than Aaron, Bonds, and Willie Mays, the only other men now in the 600-homer circle. Ruth required only 6,921 at-bats compared to the next best pace of 8,212 by Bonds. The Babe touched up Browns hurler George Blaeholder in an 11-7 win for the historic homer moments before Gehrig made it back-to-back homers, one of 19 times they connected successively; they also both connected in the same contest on 72 occasions.[68]

The Athletics, who won 107 games, their third straight season with 100 or more wins, monopolized the pennant for the third straight season. The Yankees finished second at 13½ games out, with Ruth and Gehrig tying for the league leadership with 46 home runs. This represented the last time Ruth led the league in that category.

A glance at this lethal one-two combo is in order. In 1931, Gehrig wound up with 184 RBIs, nine more than his previous high from 1927, and the second highest single-season mark ever, trailing only Wilson's 191 in 1930. Ruth chipped in with 163 more for a combined 347, the most runs driven in by teammates ever. Not only that, but their collective 772 homers as teammates stood until August 20, 1965, when Eddie Mathews of the Braves hit his 28th home run of the year to push the total of Hank Aaron and Mathews to 773.

Overall, times were tough. As the year wound down, Adolf Hitler was just weeks away from taking over as the chancellor of Germany. On the baseball scene, on December 9, 1931, major league team owners, concerned about the impact of the Depression, decided to reduce the size of their rosters from 25 to 23 players.[69] So, while the Depression finally was making a ravaging impact on baseball in 1932, the era of Hoovervilles and angst in the United States, Ruth accepted a pay cut of $5,000, taking him down to $75,000. That same year Landis' salary plunged from $65,000 to $50,000 and Gehrig, an established and underpaid star, dipped from $25,000 to $23,000.[70] Ruth and Gehrig, baseball's top run producers, wound up *losing* money. Times, clearly, were tough.

While baseball had actually prospered during the first few years of the Depression, now minor league teams began to fold. The Giants made a trip to St. Louis in which they received a check for $187 as their share of the gate—not even enough to cover their $198 hotel bill.[71]

The Yankees didn't suffer such a fate because there was no doubt Ruth's prowess and personality attracted fans to ballparks throughout the land. Yankee shortstop Roger Peckinpaugh observed that scads of people first became attracted to baseball due to Ruth. "They would be drawing 1,500 a game in St. Louis. We'd go in there with the Babe and they'd be all over the ballpark. Thousands and thousands of people coming out to see that one guy. Whatever the owners paid him, it wasn't enough—it couldn't be."[72]

Certainly Ruth knew he was magnetic when it came to pulling fans into parks. He once spoke of the time he took sick in Chicago and the newspapers announced two days before his Yankees came to town that he would sit out Sunday's game. Ruth gloated a bit when he learned of over 15,000 ticket order cancellations.[73] Inevitably, though, he had to accept his 1932 reduction in salary as a sign of the times.

The 1932 season featured the fourteenth and final season in which Ruth single-handedly out-homered at least one major league club—doing so at the age of 37. From 1918 to 1932, he accomplished this feat every season except 1925.

The Yankees took the 1932 World Series, dispatching the Cubs in four, for an astounding third straight sweep—having cruised to championships in 1927 and 1928 as well. When Ruth walked into Wrigley Field prior to Game 3, he glanced around the hitters' park and uttered, "I'd play for half my salary if I could hit in this dump all the time."

Whether Ruth actually predicted his home run that day off the Cubs' Charlie Root in his final Series is still debated, but the incident typified the enormity of the Ruth lore. The Fall Classic had begun with the Cubs and Yankees riding each other hard. The central issue in their feud revolved around former Yankee Mark Koenig. The Cubs picked him up in for part of 1932 to fill in at shortstop. A career .279 hitter, Koenig got hot, smacking the ball at a .353 clip down the stretch run. Despite his contribution, the Cubs voted to give him only a one-half share of the postseason bonus each player would receive. Ruth and other Yankees who had known Koenig were livid. They considered the Cubs to be miserly ingrates and ridiculed them in the media. Ruth stated that when he first saw the Cubs take the field for the first game of the Series, he shouted over to them, calling them a "lousy bunch of cheapskates."

In return, Cubs fans wanted a piece of Ruth, their main target, because he was both a symbol of the Yanks and seemingly the loudest of several very vocal critics of the Cubs. When he and his wife made the trip to Chicago for the third game they were "forced to run a gauntlet of two lines of hysterical, angry women" who actually spit on the Ruths.[74]

Likewise, before the game commenced, fans tried to pelt Yankees with lemons in a scene now reminiscent of the seventh game of the 1934 Series when Detroit faithful rifled fruit and vegetables at Joe Medwick, who had slid wickedly into third baseman Marv Owen and then scuffled with him. (Medwick later mused that he could understand them throwing all that fruit at him, but what he *couldn't* understand was why they brought it to the park in the first place.)

It was against just that type of backdrop that Ruth stroked a first inning, three-run seismic shot into a group of spectators in right center field. Still, the fans and Cubs bench jockeys were not to be silenced; they called Ruth "Grandpop" and worse. They relished it when Chicago roared back to knot the game, aided in part by a Ruth misplay that occurred when he dashed in on a ball then tumbled while he was trying to snag it.

They continued to torment him with a growing bloodlust when he strolled to the plate on his spindly legs in the fifth inning. Ruth recalled shouts of "big belly" and "baboon" raining down on him. Joe Garner wrote that, "Ruth gave as well as he got, shouting back at the Chicago faithful and the Cubs' bench."[75]

After Charlie Root's first four offerings, the count ran to 2-and-2. At that point, the alleged prediction/promise took place. Ruth was said to have pointed with two fingers of his right hand, as if to indicate where he planned on depositing the next pitch. Some contend Ruth was merely pointing at Root, with the two fingers standing for the two strikes on Ruth—and, more importantly, the ominous fact that Ruth was confidently indicating, "I've still got one strike left." Whatever the case, Ruth did come up big, slashing a leviathan homer, his final World Series homer, supposedly landing directly into the area he had indicated.

Despite the 1988 "premiere" of a 16-millimeter home movie of Ruth's theatrics that day, controversy lingers. The footage taken by Matt Kandle Sr., and now known simply as "the Kandle film," is baseball's equivalent to Abraham Zapruder footage of the assassination of President John F. Kennedy. Even when the film was shown on national television, it proved inconclusive, and one writer suggested that people saw what they wanted to see.

Chicago sportswriter Jerome Holtzman has no doubt as to what took place that day. He wrote, "I am enough of a baseball bibliophile to know he didn't point. It's the biggest hoax in the history of American sports." In 1991, when Holtzman informed readers of his column that he felt the "Called Shot" was a sham, his readers, who normally sent him about twelve letters a week, flooded his mailbox with hundreds of letters. How dare he utter such heresy? Holtzman noted that for baseball fans, "the Babe lives." Men such as Roger Maris and Hank Aaron caused Ruth records to evaporate with "events that should have lost the Babe in the fog of time. Instead, he is as large as ever." Fans wanted his standards to live on, and not be obliterated.[76]

Another expert pondered why, despite the army of photographers on hand, no still pictures of Ruth pointing exist and why would Ruth, who normally pulled the ball, predict a homer to straightaway center? Julia noted that the writers of the day "didn't make a big deal out of it—it was just one of the things that they might have expected of Daddy."[77]

Root has been quoted as saying there was no way in the world Ruth made a prophecy that day because if he had, he would "have put one in his ear and knocked him on his [backside]." Cubs catcher Gabby Hartnett remembered it this way: "Babe waved his hand across home plate toward our bench. . . . One finger was up. At the same time he said softly, and I think only the umpire and I heard him, 'It only takes one to hit it.'" Hartnett swore Ruth didn't point towards the bleachers. This version seems to jibe with the Kandle film.[78]

On the other hand, Ruth himself perpetuated the legend, once telling a sportswriter that his greatest game was the "Called Shot" contest. He wrote that he got the idea to predict his homer while he was fuming over the Chicago fans spitting on him and his wife. He even boasted about how it wasn't a new concept and spoke of how he had promised other homers and made good, even to the point of usually being able to place the ball in the very spot he was aiming at.[79]

Furthermore, he muddled the situation by changing his story from time to time. For example, about six months after uncorking off Root, he was interviewed by Chicago broadcaster Hal Totten. That time Ruth was quoted as saying, "Hell no, I didn't point. Only a damned fool would do a thing like that." He said he swung at the first offering, then grinned at his opponents "and held out one finger and told 'em it'd take only one to hit it."[80]

In yet another version, he said he didn't swing at Root's first pitch, but had actually held out a finger and defiantly called the pitch, "Strike one!" even before the umpire made his call. He said he took the second pitch, also right down the pipe, and once more bellowed out the call, "Strike two!" before pointing to center field and ripping the third pitch for the home run. This account is blatantly incorrect.[81] For the record, the actual pitch sequence was as follows: strike, ball, ball, strike.

Once he even confided that he "didn't exactly point to any spot." He attested that after the second strike he pointed, or "held up," one finger—this time to indicate he still had one strike coming. He concluded by saying, "Naw, keed, you know damn well I wasn't pointin' anywhere. I never really knew anybody who could tell you ahead of time where he was going to hit a baseball."[82]

The final version that Ruth, well aware of the value of perpetuating his aura, seems to have settled on is preserved on tape. It has the first pitch a called strike (as opposed to a swing and a miss in his 1933 version), causing Ruth to bark that the ball had been outside. Ruth recounted, "Well, the second pitch was another called strike and I didn't like that one very much, either. By that time they [the Cubs] were going crazy. So I stepped out of the box and looked out at center field and I pointed and I said, 'I'm gonna' hit the next pitched ball right past the flagpole.' And that's what I did."[83]

Julia commented, "He did do it, he did hold up his hand. Maybe it was one thing [gesture], maybe it was another, but he hit a home run. It was amazing the way he could come through *just* at the most critical and dramatic moment. As he said, the good Lord was on his side. Can you imagine the boos if he had struck out?"[84]

What is certain is Root came in with a slow curve, low and away and Ruth's bat lashed out as fast as the tip of a whistling bullwhip. This was Ruth's last hurrah, his final Series. He piled up 42 hits over his 41 Series contests, 33 RBIs, and hit .326 with 15 homers, most ever until Mickey Mantle eclipsed it in 1964. The Yanks won it all in 1932 and Koenig's losing team, half-share came to $2,122.50. After McCarthy's Yankees won the 1932 Series, the manager was awarded a three-year contract extension, another crystal clear message to Ruth that he would probably never guide the Yanks.

A final note on calling homers: Eleven years before the famous 1932 blast, Ruth predicted a spot where he planned on relocating a pitch. Granddaughter Linda Tosetti recalled, "On the back of a Mega Card from a series of cards they did on Babe, there was the story of Babe in Yankee Stadium during batting practice. He hit a ball into center field. The manager said he liked the direction, but could he hit it in the same spot, but higher, and Babe did just that."[85] As Julia observed, when he said he could do something, "Most of the time he came through with it."[86]

Throughout Ruth's career opponents would "ride" him unmercifully from the bench, as was typical of the times. Bench jockeys were guaranteed to jab a nerve painfully when they ridiculed his heritage; due to some of Ruth's physical characteristics, opponents accused him of being part African American. This was one subject Ruth reportedly would not tolerate. Creamer noted, "In 1932 the Cubs were calling Ruth the 'n-word' from their bench." He also said that his research never unearthed any evidence to support the hecklers' contentions. "Ruth's family," Creamer continued, "was from Pennsylvania Dutch country, and in that part of the country, interracial relations were not likely."[87] In addition, Ruth's grandfather's parents were born in North Germany and his grandmother's parents came from Havonver, Germany, meaning Babe "was a pure German on both sides."[88]

NOTES

1. Creamer, *Babe*, 351.

2. Kahn, *Beyond the Boys of Summer*, 70.

3. Pirone and Martens, *My Dad, the Babe*, 40.

4. Ibid., 67.

5. Bill Livingston, "Whatever It's Shape, a Bat Is Still a Hitter's Best Friend," *Baseball Digest*, November 1979, 85–88.

6. Stewart, *Hitting Secrets of the Pros*, 131–132.

7. Livingston, "Whatever It's Shape, a Bat Is Still a Hitter's Best Friend," 85–88.

8. Ruth, *Babe Ruth's Own Book of Baseball*, 171–172.

9. Ibid., 172.

10. Ibid., 172–174.

11. Harwell, *The Babe Signed My Shoe*, 160.

12. Eig, *Luckiest Man,* 93.

13. Miller, *The Babe Book,* 109.

14. Eig, *Luckiest Man,* 119, 189.

15. Ibid., 94.

16. Ruth and Considine, *The Babe Ruth Story*, 152–153.

17. Miller, *The Babe Book*, 125.

18. Quoted by Miller in *The Babe Book*, 126, from John Tillius' *I'd Rather Be a Yankee.*

19. Quoted by Miller in *The Babe Book*, 127, from Tom Meany's *Babe Ruth: Big Moments and the Big Fella.*

20. Ruth, *Babe Ruth's Own Book of Baseball*, 240–241.

21. Ibid., 241–242.

22. Ruth and Considine, *The Babe Ruth Story*, 154.

23. Eig, *Luckiest Man,* 122, 124.

24. Ruth, *Babe Ruth's Own Book of Baseball*, 149–151.

25. Ibid., 153–154.

26. Ibid., 187.

27. Ibid., 252.

28. Tony Gwynn, from interview with author, 1992.

29. Kelley, *In the Shadow of the Babe*, 79.

30. Pirone and Martens, *My Dad, the Babe*, 44.

31. Ibid., 42–47.

32. Ibid., 47–48, 52.

33. Linda Ruth Tosetti, from telephone interview with author, September 23, 2005.

34. Ruth, with Slocum, *The Babe and I*, 34.

35. Pirone and Martens, *My Dad, the Babe*, 52.

36. Ruth, with Slocum, *The Babe and I*, 32.

37. Ibid., 24–25, 31.

38. Julia Ruth Stevens, from interviews with author, November 2005.

39. Tom Stevens, from interview with author, November 5, 2005.

40. Smith, *Babe Ruth's America*, 214–215.

41. Julia Ruth Stevens, from interviews with author, November 2005.

42. Ruth, with Slocum, *The Babe and I*, 134–135, 138–139.

43. Tom Stevens, from interview with author, November 5, 2005.

44. Ruth, with Slocum, *The Babe and I*, 137–138.

45. Julia Ruth Stevens, from interviews with author, November 2005.

46. Ritter, *The Babe*, 178.

47. Julia Ruth Stevens, from interviews with author, November 2005.

48. Ruth, with Slocum, *The Babe and I*, 97, 101.

49. Ritter, *The Babe*, 177.

50. Ruth, with Slocum, *The Babe and I*, 101–102.

51. Julia Ruth Stevens, from interviews with author, November 2005.

52. Pirone and Martens, *My Dad, the Babe*, 53, 56.

53. From www.thedeadballera.com.

54. Enders, *Ballparks Then and Now*, 60.

55. Ruth and Considine, *The Babe Ruth Story*, 175.

56. Tom Stevens, from interview with author, November 5, 2005.

57. Eig, *Luckiest Man*, 142.

58. Alexander, *Our Game*, 140.

59. Gilbert, *Young Babe Ruth*, 158.

60. Smith, *Babe Ruth's America*, 210.

61. Quoted in Gershman, *Diamonds*, 140, from *The Glory and the Dream*.

62. From www.baseballlibrary.com.

63. Gilbert, *Young Babe Ruth*, 158.

64. Bill Gutman, *Its Outta Here: The History of the Home Run from Babe Ruth to Barry Bonds* (Lanham, MD: Taylor Trade Publishing, 2005), 43.

65. Pirone and Martens, *My Dad, the Babe*, 59, 123.

66. Linda Ruth Tosetti, from telephone interview with author, September 23, 2005.

67. From www.baseballhalloffame.org, Dan Holmes, "The Day a Girl Struck out Ruth and Gehrig," April 2, 2005.

68. From www.baseballlibrary.com.

69. Gershman, *Diamonds*, 124.

70. Eig, *Luckiest Man*, 153.

71. Smith, *Babe Ruth's America*, 230.

72. Quoted by Miller, in *The Babe Book*, 59, from John Tullius' *I'd Rather Be a Yankee*.

73. Gilbert, *Young Babe Ruth*, 158.

74. Ruth and Considine, *The Babe Ruth Story*, 191.

75. Joe Garner, *And The Crowd Goes Wild: Relive the Most Celebrated Sporting Events Ever Broadcast* (Naperville, IL: Sourcebooks, Inc., 1999), 3.

76. Ruth, *Babe Ruth's Own Book of Baseball*, v–vi.

77. Julia Ruth Stevens, from interviews with author, November 2005.

78. Creamer, *Babe*, 367.

79. Ruth and Considine, *The Babe Ruth Story*, 192.

80. Ruth, *Babe Ruth's Own Book of Baseball*, vii.

81. Ruth and Considine, *The Babe Ruth Story*, 194.

82. Ruth, *Babe Ruth's Own Book of Baseball*, vii–viii.

83. Ibid.

84. Julia Ruth Stevens, from interviews with author, November 2005.

85. Linda Ruth Tosetti, from telephone interview with author, September 23, 2005.

86. Julia Ruth Stevens, from interviews with author, November 2005.

87. Kalb, *Who's Better, Who's Best in Baseball?*, 26.

88. Harris, *Babe Ruth: The Dark Side*, 26.

THE GLORY ENDS,
1933–1935

By 1933, the ravages of the Depression finally caught up with Ruth, who was forced to take a $23,000 cut in pay from the previous year. He was still hauling in a sky-high salary of $52,000, but, in many ways, this, plus his statistical falloff in 1933, represented the beginning of the decline for Ruth.

At the age of 38, he again made history, this time in Chicago during the inaugural All Star Game. Facing southpaw Bill Hallahan, Ruth blistered the first homer, which also proved to be the game-winning hit, in All-Star history. Incidentally, the best seat in the house for the midsummer showcase was a mere $1.65 while a seat in the grandstands put a fan back just $1.10.[1]

Ruth's Yankees were an offensive machine in 1933. So much so that when Lefty Grove shut them out on August 3, it was the first whitewashing of the Yanks in 309 games, a stellar record. They led the AL in runs but thin pitching hurt, forcing them to settle for a second-place finish behind Washington.

Ruth's final pitching appearance ever took place on October 1. Nearly all of his Yankee starts occurred at the tail end of a season, as publicity stunts, and they all resulted in victories for the Bambino. This time, though, Ruth's pitching corrosion was evident when he took the ball—other than a 1930 start, his last outing had been way back in 1921.

The gimmick worked at the gate, this time pulling 25,000 fans in to Yankee Stadium despite the fact that the Yankees were mathematically eliminated from the pennant chase. Once more, as he did three years earlier in his penultimate pitching performance, Babe beat the Red Sox. He managed to turn in a complete game, which he stamped with his personal signature, a home run, in a 6-5 victory. He scattered a dozen hits, all five runs were earned, and he walked three while striking out none.

By the time he hit the showers, he had boosted his lifetime pitching log to 94-46, meaning he won nearly 70 percent (.671) of all his decisions. Ruth, who later complained that his final pitching stint left him so sore he had to eat using his right hand for a week, also finished with a career ERA of 2.28, but with a not-so-wonderful 488 strikeouts as opposed to 441 walks surrendered. On the year, Ruth hit .301 with 34 home runs, but this was his last really solid season. When he led the AL with 114 walks drawn, it was the final time he would lead the league in any major offensive department.

After the season ended, Ruth the globetrotter embarked on another tour. This one took him to the Hawaiian Islands and points west. Right about this time, the Detroit Tigers, who had just fired their manager, asked the Yankees to release Ruth so he could come to the Motor City and assume player-manager duties. Barrow granted his permission and the Tigers asked Ruth to make a trip to Detroit for a job interview. Ruth stated that he was interested, but couldn't appear until after his trip. The Tigers decided they could not wait and quickly filled the job, acquiring Mickey Cochrane from the A's. Ruth said it wasn't until he returned to the States that he learned he had lost this shot at managing.[2]

According to Ruth's daughter Dorothy, when Ruth completed the first leg of his journey to Hawaii, stopping in San Francisco, he felt it was best to phone Tigers owner Frank Navin, ignoring that it was 2:00 A.M. in Detroit. Babe issued an ultimatum, saying he had to know if Navin wanted him as his manager. "I'm leaving for Hawaii and I want an answer right now—yes or no!" Naturally, a ruffled and irate Navin spewed an emphatic, "No." Cochrane's Tigers went on to win the AL flag in 1934, topping the Yankees by seven games.[3]

An interesting historical note: In February 1934, the day before Ruth's 39th birthday, many miles away in Mobile, Alabama, Estella Aaron gave birth to a baby who, 40 years later, would break Ruth's lifetime homer record.

In 1934, the Babe's salary was slashed again, this time to $35,000. That figure was less than half of what he had earned at his zenith. Alarmingly, he had taken cuts of over 30 percent two years running, but he was still the best-paid player in the world of baseball.[4] He once described his last year in Yankee pinstripes tersely: "It wasn't a happy experience."[5]

Ruth was again able to cash in on his appeal and augment his baseball salary. For instance, in April, Quaker Oats signed him to a stunning $39,000 deal to do three 15-minute radio broadcasts a week on NBC.[6] By spring, hope was at hand for the average American, too. Construction had increased by over one-third of what it had been just the year before and the production of passenger cars was higher than it had been during any of the years in the Depression.[7]

Ruth opened the 1934 season at the age of 39 and his defensive range was diminished. McCarthy rested Ruth in the latter stages of games quite a bit, often sending Myril Hoag or Byrd in to replace him. Early in the year a pitch had drilled him in his knee, limiting his playing time, but he was still Babe Ruth, capable of garnering attention even when he failed. In the July 10th All Star Game, after the first two batters reached base, Ruth was the first of five AL All-Stars to go down on strikes at the hand of New York Giants ace Carl Hubbell. Ruth was followed by Gehrig, Foxx, Simmons, and Joe Cronin in a parade of futility.

Hubbell later confessed that striking out Ruth was "the last thought in my mind" because he was hoping to get the slow-footed Ruth to ground into a twin killing. As it turned out, Ruth never even took a swipe at the ball, looking at a fastball Hubbell wasted for a ball followed by three consecutive screwballs. "The Babe must have been waiting for me to get the ball up a little, so he could get his bat under it," Hubbell continued. "He always was trying for that one big shot at the stands, and anything around his knees, especially a twisting ball, didn't let him get any leverage."[8]

As for the regular season, well, failure there was not acceptable. In June, a sports columnist surveyed the Yankees and revealed that the players had unanimously voted "that Ruth ought to be taken out of the lineup for good." By June 24, he was in the midst of an anguishing 0-for-24 slump. It reached the point where some of the younger players made it clear that they were not impressed with, nor could they relate to, an over-the-hill player who dated back to the nineteenth century. But that day, displaying his flair for drama, Ruth took Chicago's Sam Jones yard for a grand slam and the Yanks topped the White Sox.[9]

His 700th lifetime home run came on July 13 versus Tommy Bridges of the Tigers. Ruth, at 39 years and 157 days reached the 700 club faster than the only other men in that group, Henry Aaron and Barry Bonds. He also did it in almost 1,000 fewer at-bats than Bonds required.

On August 12, Ruth made his final appearance as a Yankee against the Red Sox in Fenway Park. It was reported that a record Fenway crowd of 46,766 fans, with an estimated 20,000 turned away, packed the park. In the first game of a twinbill, Ruth came up with two hits; in the nightcap, he had just one official trip to the plate and he left "the field to standing cheers in the eighth inning."[10] Just over six weeks later, he put the finishing touch on his glamorous Yankee career when, on September 29, he powered his last circuit shot while in Yankee pinstripes. The next day, his last as a Yankee, Ruth was hitless against a fellow Baltimorean, Sid Cohen, a rookie southpaw.

In the autumn, Ruth trekked to baseball-crazy Japan. The ballpark in Tokyo, seating 60,000 fans, sold out three weeks before it hosted the opening game of the tour and Osaka's 80,000 capacity stadium also sold out early. Japan's first pitching standout, Eiji Sawamura, a mere 18-year-old, retired Ruth on strikes on two occasions in an exhibition contest. He also struck out Charlie Gehringer, Ruth, Foxx, and Gehrig in a row, losing the game only when Gehrig's ninth-inning homer gave the American squad the nod 1-0. Overall, the major leaguers went an unblemished 17-0 on the 12-city trip with Ruth, acting as the field general of Connie Mack's touring team, leading the way with 14 home runs, after being held homerless in the first four contests. Ruth's tour spawned the first pro league in Japan and the schoolboy pitcher was its first star, engineering three no-hitters before he went into the army where he was killed. To honor their hero, the Japanese named their version of the Cy Young Award after him.[11]

After returning to the United States, and until the day he passed away, according to his wife, Claire, "... Babe Ruth, figuratively, sat by the telephone waiting for a call everybody but he knew could never come." Sometimes he would rationalize his failure to become a big league manager, "To hell with 'em, I'm having more fun and making more money than any of 'em!" Other times he was filled with "bewilderment and pain. And, now and then, there were hot tears of frustration." His anguish over being ignored as managerial timber was as deeply intense and as clearly evident as the emotion portrayed in Munch's *The Scream*.[12]

Ruth did receive an offer from Yankees owner Jacob Ruppert, an opportunity to guide the minor league Newark team, but he refused. He saw himself as being above that type of position and felt he needed no time in the bush leagues to learn a new trade. Basically, it would have been his first training since he learned shirt-making back at St. Mary's, and Ruth would have none of that. He simply wanted the same opportunity given to the likes of the volatile Rogers Hornsby and Ty Cobb, who managed in the "Bigs" without first being relegated to the minors.

Finally, in 1935, Boston Braves owner Judge Emil Fuchs made Ruth an offer that would bestow several titles upon him, but little real authority or clout. While Ruth would be considered a team vice president and an assistant manager, and while Fuchs held out a vague hint of a promise about Ruth later becoming the team's manager, Ruth's actual value to the club would be to draw spectators, especially on days when he played in the outfield. Fuchs realized NL fans, who had seldom if ever seen the Bambino, would turn out to catch a glimpse of the aging legend.

Ironically, Fuchs, who never would hire Ruth to manage, had made himself the team's manager in 1929. His squad lost 98 times and finished last, 43 games out of first place. He was one of just six men who became big league managers with no pro ball experience at any level—the others included Ed Barrow and Braves owner Ted Turner in 1977, for one contest. Mercifully, it was Fuchs' only venture as a big-league manager.

On February 26, 1935, when Ruppert gave Ruth his release from the Yankees, he did so without charging Fuchs a penny. Ruppert, however, wasn't being noble; by this time Ruth, with little punch and limited mobility, was considered a liability. Ruth's salaries late in his career are noteworthy in that as late as 1935 only seven men had earned $30,000 or more at any time during their playing days: Cobb, Speaker, Hornsby, Wilson, Simmons, Gehrig, and Ruth. Thus, Ruth's Braves contract for $25,000 was relatively astronomical.[13]

Canadian-born George Selkirk was the Yankees replacement for Ruth in the outfield. He went on to have a respectable career, but his output marked a precipitous drop off from what Ruth had given the team. Selkirk hit .312 in 1935 and provided 94 RBIs, but with only 11 homers. Now best known to trivia lovers, Selkirk hit .290 in his nine big-league seasons, hitting over .300 five times and driving in 100 or more runs twice. The Ruth-less Yankees went on to win 89 contests, but that was only good enough for a second-place finish.

The Braves, meanwhile, saw a jolt in attendance right away, as they pulled in some 6,500 fans to watch Ruth's NL debut, albeit in an exhibition game in St. Petersburg, Florida, also the home of the Yankees camp. That same day, the Yanks played a game in nearby Tampa and attracted a measly 384 spectators.[14] Ruth's manager, Bill McKechnie wasn't thrilled with it all, noting Ruth had become too old and slow for outfield play and lacked the nimbleness to handle the job at first base. Nevertheless, as Boston headed north and took on the Yankees farm team at Newark, New Jersey, Ruth handled the bat with skill, twice homering mightily.

His bat continued to sizzle in the regular-season opener on April 16. Facing "King Carl" Hubbell, Ruth almost single-handedly won it for the Braves in his official NL debut. Ruth, the drama king, didn't disappoint, starching a single and a 430-foot homer, much to the delight of the 25,000 in attendance, a team record for a home opener. He drove in three of Boston's four runs as the Braves scratched out a win over the Giants. He added two safeties the next game.[15]

If the previous year wasn't a pleasant one for Ruth, he soon found 1935 to be "pretty much of a nightmare." He even went so far as to say if he could have replayed his life, his final 28 games with the Braves would never have occurred. Ruth never played through an entire contest over that 28-game span and struck out 24 times over just 72 at bats. Had he not played with the Braves, he would have retired with 708 homers, bowing out as a Yankee.[16]

At the age of 40, Ruth quickly discovered conditioning and playing were sheer torture. After his rousing start came the nearly total demise of his stats; hits

BABE RUTH

and homers became scarce. Over the rest of April, he produced two hits, one a
homer for his lone RBI. Further, Ruth became disenchanted with Fuchs who
was apparently trying to squeeze out every penny he could by exploiting Ruth's
name. Claire wrote that Babe "fell out completely when the Judge ordered him
to appear at the opening of a cheap clothing store in Boston." With a sense of
dignity and a dawning awareness of the terms of his contract, Ruth refused to be
a shill for the store.[17]

The Braves, doomed to lose well over 100 games that year, kept stringing Ruth
along, encouraging him to hang in there. When, shortly into the season, he
informed Fuchs he was ready to retire, the Braves owner asked him to stick it out
and accompany the team on their first swing out to cities that had special Babe
Ruth days planned, including events in Cincinnati and in Philly on May 30.

Ruth consented to make his last road trip and, as he put it, "For one brief day
I again wore the crown of the Sultan of Swat."[18] That grand afternoon came
when he visited Forbes Field on May 25, 1935, one day after the first night
game ever held in the majors (Philadelphia at Cincinnati). Even though Ruth
was a mere five days away from hanging up his cleats, he reached back for one
last pyrotechnic display.

Underestimating Ruth was a mistake. Even in his fading days it was folly to
dismiss him entirely as an old, fat man who could no longer catch up to a
fastball. It is reminiscent of a line from the colorful Damon Runyon who once
wrote, "It may be that the race is not always to the swift nor the battle to the
strong—but that is the way to bet." Ruth was still strong.

His day began when he faced Pirates starter Red Lucas who served up a pitch that
Ruth promptly launched into the cozy right field stands. That, despite a sportswriter having earlier told Pirate manager Pie Traynor that Ruth would do no
damage—he had just been out all night and rendered useless. Later, reliever Guy
Bush, who had been among the Cubs hecklers of Ruth in the 1932 Series and who
had plunked him with a pitch the last time they had squared off, made the mistake
of giving Ruth not just one or two good pitches to smoke, but three. Additionally,
Ruth made good on those three offerings, spanking a single sandwiched between
two home runs, for a splendid swan song.

In the seventh, with no runners on, he vaporized the ball, giving him his sixth
RBI and his final homer. The ball didn't follow the path of the two he had
previously crushed by going *into* the right field grandstand of Forbes Field, it
flew *over* the double-decked right field roof which stood a lofty 186 feet high.
The roof blast was something that had never occurred since the park opened on
June 30, 1909, and would be matched only by a few men in the park's history.

The homer represented the fourth time he had amassed three homers in a
game, twice in regular-season play and twice in the World Series, and this home

108

run made him the first man to swat three in a game in both leagues. His Herculean outburst was the 72nd time Ruth racked up a multihomer game, which is still a record. Exaggerated reports had his last bash sailing 600 feet as astonished fans and players alike gaped at the veritable moon shot. Hype aside, through the final day of Forbes Field's life, June 28, 1970, that prodigious hit was said to have been Forbes' longest ever.

Pittsburgh's Gus Suhr remembered the game well. "He didn't play the whole game, either. He got three home runs and played to the eighth, I think." Ruth pulled himself from the game even though it meant possibly missing a chance to author a fourth homer. Suhr added respectfully, "The old boy, he must've been something to see 'cause I saw him when he was through and he still hit three home runs."[19] Suhr was one of only about 10,000 people who witnessed the event, but the crowd roared with the force of 20,000 as Ruth minced his way around the bases after number 714, the final hit of his illustrious career.

Bush, who noted Ruth still had his great swing, believed the homer was the longest one he ever dished up. In a classic case of mixed emotions, Bush was awestruck by what Ruth had done, but at the same time, he also felt some pity for him, saying that the "poor fellow" could barely "hobble along." When Ruth rounded the bag at third, Bush tipped his cap at the Babe. In return, said Bush, "He looked at me and kind of saluted and smiled."[20] Bush was the 216th pitcher to serve up a homer to Ruth, providing a coincidental touch of unity, in that 216 was also the address of the building where Babe was born.

Ruth's daughter Julia commented, "He really didn't talk much about [his feats]. He didn't really bring the game home. When he hit the last three in Pittsburgh, I thought it was great, but it wasn't as though he hadn't done it before. To me it was Daddy and that was the kind of thing that Daddy did." Ruth later stated that he wished he had walked away from the game after drilling his 714th. Because he had removed himself from the game after his final heroic blow, the timing would have been impeccable. But, recalled Julia, "When he made a promise, he kept it no matter what, and he had promised Judge Fuchs that he would finish the particular [road trip]."[21]

So, a few more NL cities got their opportunity to honor Ruth. For instance, in Cincinnati on May 26, the Reds held their "Babe Ruth Day." However, it was hardly a showcase for the aging Ruth. He fanned three times in a loss. He coaxed a walk when he pinch hit on May 27, but the next day his 40-year-old legs failed him as he stumbled about and sustained an injury, leaving the game in the fifth inning.

It was on to Philadelphia and another "Babe Ruth Day" on May 29; he walked twice and whiffed twice. His finale came on May 30 at Philly's bandbox of a park, Baker's Bowl. It required a meager poke of 280 feet to reach the foul pole in right, but Ruth could muster nothing. That day he was in the starting line-up of the first game of a twin bill. The occasion was far from auspicious as he played only the first inning. Babe opposed the obscure Jim Bivin, grounded out routinely to first baseman Dolph Camilli, hurt his knee in the field, then banished himself to the dugout. Hal Lee replaced Ruth in left field and that was that. No fanfare, no farewell; it was over. The June 1 issue of the *New York Times* wrote that Ruth had missed a Memorial Day double-header versus the Giants. "He fears he has a touch of water on the knee and, likewise, that he will be unable to get into the series."

Ruth had experienced a solid, but hardly Ruth-like season in 1934 (.288, 22 HR, 84 RBIs), but 1935 was an entirely different story. Struggling under the oppressive weight of his miserable .181 batting average, Ruth called it quits. Interestingly, his six homers in just 72 at-bats worked out to a home run percentage of 8.3; his lifetime percentage was 8.5—even at the age of 40 he still managed to hit his share of home runs.

The most stunning career in sports history officially came to an unceremonious end on June 2, 1935. Confusion remains on whether Emil Fuchs fired Ruth or whether Ruth announced his retirement first. Both men issued statements to the press concerning Ruth's termination shortly after they had argued over Ruth's request to leave the team for a few days to attend a New York reception for the ocean liner *Normandie*, a huge social event. It was also reported that when Claire and Babe drove home from Boston that day, he wept for much of the ride home.[22]

The Braves, who had played .270 ball with Ruth on the team, posted a won-loss percentage of .241 the rest of the way, dropping a mortifying 115 decisions. When he retired, Ruth had more than double the total of the second man on the all-time home run list. Fittingly, that man was Lou Gehrig; other than Ruth, only Gehrig and Hornsby, with 300 on the nose, had reached the 300 plateau.

On September 4, Ruth received a gift from NL president Ford Frick, a lifetime pass for any NL game played. The lifetime pass was indeed a token of respect, but, either the next season or in 1939 (sources differ), when Ruth called the Yankees requesting tickets for their home opener, he was told by a worker that they would mail the tickets out, after he send a check to them.[23] According to a Hall of Fame display, Ruth sat in the grandstands, having paid his own way into the 1939, not 1936, Yankee Stadium opener.

Looking back, Elbie Fletcher, a rookie with the 1935 Braves, recalled Ruth's final days as a ballplayer. He stated that while Ruth's teammates were in awe of him and his "marvelous swing," he was a sad figure. "He couldn't run, he could hardly bend down for a ball . . . to see Babe Ruth struggling on a ball field, well, that's when you realize we're all mortal and nothing lasts forever."[24]

NOTES

1. Miller, *The Babe Book*, 115.
2. Ruth and Considine, *The Babe Ruth Story*, 200–201.
3. Pirone and Martens, *My Dad the Babe*, 168.
4. Creamer, *Babe*, 375.
5. Ruth and Considine, *The Babe Ruth Story*, 202.
6. See www.baseballlibrary.com.
7. Smith, *Babe Ruth's America*, 269.
8. Thorn and Holway, *The Pitcher*, 74–75.
9. Smith, *Babe Ruth's America*, 271.
10. See www.baseballlibrary.com.
11. Thorn and Holway, *The Pitcher*, 68.
12. Ruth, with Slocum, *The Babe and I*, 176, 182.
13. Eig, *Luckiest Man*, 194.
14. Smith, *Babe Ruth's America*, 282.
15. Ibid., 283.
16. Ruth and Considine, *The Babe Ruth Story*, 210.
17. Ruth, with Slocum, *The Babe and I*, 179.
18. Ruth and Considine, *The Babe Ruth Story*, 211.
19. Kelley, *In the Shadow of the Babe*, 90.
20. Ruth and Considine, *The Babe Ruth Story*, xiv.
21. Julia Ruth Stevens, from interviews with author, November 2005.
22. Ritter, *The Babe*, 242.
23. Ibid., 245.
24. Ibid., 214.

AFTER THE LAST HURRAH,
1936–1948

Ruth kept busy after retirement, often golfing, bowling, hunting, and fishing. He listened to his favorite shows on the radio, *The Lone Ranger*, *The Green Hornet*, and *Gangbusters*. His daughter Julia outlined a typical day: "He followed pretty much the same routine. He'd get up in the morning and eat a good breakfast, and then he'd go off and we would not see him again until 5:00 generally. Like any other father, he'd come home and he'd say, 'Anybody coming over tonight? If not, I'm going to get into my pajamas and relax and be comfortable.' After dinner, lots of times we'd play cards and Daddy was so good at anything that he did. Some celebrities' kids resent their father being monopolized; I never did. I just thought it was wonderful: they can like him, but he's *my* dad."[1]

Ruth was not much of a reader, but the headlines of the era included such events as the explosion of the *Hindenburg* in New Jersey, claiming the lives of thirty-six people. He would glance through the newspaper, but mainly to pore through box scores. What he wanted most was a spot in the game again. Crestfallen, he soon bitterly realized that there was no job for him in baseball. Not even after he was bestowed with baseball's greatest honor.

In January 1936, the first Hall of Fame election was held to determine the charter members of that august organization. On February 2, the results were released and the elite five men receiving the mandated 75 percent of votes cast were Ty Cobb, Honus Wagner, Christy Mathewson, Walter Johnson, and Ruth. The actual induction ceremony didn't take place until 1939. Julia observed, "He hated ties. If you've ever noticed that 1936 Hall of Fame picture [of the original five members], he is the only one there with an open shirt."

Ruth was out of the game, but juggernaut Lou Gehrig rolled on, with his longevity streak alive. Once, when asked about Gehrig's astounding ability to play day after day, Ruth replied with cynicism and, perhaps, a touch of jealousy. "This Iron Man stuff is just baloney. . . . The guy ought to learn to sit on the bench and rest. They're not going to pay off on how many games he's played in a row."[2]

Ruth continued life as a celebrity, but it was rather hollow. Joe Garner wrote, "He made personal appearances, awarded trophies to beauty queens, and showed up at Yankee Stadium as a spectator. But he seemed lost, a man in search of a purpose."[3] In early December 1936, Ruth had refused an offer to manage a minor league team in Albany, New York. Later, though, he relented to overtures from the Brooklyn Dodgers and on June 18, 1938, accepted a coaching job that was to run for the rest of that season. The next day he donned a very foreign uniform and jersey number (35), and assumed duties that included giving batting tips and coaching first base as a figurehead. As a ploy to draw fans, the Dodgers also had him take batting practice and appear as their first baseman in exhibition games, despite the fact that he looked painfully old and rusty.

Once again, Ruth was under the delusion that this position could lead to him winning a managerial job. About the only goal the insatiable Ruth desired but didn't get to "devour" was managing at the big-league level. A token job as a coach–fan magnet or a managerial gig in the minors wasn't satisfying and he remained bitter. Still, by and large, Ruth seemed to enjoy his role on the team. However, when the volatile Leo Durocher was named to manage the 1939 Dodgers, it was as if the writing was boldly spray painted on the wall due to bad blood between them: Leo "The Lip" was in and the Babe was out.

After all, this was the same Durocher who had once scuffled with Ruth and whose name was soiled by Ruth a decade earlier. Baseball Library's Web site stated that there were "whispered rumors" on the club, almost certainly untrue ones, contending "that Leo was stealing money and jewelry from his team-mates."[4] Another version stated that one night Ruth came back to his hotel under the influence of alcohol and asked for help getting to his room and into bed. Durocher gave him a hand but when Ruth discovered his watch missing the next morning he assumed, with no solid proof, that Durocher was guilty of the crime. Ruth's wife Claire wrote that Durocher had undermined Ruth in 1938, revealing to the public that Ruth, never known for his keen memory, had missed a sign in a key spot that cost the Dodgers a win.[5] This story is certainly suspect because first base coaches don't flash signals.

In any event, Durocher, who had been drummed out of the Yankees organization and waived in February 1930, went on to guide the 1939 Dodgers as a rookie skipper and captured his first of three pennants two years later. Ruth, on the other hand, languished at home, never again to actively don a uniform on a baseball field as a coach or manager. It must have further galled Ruth that Durocher became a big-league manager even though he couldn't carry Babe's proverbial jock strap and he had no experience (even in the minors) as a manager, a factor some teams had claimed went against Ruth's chances for being hired to lead a major league club.

Over the course of Ruth's career, more than twenty of his contemporaries did get managerial positions with no previous experience. The list included Walter Johnson, Bill Terry, Cochrane, and, said Julia, "Everybody. Everybody it seemed that ever held a bat got a chance to be a manager, but not Daddy. He didn't think it was fair. It was too bad because I think he deserved the chance. He might have fallen flat on his face. I don't think so because he really knew baseball and he got along great with the players. I think they would have been right behind him."[6] He had asked for a managing job, had begged for it, and, in 1935, had even notified the Yankees that he'd do the job for a token salary of one dollar—all to no avail.[7]

Right around this time period Ruth was forced into the role of a disciplinarian when his daughter Dorothy began dating. Ruth the Lothario became Ruth the Terrible; he, of all people, knew what boys and men were like. He would meet Dorothy's boyfriends at the door and immediately established a midnight curfew—this coming from a man who had reveled in staying out all night.[8] Julia also remembered her father "was very much in favor" of discipline *as a father*. "He was never mean about it, he just said, 'I want you in the house by midnight,' and that was that even though all my friends might still be partying and so forth. He was very protective."[9]

When Ruth discovered Dorothy had been "playing hooky," once for two weeks running, he and Claire imposed the parental version of a suspension by grounding Dorothy for a month. By the following year, shortly after turning 18, Dorothy rebelled and left home. She found it ironic that her father's fans were "more his 'family' than his real family ever was."[10]

Ruth once observed, "If it wasn't for baseball, I'd be in either the penitentiary or the cemetery."[11] That may have been true of the young Ruth, but it wasn't entirely true for the aging Ruth who had no choice but to stay busy while also waiting for another job opportunity. Not long after Durocher began his managerial career—something that continued to rile Ruth—Babe received more bad news: Lou Gehrig was dying. Everyone knew, of course, that "The Iron Horse" had suffered through a bad 1939 spring training and knew that he was forced to make a trip to the Mayo Clinic. Then, when word leaked that he had a rare form of infantile paralysis that ended his endurance skein at a staggering 2,130 games, the shock set in—Lou was mortal. His streak ended on May 2,

1939; not long after that, it was announced that his uniform would be retired in two months, a first in big-league history.

Ruth found it difficult to witness the weakened Gehrig, a man once able to seemingly snap "an oak tree in two with his hand," now shuffling along, losing his balance and "in the end, becoming too weak to light a match."[12] When Gehrig bade his farewell to Yankee Stadium, giving his "luckiest man in the world" speech on the Fourth of July, 1939, Ruth's emotions crashed about him. He approached his former teammate, hugged him, tried to make him smile, but instead, began sobbing as if he were a baby.[13] Ruth also stated that he felt such a tragedy should never again happen, yet he was fated to make a similar adieu only about seven years later and under eerily similar circumstances.[14] Few, if any, could have imagined the rollicking Ruth would outlive the wholesome, robust Gehrig, but he did.

Gehrig, who was honored by being inducted into the Hall of Fame without having to wait the customary five-year period, died on June 2, 1941, from amyotrophic lateral sclerosis, now most commonly known as Lou Gehrig's disease. On the day Gehrig was put on view at the Church of the Divine Paternity in New York, Ruth popped in, cut to the front of the line, and cried as he gazed down at his former teammate.[15] Incidentally, according to Frank Ardolino, catcher Bill Dickey, a former Yankee teammate, contended that the hug Ruth initiated "was one-sided on the Babe's part" and Gehrig "never forgave him."[16]

On June 12, 1939, the official opening of the Hall of Fame took place. While Ruth didn't receive as many votes as Cobb, he did receive the loudest applause from the crowd that day. On January 7, 1940, Dorothy was married to Daniel Sullivan. Ruth's granddaughter, Linda Ruth Tosetti, said a wedding had been planned but "three days before my mom ran off and eloped with Daniel."[17] In October, Dorothy gave Babe his first grandchild, a boy named Daniel Jr. The union lasted only five years, producing two more children, Genevieve and Ellen. In retrospect, Dorothy conceded that she got married because she needed security and companionship. So, another parallel existed in the lives of Babe and Dorothy in that both of their first marriages failed. Dorothy's second marriage to Dominick Pirone resulted in three other children: Donna, Richard, and Linda.

The United States officially entered World War II on December 8, 1941, one day after the infamy of the sneak attack on Pearl Harbor. Ruth was, of course, excused from serving his country, this time due to his age, 46, but he did sell war bonds and raise funds. He also, according to Dorothy's biography, felt betrayed by the Japanese who had treated him so warmly during his visits there. When he heard the news of the Pearl Harbor attack, he became outraged and stomped through his apartment destroying mementos and trophies from Japan.[18]

Just over a month after Pearl Harbor, Commissioner Landis wrote a letter to President Franklin D. Roosevelt asking if he felt baseball should be played while a war raged. On January 15, 1942, Roosevelt wrote back affirming, in the now-famous "Green Light" letter, that the game should continue. The President stated that it was Commissioner Landis' call, but that his "personal and not an official point of view" was that baseball would help the nation "have a chance for recreation and for taking their mind off their work even more than before." He even encouraged more night contests because those games gave "an opportunity to the day shift to see a game occasionally." Roosevelt continued, "As to the players themselves, I know you agree with me that the individual players who are active military or naval age should go, without question, into the services. Even if the actual quality to the teams is lowered by the greater use of older players, this will not dampen the popularity of the sport."[19]

There were those who objected to Roosevelt's stance; some even wrote what were termed "Red Light" letters to the president, but Landis concurred and the season went on as planned. A 2005 ESPN report stated that 95 percent of major league players wound up spending time in the armed services. While the quality of play did suffer—after all, this was an era featuring a one-armed outfielder—baseball didn't vanish.

In a round about way, the war led to Ruth's final appearance in a Yankee uniform in "his" stadium. On August 23, 1942, Walter Johnson and Ruth took part in an exhibition for the benefit of the Army Navy Relief fund. On the eve of the game, Ruth had the nervous energy and anticipation of a kid, worrying about his uniform's appearance and fretting that he wouldn't perform well. Although both Ruth's bat and Johnson's arm were both full of corrosion, they gamely took to the field. Johnson fed 21 pitches to the Bambino and Ruth lifted the third offering for a "homer" into the lower right field seats and nearly propelled the final offering into another time zone, high and deep into the third deck in right field. The ball actually landed in foul territory by a scant couple of feet, but Ruth, with his regal air, ignored that technicality and made his final trot around the bags on his way to touch Yankee Stadium home plate for the final time.[20]

The next few years were uneventful; they were spent making appearances, golfing, hunting, and fishing. In 1943, Ruth took part in several baseball games, benefits for the armed services. In 1945, the world around Ruth was abuzz with activity. May 7, V-E (Victory in Europe) Day, was celebrated by ecstatic Americans everywhere. Almost exactly eleven months after the D-Day invasion of Normandy by 176,000 Allied troops, the war in Europe ended when the Germans surrendered in far off Rheims, France. Then, on August 6, the American bomber "Enola Gay" dropped the atomic bomb called "Little Boy" on Hiroshima, Japan. Peace was then just eight days off.

Days earlier, in Ruth's circles, Mel Ott hit his 500th homer on August 1, allowing him to join Ruth and Foxx as the only men with 500-plus home runs. Ott had once said he didn't want anyone to break Ruth's home run record, "It just wouldn't seem right."[21] In New York, the Yanks were sold to Del Webb, Dan Topping, and Larry MacPhail, the man who had hired Ruth to coach the Dodgers. Ruth quickly contacted MacPhail regarding a job, but was eventually told to "Sit tight."

On September 30, 1945, Ruth consented to appear in a game for the Savitt Gems, a semi-pro team. With the sun beaming down as he took batting practice, he did what he did best, lifting six pitches out of the park. The *Hartford Courant* stated, "It is believed that Babe Ruth, pinch hitting for [Cliff] Keeney, took his last swing in a game...at Bulkeley Stadium in Hartford, Connecticut." The article quoted Kenney as saying, "Now Babe was 50 and he certainly wasn't in playing shape. So he was given some nice pitches to hit out." During the actual game, Ruth, at around 250 pounds, squeezed into "a specially-stitched Gems uniform," tapped out to the pitcher. His name never again graced a box score.[22]

More baseball history was made on October 30 when Jackie Robinson signed a minor league contract, making him the first African American player in organized baseball in the modern era and the first overall since 1884.[23]

The introduction of ENIAC, the world's first "electronic digital computer," was unveiled in 1946. Even though it weighed in at a cumbersome 30 tons, and it contained 18,000 vacuum tubes spread out over a sprawling 1,800 square feet, its use let the world know that the age of the computer was dawning, just as baseball fans soon became aware that the era of Ruth was waning.[24]

In the early days of 1946, an old ache, the rejection of Ruth as a manager, struck once more. MacPhail, who was running the Yankees organization, continued brushing Ruth off, then filled the managerial position with another candidate. The Yanks ran through three managers and wound up 17 games out of first.

On September 20, Babe wrote a letter to MacPhail, pleading for *any* position on either the Yankees or their Newark farm team. Money, he wrote, wasn't important, he simply wanted to don the uniform once more, to be around the guys, to work. In MacPhail's response, dated October 8, he informed Ruth that the Yankees were in a rebuilding phase and that type of club required an experienced skipper. He then offered to discuss a job in the New York area dealing with promoting sandlot baseball, a position light years away from the Bigs.[25] Ruth's appeal to MacPhail was to be his last effort to latch on to the job that had eluded him for so long.

Julia recalled how the failure to achieve a big league managerial position affected her father.

He always read the box scores. He did follow baseball and he did go to games. He was always hoping to get a call about a manager's job; it was the biggest disappointment of his life. I know he died of cancer, but I sometimes think a broken heart had a great deal to do with it. By the time he reached that point, I guess he had just given up; they were never going to ask him to be a manager which is what he had wanted so much to really top off his career.

I have been told by various reporters that another reason he never received an offer to manage a major league team was because they were afraid he was going to raise their salaries. He was all for ballplayers getting [better] salaries. He also wanted an association to help ballplayers—they have it now, but he wanted it way back then—who had not made enough in their lifetime as players to be able to support themselves. He very likely would have gone to bat for his team, saying, "Well so-and-so had a good year, he deserves [a raise]." It was all in what they figured was *their* best interests. Actually, their best interests would have been served very well if they had put Daddy in as a manager.[26]

In September 1946, Claire and a number of Ruth's friends first began commenting on how hoarse his voice sounded. Ruth attributed it to the nitrate of silver treatment he had received years earlier. Even when sharp pains over his left eye started to badger him, he dismissed the seriousness of the warning signs.

This was the same Ruth who, during his playing days, worried about his eyes so much he avoided reading and attending movies, holding to an old, common belief that such activities could harm the eyes. Now, Ruth's "solution" for his symptoms, merely popping aspirins, didn't help. The pain lingered and, by November, intensified. He then took his doctor's advice and entered French Hospital in New York on November 26 for observation. He made his entrance in a wheelchair, quite a decline for a man who once roamed the outfields of ballparks throughout the nation.

Dorothy wrote that by about this time his "despondency" reached its nadir.[27] Said his granddaughter, Linda Ruth Tosetti, "Towards the end of his life, I think he lost spirit. Babe was very much a people person—one thing Babe liked was to be with people and touch people. Towards the end, he became 'Mister Babe Ruth, don't go near him.'" It got to the point where Ruth "could no longer touch the people, the people could no longer touch him.

"He still did do some appearances certainly, but I think he changed from being 'one-of-the-crowd' to a more revered status. I don't think anyone 'kept' him from the fans, just that they started thinking of him differently. That was sad. My grandfather had a zest for life that measured tenfold more than the normal person."[28]

At first, X-rays revealed nothing, and Ruth later recalled that his health worsened to the point where he had difficulty speaking, his left eye "drooped shut" and he couldn't swallow. Finally, a malignancy was spotted and surgery was ordered. Ruth, who had long strayed from the Catholic Church, made his confession and asked to take Holy Communion the morning of the operation.[29]

Ruth spoke of his hair falling "out in hunks when the nurses tried to comb it" due to his receiving what seemed like endless radiation treatments. He had lost 80 pounds and felt as if death was imminent.[30] When news of Ruth's weak condition hit the newsstands, he was inundated by an estimated 30,000 pieces of mail, including one from Brother Gilbert, writing shortly before his own demise.[31]

After Ruth was released from the hospital on February 15, 1947, he had exactly a year-and-a-half left to live. He continued to puff his cigars and often punctuated his speech with hacking coughs. Fellow slugger Hank Greenberg paid a visit to Ruth and commented that "he was very disappointed by the way he had been treated." Greenberg acknowledged that Ruth did receive a lot of attention from fans, but his gripe was with team owners. Greenberg continued, "the owners should have appreciated what he contributed to the game and made an effort to ease him out of baseball with a little more dignity."[32]

Baseball Commissioner Happy Chandler declared April 27, 1947—just a dozen days after Jackie Robinson broke the big league color barrier—to be "Babe Ruth Day" in every ballpark throughout organized baseball, a day to celebrate Ruth's career and to unite in prayer. Chandler called the event a display of affection for Ruth and his numerous contributions to baseball.[33]

The biggest ceremony that day was, of course, in the Bronx, where Yankee Stadium listened in admiration mixed with gloom as Ruth, his hair Boo Radley white, said farewell to his fans. Mel Allen introduced Ruth who slowly approached a cluster of microphones and, his voice raspy and ghostly faint, feebly began his speech. "You know how bad my voice sounds? Well, it feels just as bad." Ruth's words were floating out via a national broadcast while also being heard over public address systems throughout all major league parks.

Ruth touched on two of his loves, "You know, this baseball game of ours comes up from the youth." He later added, "The only real game, I think, in the world is baseball." Soon, after a few more comments, including how youngsters are bound to succeed if they try hard enough, he swiftly concluded, "There's been so many lovely things said about me, I'm glad that I've had the opportunity to thank everybody. Thank you." The 58,339 in attendance cheered as Ruth received gifts, including a plaque bearing his image on it from the AL, and from the NL a book with signatures from every player in that league.

Shortly before the festivities, the *New York Times* had located Johnny Sylvester, the boy Ruth had dedicated a homer to years earlier, and taken him to Ruth's apartment. Sylvester greeted his hero with a heartfelt, "I'm grown up now, thanks to you." Julia recalls Sylvester saying, "I wish I could do for you, Babe, what you did for me." It was fitting for Sylvester to return the visit Ruth had paid him so long ago.[34]

On June 29, 1947, Ruth began receiving daily injections of an experimental anti-cancer drug, teropterin. Ruth was also one of the first patients to undergo experimental chemotherapy, and perhaps the first ever to get both chemotherapy and radiation therapy for his type of cancer. At first, the chemotherapy succeeded, giving him some false hope.

Another summer broke in New York in 1948, this one bringing back the searing pain to Ruth. His jaws ached when he ate, and he knew he had to visit his doctors once again. He wrote about his weight loss, recounting how, at his worst, his frame resembled a "rattling skeleton" and how, when he had recovered enough to stand up, he was surprised that he could gaze down directly to see his feet.[35]

A ceremony was held on June 13, 1948, as the Yankees retired Babe Ruth's jersey on the twenty-fifth anniversary of Yankee Stadium. This was to be his final appearance on his team's field of play. As the top-coated Ruth doffed his cap to the adoring crowd, he beamed at them, but physically appeared frail, a shocking contrast to the mighty Ruth his fans remembered.

Pitcher Bob Feller, whose Indians were playing in New York that day, recalled the moment. "Babe came walking out of the runway. He was dying of throat cancer. He was very feeble. He probably only weighed about 145 to 150 pounds. He reached in the bat rack. . . . He grabbed a bat at random to use for a cane and to lean on."[36]

Heywood Hale Broun mused, "Even though, by that time, he was wasted away, somehow, on that day, he filled the uniform to be once more, for some last gasp, a heroic figure. You had just this moment that you tried to hold and keep." Perhaps it was the Broun version of Ruth fans wanted to see, to remember, and to cherish.[37] In reality, Ruth looked terrible; reportedly his weight had tumbled from 278 pounds to a cadaverous 150 in a few weeks.[38]

Many of Ruth's former teammates were on hand, and when Ruth first entered the clubhouse they marched over to him "to shake hands, touch him, put their arms around him, straining to hear his gravely whispers." The chill in the air at Yankee Stadium must have matched their emotions; they *knew* this would be their final chance to be with their buddy, the Babe. When Joe Dugan sat next to Ruth and asked how he was, Ruth ruefully replied, "Joe, I'm gone. I'm gone, Joe."[39]

Ruth had his Last Rites on July 21, and on July 26, made his final public appearance. Newborn-kitten weak, Babe left the hospital and showed up at the New York premiere of the film *The Babe Ruth Story*. Dorothy later wrote that Babe had to be carried out of the hospital to view the premiere and was so heavily drugged he wasn't even aware of his surroundings. Julia stated, "He was under sedation, with an attendant on either side of him, holding him up because he couldn't walk into the theater. That was so sad. When I think of Daddy, I think of him in all the years when he was big and strong."[40] Dorothy recalled his eyes as being expressionless and detested the exploitation, calling it "one of the cruelest scenes" she ever saw.[41]

The day before he passed away, Babe and Dorothy spoke. Only once before had Ruth told her that she was his real daughter, and that came during an argument, leading Dorothy to feel he may have simply been telling her what she wanted to hear. So, now, once more needing reassurance that she was not adopted, Dorothy asked the vital question, he nodded, and her doubts were over.

By 6:30 P.M. the next day, the doctor gravely informed Ruth's family that he was "sinking rapidly." The assessment was correct; Ruth would linger awhile, but the official time of death was listed as 8:01 P.M. on August 16, 1948. Ruth lost his battle to throat cancer at the age of 53 in Memorial Hospital, later to be known as Sloan-Kettering, in New York City.[42]

Some sources say that the writers of the day never printed the truth about Ruth having cancer and that Ruth himself was spared of knowing his exact condition. Julia quoted Jack Lait, a *New York Daily Mirror* editor, "Every newspaperman in New York knew for years that Babe Ruth had cancer of the throat. Yet that was never written. We knew he did not suspect and [we] feared that the dreaded word would break him down."[43]

However, Dorothy wrote that, at the very latest, by the time he checked into the hospital for the final time, he was cognizant of his illness.[44] Tosetti confirmed that, "My mother said, 'He most definitely knew.' I don't care what anybody else says or how close they were, my mother said *he knew*. How could he offer himself for experimentation if he didn't know. The man's hair was turning white and he was losing weight, he was no dummy, he knew. He was a smart man. Maybe he didn't let anybody else know, but he knew."[45]

Additionally, Claire said that shortly before Ruth's demise a visitor to the hospital asked him how he felt. Ruth replied, "Lousy. And they think they're kidding me. But they aren't. I know what I got." She also wrote that the night before he died, right after kissing him goodnight, he said, "Don't come back tomorrow. I won't be here."[46]

According to the *Baltimore News-Post* of August 17, 1948, the chalk-white Ruth's final moments came when "he sighed ever so slightly, one hand plucked feebly at the coverlet for a moment—and he was still." It concluded, stating Mrs. Ruth's "bedside vigil was ended. . . ."

An autopsy revealed the cancer's origin was in a part of the ear passage behind his nose and spread until it pressed on nerves which resulted in paralysis and caused Ruth's hoarseness and difficulty in swallowing. The insidious disease spread to his lungs and liver as well.

It was decided that his body would be put on display in an open mahogany coffin, blanketed with orchids and red roses at the main entrance of Yankee Stadium, its flags at half staff. It was his final visit to the house he had "built." During the time of mourning there, from 5:00 P.M. on August 17 until 7:00 A.M. on August 18, it was estimated that at least 100,000 people—a fitting number, about the amount of two days' worth of standing room only at a ballpark— queued by his coffin. Even in death, Ruth remained, so to speak, a potent drawing card. The line moved quickly, but his admirers had the opportunity to peer down at the Babe, lying in state like a dignitary and attired in a double-breasted blue suit. He clutched a set of rosary beads in his left hand.[47]

Presiding over Ruth's funeral was a distinguished friend of the Babe, Francis Cardinal Spellman, Archbishop of New York. In front of 6,000 mourners inside the gothic St. Patrick's Cathedral he spoke of "the divine spirit that inspired Babe Ruth to overcome hardships and win the crucial game of life" and praised Ruth for his contributions to "generations of American youths" who learned "from the example of his struggle and successes." He lauded Ruth for "his generous-hearted soul" and asked God for a "final scoring" of Ruth's "good deeds."

Outside an estimated 75,000 additional mourners stood by despite rain, with thousands more lining the cortege route and at the cemetery. After the church proceedings, some spectators took flowers, coveting a final souvenir of Ruth. One flowery writer observed, "Even the heavens wept at the passing of Babe Ruth." A newspaper account stated that the fifteen-minute downpour "suddenly stopped as the casket was placed in the hearse at noon." Police held back the throng as "Babe began his last journey."[48]

That trek went a few blocks east of Yankee Stadium and arrived at the cemetery at 1:40 P.M. Ruth was laid to rest in Gate of Heaven Cemetery located in Hawthorne, New York, 25 miles, or around 330 of Ruth's 400-foot homers, from Yankee Stadium. After a service was held beneath a canopy, the coffin was placed in a receiving vault and a floral display with a baseball motif was situated in front of the tomb. "It had been a quiet and fitting farewell to the Babe," wrote one reporter, "but hardly had the family left the cemetery when the inevitable horde of souvenir hunters broke through a rope barrier and began picking at the remaining mass of floral tributes."[49]

There were 57 honorary pallbearers from all walks of life including politicians, former players, and even Sylvester and actor William Bendix. One of his eight official pallbearers, all former teammates, was Dugan who, at one point, turned to fellow pallbearer Hoyt and muttered, "I'd give a hundred dollars for a beer." Poignantly, and quite correctly, Hoyt replied, "Joe, so would the Babe."[50]

Over a four-day period, Manhattan newspapers published 490 eulogistic columns. *The Pittsburgh Press* basically felt that Ruth, had he still been alive, would not have bothered to read them. Young fans still leave notes on his grave including a touching one displayed at the Babe Ruth Museum: "You are my favorite baseball player . . . say hi too [sic] God for me."

Julia said Babe's death devastated Claire. "Oh, my goodness did she ever look after him. As far as Mother was concerned, the sun rose and set on Daddy. And for him to have died so early, Mother was never really the same after that."[51]

America wasn't through paying tribute to Ruth, though. On April 19, 1949, during pregame ceremonies for the Yankees home opener, a granite monument to Ruth, placed then on the playing field, sitting on the warning track about 10 feet in front of the wall, was unveiled in dead center field, joining monuments for Gehrig and Ruth's late manager Miller Huggins.

NOTES

1. Julia Ruth Stevens, from interviews with author, November 2005.
2. Ardolino, "Lou vs. Babe in Life and in *Pride of the Yankees*," 17.
3. Joe Garner, *And the Fans Roared: The Sports Broadcasts that Kept Us on the Edge of Our Seats* (Naperville, IL: Sourcebooks, Inc., 2000), 7.
4. From www.baseballlibrary.com.
5. Ruth, with Slocum, *The Babe and I*, 186–187.
6. Julia Ruth Stevens, from interviews with author, November 2005.
7. Pirone and Martens, *My Dad, the Babe*, 172.
8. Ibid., 121.
9. Julia Ruth Stevens, from interviews with author, November 2005.
10. Pirone and Martens, *My Dad, the Babe*, 122, 124.
11. From www.baseballalmanac.com.
12. Ruth and Considine, *The Babe Ruth Story*, 219.
13. Ruth, with Slocum, *The Babe and I*, 165.
14. Ruth and Considine, *The Babe Ruth Story*, 218–219.
15. Eig, *Luckiest Man*, 357.
16. Ardolino, "Lou vs. Babe in Life and in *Pride of the Yankees*," 17.

17. Linda Ruth Tosetti, from telephone interview with author, September 23, 2005.

18. Pirone and Martens, *My Dad, the Babe*, 174.

19. From www.baseballalmanac.com.

20. Ruth and Considine, *The Babe Ruth Story*, 220–221.

21. Harold C. Burr, "He Hits Off One Foot," *Baseball Magazine*, May 1939, 537–538.

22. From www.courant.com.

23. Gershman, *Diamonds*, 125.

24. Ibid., 158.

25. Ruth, with Slocum, *The Babe and I*, 194.

26. Julia Ruth Stevens, from interviews with author, November 2005.

27. Pirone and Martens, *My Dad, the Babe*, 174.

28. Linda Ruth Tosetti, from telephone interview with author, September 23, 2005.

29. Ruth and Considine, *The Babe Ruth Story*, 232–233.

30. Ritter, *The Babe*, 238.

31. Ruth and Considine, *The Babe Ruth Story*, 234–235.

32. Quoted by Miller in *The Babe Book* (185), from Hank Greenberg's *The Story of My Life*.

33. Ruth and Considine, *The Babe Ruth Story*, 237.

34. Ibid., 239.

35. Ibid., 244.

36. John McMurray, "Pitching Great Bob Feller Has Fond Memories of Many Hall of Famers," *Baseball Digest*, July 2005, 68.

37. Garner, *And the Fans Roared*, 9.

38. Gilbert, *Young Babe Ruth*, 177.

39. Creamer, *Babe*, 423.

40. Julia Ruth Stevens, from interviews with author, November 2005.

41. Pirone and Martens, *My Dad, the Babe*, 179.

42. Ibid., 184.

43. Stevens, with Martens, *Major League Dad*, 112.

44. Pirone and Martens, *My Dad, the Babe*, 178.

45. Linda Ruth Tosetti, from telephone interview with author, September 23, 2005.

46. Ruth, with Slocum, *The Babe and I*, 197, 208.

47. Quoted by Miller in *The Babe Book* (190), from Bill Koenig's "Frail from Cancer, Ruth Was Last to Know He Was Dying," *USA Today Baseball Weekly*, August 1998.

48. From Babe Ruth Museum archives.

49. Ibid.

50. Widely quoted.

51. Julia Ruth Stevens, from interviews with author, November 2005.

Babe Ruth Birthplace and Museum in Baltimore, Maryland. *Courtesy of the author.*

RUTH AND THE RECORD BOOKS

According to sportswriter Bob Broeg attempting "to capture Babe Ruth with cold statistics would be like trying to keep up with him on a night out." Infielder Toby Harrah uttered the classic line, "Baseball statistics are like a girl in a bikini. They show a lot, but not everything." Both quotes ring true; but in Ruth's case, stats pretty much do tell it all. His numbers are phenomenal.

No discussion of Ruth's lasting impact on the game can take place without touching on his myriad records—attention *must* be paid to his stats. When he retired, he tied or owned nearly 200 AL standards and possessed 64 major league records, which is in itself yet another record. Astonishingly, many of Ruth's marks still stand.

Long after his death, Ruth remained in the news. For example, every time one of his records was threatened, the name Ruth would again be splattered over the sports pages from coast to coast. A few of the more impressive records included the most lifetime runs driven in (a total, since broken, that varies according to the source used; more on this later), the most years leading the AL in RBIs (6), the most seasons with 100-plus RBIs (13), the most years leading his league in runs (8), the most years with 150 or more runs scored (6), the most years leading the league in walks (11), the most times compiling 100 or more walks in a year (13), and, naturally, his 60 homers in a single season as well as his 714 lifetime home runs.

In 1920, Ruth became not only the first man to hit 30 homers, but the first to reach 40 and 50 as well. He even attained the 50 home run strata twice before anyone else had managed to swat 30, and he set the bar high with the most extra inning homers at 16. Not only that, from 1926 through 1931 he averaged just over 50 home runs a season with 302 round trippers over that span. He even averaged 40 or more over 17 consecutive seasons, and, from 1926 through 1932, piled up 40 or more each year, which is still a record. Ruth also established undying records with his 457 total bases in 1921 and his combined total of 375 hits and walks in 1923.

Ruth didn't merely break records; he absolutely annihilated them. Take the record for the most home runs in a single season—it had stood at a mere 27, a far cry from his eventual 60, from 1884 until 1919. Further, when he set records, they tended to last for a long time, many lasting into the 1960s and beyond. His three most cherished records, the ones he said he felt would never be broken, did last a long time, at least by baseball measurements. Ruth's coveted 60 homers in a single season stood the test of time until another Yankee, Roger Maris, nudged by him with 61 in 1961.

Next was a mark Babe set as a pitcher. Over the course of three 1916 and 1918 World Series outings, he recorded 29 2/3 consecutive scoreless innings. His daughter Julia said, "Any time he did an interview with a reporter who had not done his homework and didn't ask a question about his pitching, he'd bring it up. He'd say, 'Well, you know, I was a pretty fair pitcher, too!' "[1] His Series record skein stood until yet another Yankee, Whitey Ford, usurped it on October 8, 1961, a week after Maris hit his 61st homer. That coincidence allowed Ford to quip, "It's been a tough week for the Babe."[2]

Finally, Ruth's career home run total survived until April 8, 1974, when Hank Aaron of the Atlanta Braves took an Al Downing pitch for a ride in Atlanta's Fulton County Stadium. Thus, of his three greatest feats, Ruth's 714 lifetime home runs remained a record deeper into the twentieth century than his others, although his shutout inning streak in Series play stayed on the books for the longest time, 43 seasons.

Interestingly, Ruth has been so beloved and venerated over the years that many members of the media, many fans, and even a commissioner of baseball tried to protect his records. Those in Ruth's corner would downplay or disparage men who broke Ruth's marks. The "protection" even came in the form of hate mail to Aaron. Filled with arguments that bordered on tirades, this mail was as venomous as it was voluminous.

The most glaring example of guarding Ruth's feats took place when Maris neared the 60–home run record. Much was made of the fact that he was playing a 162-game season while Ruth had always played 154-game schedules. And, due to a tie, Maris' 1961 Yankees played in 163 games (Ruth's 1927 Yankees also played in a tie contest in which the stats counted). At any rate, it took Maris until the season finale on October 1, 1961, to exorcize the ghost of Ruth when he connected for historic home run number 61. Incidentally, Sal Durante retrieved the home run ball and sold it for $5,000. In October 2004, a memorabilia enthusiast forked over nearly $800,000 for ownership of Bonds' 700th home run ball. Imagine what Ruth's 60th or 714th would fetch today.

It clearly was an advantage to shoot for records with eight additional games on the schedule. However, some people, including Maris himself, argued that a "season is a season," and if a player sets a record over the course of a single year, he should own that outright. Also, when Ruth collected his 60th home run, he had only six plate appearances less than Maris had in 1961. However, on July 17, 1961, Commissioner Ford Frick, who had been both a friend and a biographer of Ruth, had decreed that Ruth's record "cannot be broken unless some batter hits 61 or more within his club's first 154 games." Several days later Frick added that if a player surpassed Ruth after the season's 154th contest, the record would go in the books, but with an asterisk attached to it like a scarlet letter.[3] In other words, Frick pontificated, Maris would not "be considered the official record holder." Alan Schwarz wrote that "two-thirds of baseball writers supported the decision." He added that famous columnist Shirley Povich "called any 162-game record 'artificial' and 'synthetic.'"[4]

A logical proposal to end the debate would be to list two sets of records, those set in 154-game seasons and those created under the 162-game format. If that were the case, George Sisler would still be honored for his record 257 hits from 1920, and next to his name, in a separate column, would be that of Ichiro Suzuki with his 262 base hits from 2004. Likewise, Ruth would still own the 154-game season record. Why penalize men such as Sisler and Ruth for having played under the conditions of their era?

Even when Ruth's single season record was surpassed by Mark McGwire and Sammy Sosa in 1998 and then again by Barry Bonds in 2001, detractors were still vociferous. Ominous clouds of controversy and allegations swirled when the seedy world of steroids became exposed around, and into, the twenty-first century. "Sure," the argument went, "they beat Babe, but they needed steroids to surpass him." Jose Canseco alleged that "McGwire was right there with me as a living, thriving example of what steroids could do to make you a better ballplayer."[5] On the CBS program *60 Minutes*, Canseco told interviewer Mike Wallace that steroids make "an average athlete a super athlete. It can make a super athlete incredible. Just legendary." Bud Shaw of Cleveland's *Plain Dealer* wrote that "the former mistress of Bonds says that not only did he tell her he used steroids but fretted someone would find out about him."[6]

Many experts felt that baseball's sudden surge in power stats during the 1990s was highly suspicious, and consequently tainted. After all, they pointed out, Ruth's home-run percentage of 11.79 (54 homers over his 458 at bats in 1920) stood for an eon as the game's best ever. Then, during baseball's alleged steroid period, that record was bettered not once or twice, but *five* times; Bonds eclipsed the old record twice with a new all-time high of 15.34 in 2001 and McGwire exceeded Ruth's record three times.

In 2005, Tom Stevens stated that if Bonds breaks his godfather's (Willie Mays) home-run total and if it is proven that Bonds cheated, an asterisk should be placed next to his name. "How else are you going to deal with it? And, when you compare Bonds with Babe, he exceeded Babe's [career] at bats a couple of seasons ago."[7]

In baseball it seems unnatural for a long standing, venerable record to be utterly destroyed—surpassed sometimes, yes, but wiped out, no. For instance, when Maris first broke Ruth's record, he did so by a lone home run, less than 2 percent beyond the former record. When McGwire breezed by Maris' 61 home runs by hitting 70, he did so by an astounding improvement of nearly 15 percent. That would be similar to someone coming along and breaking Hack Wilson's single-season RBI total of 191 by almost 30. While most fans enjoyed the McGwire-Sosa Show in 1998, there were rumblings about the wild offensive eruptions by the game's biggest sluggers.

In a *Baseball Digest* article, Bob Nightengale quoted Cy Young Award winner Steve Stone as observing, "Baseball is a game of records. We live and die by them. You want those records to mean something. You want to know that what players accomplished in the game is because of their ability and not because of the work of a chemist." Bob Costas added, "Bonds is a historic figure, and no one knows how much of what he has accomplished can be attributed to cheating. Everything he's done, as magnificent as it is, will be viewed with skepticism." Meanwhile, of course, Ruth's record remained untouched by the criticism that riddled Bonds and McGwire and even, in a different vein, Maris.[8]

Ruth's career home-run record didn't go away quietly, either. As Aaron approached the 700-home run plateau, Ruth backers often seemed to take it personally that Ruth's lifetime record was about to fall. Harry "the Hat" Walker, former batting crown winner, defended Ruth. "Here's a guy who went to bat [almost exactly] 4,000 times less than Hank Aaron. Four *thousand* times. Hank was great, but 4,000 times less does make a lot of difference. Hank was great, don't get me wrong," he emphasized, "but Ruth was so super."[9]

Many experts agreed with Walker and argued and assumed that if Ruth had been given an additional 4,000 trips to the plate, he would have continued to rack up homers at his lifetime rate of one home run for every 11.76 at bats, second only to McGwire. That being the case, Ruth's projected home run total would have ballooned to almost exactly 1,050.

Ruth's daughter Dorothy was upset when Maris and Aaron topped her father's records. Ruth's wife Claire allowed that her husband's records might fall, but commented that the person who initially sets records remains special. "Charles Lindbergh was the first one to fly the Atlantic alone. Who was the second?"[10]

Aaron supporters pointed out that Ruth would've had more at bats if he had taken care of himself better. They noted that Aaron's longevity, consistency, and durability were worthy of respect and that he deserved his status as the reigning home-run king. The two points may not be contradictory: Ruth is probably still seen by the consensus of experts as the most memorable and wondrous player ever while Aaron, irrefutably, remains the all-time home-run king with his 755 homers.

However, as Barry Bonds approached Ruth's home-run total at the end of 2005, Ruth's ancestors were ruffled by Bonds' words and behavior, especially when, during the 2003 All-Star break, he said the following about Ruth:

> If there is a record you want to go after, it's Babe Ruth. Because Babe Ruth is Mr. Baseball, right? He's considered the greatest baseball player, and if you want to compare yourself, you want to compare yourself to the greatest player. Because as a left-handed hitter, I wiped him out. That's it. And in the baseball world, Babe Ruth's everything, right? I got his slugging percentage, and I'll take his home runs and that's it. Don't talk about him no more."[11]

Many of the other notable records of the Colossus of Clout also eventually fell. Even Ruth's seemingly insurmountable record for slugging percentage in a season toppled, though it stood for a long 81 years. No one matched his slugging average of .847 in 1920 until 2001, when Bonds, while establishing the most recent record for most homers in a single season (73), posted a simply stupendous slugging percentage of .863, although Ruth still owns two of the top three seasons in this realm.

In addition, as far as career slugging goes, Ruth's inviolate record of .690 makes Ted Williams' .634 a very distant runner-up and even Bonds can only envy Ruth here with his .611 through 2005, fifth best all-time. Beyond that, Ruth still owns the record for the most times leading his league in slugging, 13, topping the circuit every season from 1918 through 1931 except in his off season of 1925. Also, only he and Bonds eclipsed the single season .800 slugging percentage figure twice. Stevens noted that although Babe hadn't worn a uniform in 70 years his .690 "is as unassailable as Cobb's lifetime batting average. There are a lot of ballplayers who never see .600, and good ballplayers, like

Frank Thomas [.568 lifetime]." Some decent players won't even "see .600 in a single season in their heyday."[12]

To this day, only three men with 3,000 or more plate appearances retired with a slugging percentage over .600, a lifetime batting average of .330 or better, as well as an on-base percentage over .400. Those men were Lou Gehrig, Ted Williams, and, of course, Ruth.

At one time Ruth also held such illustrious records as most career walks drawn (broken in 2001 by the ageless Rickey Henderson and more recently by the widely feared Bonds with 2,302); most bases on balls in a single season (170; Bonds topped that three times with his high of 232 in 2004); lifetime runs driven in (the figures vary here from around 2,192 to 2,213, trailing only Aaron, but he's still the top RBI man in AL history); and the highest career home run percentage (8.5; second now to McGwire's 9.42).

By his career's end, Ruth had carved out the record for the highest lifetime on-base percentage, .474, which stood until Ted Williams retired at .482. Likewise, Babe's 345 homers hit in his home park and his 367 road homers were baseball's bests until Aaron snagged them from Ruth. Only Henderson and Cobb scored more lifetime runs than Ruth with only Aaron and Stan Musial possessing more career extra base hits. The Babe, Gehrig, and Jimmie Foxx are tied for the most 100-RBI seasons with 13, and only Ruth and Gehrig strung together three consecutive seasons with 150-plus runs driven in. Ruth also now shares with Sammy Sosa the record for producing four seasons with 50 or more homers.

Julia recalled that one of Dorothy's daughters, Donna, said, "When I meet the one man who can break *all* of Babe's records, that'll be [amazing]."[13] As Tom Stevens pointed out, while many of Ruth's records crumbled, it took many men to break them, from speedsters such as Henderson to sluggers such as Aaron and hurlers such as Ford. And there are yet other records Ruth shares with no man. In all, Ruth topped his league in home runs a record 12 times, fully 50 percent more times than the NL's best of 8 titles by Mike Schmidt.[14]

By the end of his career, Ruth had amassed more home runs than an entire club for a given season 91 times. In 1927, he out-homered 12 teams, including every AL team but the Yankees. Nowadays, as Gabe Costa put it in *The Baseball Research Journal*, "It is unthinkable to envision any recent slugger rivaling this kind of dominance. McGwire, Sosa, or Bonds would have to hit in the neighborhood of 200 homers to surpass another team's home run total."[15]

Even when Ruth struck out, crowds ooh'ed and ahh'ed in the same collective tone of voice as spectators at a fireworks display. It's certainly true that Ruth took enormous cuts. "Characteristically," wrote Charles C. Alexander, "he spun 360 degrees when he missed the ball." He also noted that in 1920 a physicist determined that when Ruth took a cut it "generated 24,000 foot-pounds per second—about forty-four horsepower."[16]

In a much less scholarly fashion, Grantland Rice wrote, "To watch Ruth go down, swinging from the heels, often sprawling from the sheer violence of his cut, was almost as exciting as seeing him blast one out of the park."[17] Phil Rizzuto's take on Ruth was simple: "Not many guys looked good striking out, but the Babe did."[18] Yet few fans today realize he never once fanned more than 93 times in a season. By contrast, Reggie Jackson went down on strikes 100 or more times in a record 18 seasons. Ruth's lifetime total of 1,330, while high for the early Twentieth century, was almost half of Jackson's 2,597 career K's. Ruth's strikeout total doesn't even place him in the top 50 of all-time.

In baseball today it is not rare to see middle infielders fanning 150 or more times in a season (e.g., Jose Hernandez with 185 and 188 in 2001 and 2002 respectively, or Mark Bellhorn with 17 homers and 177 strikeouts in 2004). As for pure sluggers, Sosa has struck out 150 or more times in six seasons, and, on two occasions, Bobby Bonds whiffed twice as many times as Ruth did in his worst year for strikeouts. In 2004, Adam Dunn surpassed Bonds' single-season strikeout record when he fanned 195 times. Even when striking out, the Babe was productive—that is to say, five times he led his league in strikeouts and homers in the same year, the most ever.

Beyond being the greatest slugger of all-time, Ruth was also the greatest hitting pitcher ever. A lifetime .304 hitter as a pitcher, Ruth, during a 1918 start, accumulated a record 10 total bases on three doubles, a single, and a triple.

Ruth's records would crop up and some even be altered long after he last hung up his spikes. For example, in April 1969, the Baseball Records Committee discovered that Ruth deserved to be credited with 715 home runs, not 714, because a triple he had cracked back on July 8, 1918, should have been ruled a home run. Nothing came of the recommendation, though, and his 714 total is still on the books. However, that same committee acted in February 1976 to revise Ruth's career RBI total to 2,204.[19] As George Vass wrote, "Even the lordly *New York Times* on May 4, 1975, three days after Aaron reached 2,010 [RBIs], admitted it was as confused as everyone else. 'How many runs batted in did Ruth have in his career?' the *Times* asked. 'Nobody really knows....' "

Part of the problem in ascertaining Ruth's true RBI total is because that statistic wasn't officially kept until 1920, Ruth's seventh year of play, so records up to that point were suspect.[20] It seems a shame, especially to baseball purists who like their statistics in unwavering black and white, that some stats from the early eras of baseball cannot be nailed down definitively.

Ruth's pitching statistics cannot be ignored. He not only led the league in ERA in 1916, he also posted the lowest batting average allowed when he held enemy hitters to a paltry .201. Furthermore, his lifetime ERA was an inconceivably low 2.28. Of course, that total was obscenely high compared to his career ERA in World Series play—a miserly 0.87, still the third lowest ever. His lowest won-loss percentage for a season was a robust .643 while his best full season produced a .692 mark.

Among Hall of Fame pitchers, only Bob Feller won more games than Ruth did before the age of 23. A comparison with Walter Johnson is also fitting. In fact, in 1916 and 1917, Ruth's finest years on the mound, he carved out a 47-25 record with a wonderful ERA of 1.88. Over that same span, Johnson went 48-36 with an ERA of 2.04. By the way, against top hitters, Ruth was stingy with the gopher ball, giving up only one homer to a future Hall-of-Famer, Sam Rice.

One puzzling aspect of Ruth's career is how a handful of Hall of Fame voters perceived him. Tom Seaver gained a higher percentage of votes when he was elected to the Hall than any man who ever played baseball, garnering 98.84 percent of all votes cast. This is not to diminish Seaver's status, but it is difficult to fathom that he topped Nolan Ryan's 98.79 percent (second best), Ty Cobb's 98.23 percent (third all-time), and Hank Aaron's 97.83 percent (fifth best, one behind George Brett). In fact, Babe Ruth's percentage of 95.13 is stunningly low, only ninth best all-time as 11 voters inexplicably left him off their ballots. One would think that surely among Cobb, Aaron, and Ruth, there should have been at least one unanimous pick to Cooperstown.

NOTES

1. Julia Ruth Stevens, from interviews with author, November 2005.

2. Widely quoted.

3. According to sportswriter Jack Lang, the Frick asterisk is a fallacy. Another New York writer, Dick Young, brought up the concept of the asterisk in a September 1961 meeting in frick's office. Lang, who also attended the meeting, stated "the asterisk never appeared," but instead the *Elias Sports Book of Records* published both the Ruth record for 154 games and the Maris mark. Quoted from Jack Lang's letter to the editor of *Baseball Digest*, August 2005.

4. Schwarz, *The Numbers Game*, 166.

5. Steve Wilstein, *Associated Press*, February 13, 2005.

6. Bud Shaw, *The Plain Dealer*, January 16, 2005.

7. Tom Stevens, from interview with author, November 5, 2005.

8. George Vass, "Baseball Records: Fact or Fiction?" *Baseball Digest*, June 2005, 22–23.

9. Harry Walker, from interview with author, June 28, 1997.

10. Julia Ruth Stevens, from interviews with author, November 2005.

11. Barry Bonds, Associated Press.

12. Tom Stevens, from interviews with author, November 5, 2005.

13. Julia Ruth Stevens, from interviews with author, November 2005.

14. Tom Stevens, from interview with author, November 5, 2005.

15. Gabe Costa, "Babe Ruth Dethroned?" *The Baseball Research Journal*, May 2003, 103.

16. Alexander, *Our Game*, 136.

17. Quoted by Miler in *The Babe Book* (37), from Grantland Rice's *The Tumult and the Shouting*.

18. Ibid., 62.

19. From www.baseballlibrary.com.

20. Vass, "Baseball Records: Fact or Fiction?" 25–26.

RUTH AND THE GAME TODAY

Although Babe Ruth has been dead for more than fifty years, discussions of him crop up even now among writers, fans, and even ballplayers. Clearly, Ruth was special; his status and his legend require no hype. Unfortunately, at times it's nearly impossible to distinguish between fact, semitruths, and fiction when it comes to the lore of Ruth. Many true things were written about him, yet they sounded so far fetched as to be scoffed at. Likewise, many inaccuracies and downright falsehoods were written about Ruth, but have been repeated so often and were so typical of Ruth that they are now accepted as truths. Even respected writers of Ruth's era perpetuated and embellished Ruthian myths and epic feats. Still, Ruth was multitalented. Many writers accurately talked of Ruth not only as a great hitter but also as a fine base runner and fielder, especially with his gun of an outfield arm.

Former third baseman Rube Bressler said that Ruth "was like a damn animal. He had that instinct," and that Ruth *never* made a mistake in throwing to the wrong base.[1] Johnny Vander Meer went further, "He never threw to the wrong base or missed a cutoff." And Yankee outfielder Ben Chapman added that he had never seen Ruth commit a mental error.[2] Waite Hoyt was more realistic in saying, "It has been said that the Bambino never made a mistake on a ball field. Of course, that's exaggerated."[3]

Defensively it would be folly to compare him to a Roberto Clemente or an Ichiro Suzuki. Ruth spent 1,131 games in right field, 1,062 in left, and even roamed center field for 64 games—his 1920 Yankee debut was as a center fielder, but he never played center after 1924. In addition, he was positioned at first base in 31 games (mostly in the late 1910s and into the early 1920s) and, of course, he pitched in 163 games and also pinch hit 67 times.[4]

In an effort to protect his eyes, Ruth made it a point to avoid a park's sun field. He tended to play in right field at Yankee Stadium because left was the troublesome field there and the Hall of Fame officially lists him as a right fielder. Interestingly, when he retired, he ranked number one for homers recorded by right fielders *and* by left fielders.

Over his career, Ruth committed 179 errors, with alarmingly high totals of 18 in 1918, the year he began splitting duties between the outfield and the mound, and 20 in 1920 when all but 3 of his 142 games played were in the outfield. He compiled double figures for errors seven times. To be fair, Clemente reached double figures in that realm six times. Of course, through Suzuki's first four major league seasons, he had only nine *total* errors. So, Ruth's defensive statistics are far from perfection.

Fellow Boston outfielder Harry Hooper recalled the early days of Ruth. He said while Ruth may well have been "a natural as a pitcher and as a hitter . . . he sure wasn't a born outfielder." Hooper was stationed in center field with two suspect outfielders flanking him, Ruth and Braggo Roth. According to Hooper, it got to the point that he began to fear for his life. He said the Ruth-Roth duo was "galloping around that outfield without regard for life or limb, hollering all the time, running like maniacs after every ball."[5]

While in pursuit of fly balls Ruth had been occasionally known to run recklessly into walls and once even crashed into a palm tree located in fair territory at a Florida park, that time knocking himself out. Ruth's daughter wrote that he was constantly injuring himself, and that he could have "won a few awards for acting."[6] Once he hurt his hand yet melodramatically *limped* off the field. It was written that "no player in big league history was carried off the field on his shield as often" as Ruth.[7] Nonetheless, some of Ruth's peers later considered him to be a good or even great outfielder. Ty Cobb called Ruth "an amazingly graceful fellow for one so huge."[8]

Former major leaguer Tot Pressnell attested to the accuracy of Ruth's arm, "He had a spot in the Yankee Stadium about halfway between first and home where the ball hit so regular that it had the grass tore up—where he was throwin' balls into home plate."[9] Former Yankee third baseman Joe Sewell told a similar tale, saying that on pegs to his bag from Ruth, he would merely place his glove low, between his feet and Ruth's perfect throws would nestle in his glove after taking one hop. Sewell said that Ruth's outfield arm was the best of all the teammates he ever had, including the great Tris Speaker. Some other outfielders, conceded Sewell, had stronger arms than Ruth, but none as accurate.[10]

Other experts have gushed about Ruth's base-running acumen, suggesting the same infallibility some had mentioned about his glove work. However, no player who lasts as long as Ruth did—some 2,503 games over 22 seasons—escapes an occasional blunder. After all, he *was* human, and his attempted stolen base misadventure to end the 1926 World Series was monumentally infamous. However, as a rule, he did run the bases well.

Many modern fans conceive of Ruth as a bloated "swing from the heels and just trot around the bases" kind of guy. While he did get hefty in his later years, there were many times when he could "steal you a base" over his career. He even teamed up with Lou Gehrig on double steals, sometimes with a steal of home. Gehrig, incidentally, still owns the Yankees record for stealing home, but Ruth wasn't far behind with 10 thefts of the plate, and only 31 men stole home more times than Ruth did, although both Gehrig and Ruth trailed Cobb's 54 by several laps.

However, when it comes to measuring a base stealer, one must concentrate on the percentage of times he swiped a bag. Ruth's 117 times caught stealing dragged his success rate down to a miserable .513. Great burglars such as Willie Wilson or Rickey Henderson were successful around 80 percent of the time. A good stolen base artist should be successful around 67 percent of the time; anything around 50 percent is simply not acceptable, a veritable crapshoot on the diamond. So, while Ruth wasn't a pure five-tool player, it seems like a case of carping to minimize his talent.

By way of comparison, consider Brooks Kieschnick, a marginal player for the Milwaukee Brewers in 2003 and 2004, who performed as both a relief pitcher and a sometime outfielder-pinch hitter. Fans were fascinated by such an oddity and relished it when he came through with a victory or a hit. However, the attention he received was disproportionate to his output—a 2-2 record as a pitcher and a two-year batting average of .286 in very limited at-bats, raising his lifetime average to a mediocre .248 (the Brewers released him in April 2005). If Kieschnick could cause a stir, imagine the furor a modern Ruth would create in today's game.

Yankees great Don Mattingly observed, "It's hard to compare different times; the game changes and evolves."[11] In his era, Ruth never dealt with jet lag, didn't have to play night games, or any grueling day games after a night game. He didn't face African-American pitching other than exhibition games or a pitcher with a pure Bruce Sutter–like splitter, and there were no pure sliders. There were no bullpen specialists like Trevor Hoffman or Billy Wagner around back then, so a batter often had four "looks" at the starting pitcher who may have been tiring by Ruth's third or fourth at-bat. All that aside, Mattingly believes Ruth would hit today as well as, say, Barry Bonds.

> Oh, definitely. He'd probably hit 714 homers or more because now
> the training methods are better so he'd probably have been stronger,

and obviously he was kind of bull strong anyway, but with the evolution of weight training, I think [improvement] just grows.

I think the biggest difference you get now is there's a lot more specialty guys ... if Ruth came up, we'd get a lefty out of the pen for him each time he got there. So he may face two lefties a day—you're not going to get four or five at bats off the same guy. I just think that [with] great players—they were great in the past, they're great players now."[12]

Atlanta manager Bobby Cox opined, "What he did in those days had to be impossible. I think the Babe would have hit, probably, 70 nowadays—every year. He was doing it [fantastic feats] when nobody else was doing anything."[13]

Ruth's daughter Julia agreed, adding, "Daddy had at least five years of pitching when he didn't come to bat [much] at all."[14] That, of course, cost him additional homers.

As for the issue of a Babe Ruth playing today and being handcuffed by pitches such as sliders, former catcher Elrod Hendricks scoffed, "It didn't bother Ted Williams once he figured it out, and he made it his business to figure it out—to learn to hit that pitch and hit it well. Those guys are good because they make adjustments to the game."[15]

A twenty-first-century Ruth would benefit from modern equipment, permitting him to scrutinize his swing on video. Modern players also have the advantage of employing sophisticated skill-improving techniques and equipment. Further, today's training methods and sports medicine are to those of Ruth's era as biochemistry is to alchemy. Hall of Fame pitcher Jim Palmer believes Ruth would definitely take advantage of nutritionists and trainers to get in top shape. "He'd have his own personal trainer and that would all be taken care of." Ruth, he believes, would go along with such a regimen. "I think it's in vogue now, isn't it?"[16] Ruth, Mattingly supposed, might even take better care of himself, adding with a chuckle, "Probably—a *little* bit."[17]

However, Ruth's granddaughter Linda Tosetti disagrees, "Babe is just Babe— he wouldn't. He would do it just like it did it then, when coerced to do it, when told he had to do it, or when he was being bad. It took a whole city of New York to rein him in when he was a good time Charlie. The original health food guy, in-bed-by-ten, was Lou [Gehrig]. That didn't seem to rub off on Babe, so I doubt nowadays it would have. He'd be out at the latest hot spot having a ball, breaking curfews because he only needed two or three hours of sleep."[18]

Former Yankees pitcher Steve Karsay succinctly stated, "If he put up the numbers and did the same things he did back then, today, then I don't think anybody would say a word to him. They'd let him do whatever he wants and let him succeed the way he knows how."[19]

Ruth would probably have loved to play in the modern era as he would have fit in comfortably in our world of "super-sizing." One could argue that phrase should have been coined for Ruth. This is an age of hype and that, too, would have suited the Babe just fine. After all, he may have played decades before the massive media frenzy that is a part of the baseball scene today, but Ruth did quite well in promoting himself. He loved to pan for the cameras and "play it up big" for the reporters. His daughter Julia acknowledged that he had a bit of ham in him. "He'd do anything for a laugh. Have you ever seen a picture of him with a baby bonnet on? No one could have been any more down to earth than he was."[20]

Ruth clearly had a presence. He was last century's equivalent of Shaquille O'Neal. Ruth did a ton of endorsements and would certainly rival O'Neal on Madison Avenue today. He even appeared in a handful of movies where he clearly showed that his acting was a light year or two behind his athletic ability. Perhaps a comparison to Muhammad Ali is more apt because it would hold true on many levels. There was a degree of braggadocio about both men. Moreover, like a Walter Brennan line from an old television show, both men backed up their words: "No brag. Just fact." Like Ali, Ruth was a superlative self-promoter. From playing the vaudeville circuit to barnstorming across the country and overseas— much like Ali's fighting some bouts in far away lands—Ruth, wasn't content merely to appear on the diamonds of big-league cities from April into October.

Another interesting question is this: Would a modern Ruth get in more or less scrapes with the front office? John Olerud, who, like Ruth, played for the Red Sox and Yankees, commented that today, "You don't see a whole lot of fines and suspensions coming from teams as much as you do from the Commissioner's Office. If guys are playing well, some of the other stuff kinda' gets overlooked, but if you're not playing well, the manager's not going to have a whole lot of patience for you."[21] That sounds much like what happened when Yankees manager Miller Huggins confronted Ruth in 1925.

Julia felt Babe wasn't the least bit mean-spirited or defiant, he just didn't heed managers much. She laughed, "Obviously, I don't think he paid much attention to them. I think he just felt that whatever he did would be all right because he was producing. He didn't think all that much of himself in that respect, but he always was trying to do his best when he was out in the field. And when that was over, he wanted to go out and have a good time, and he didn't want anybody telling him not to do it."[22] Terry Francona agreed, "When you get a pretty good player, you can turn your head a little bit. He's hitting 40 home runs, driving in 140, then [you can ignore even more.]"[23] So, if Ruth played today, much would hinge on his numbers, but with Ruth and his stats, much could be forgiven.

Former Pirates manager Lloyd McClendon commented, "As a manager you try to treat all your players the same. Obviously your bigger names are certainly different in some respects, but you're going to lose respect as a manger if you start treating players differently."[24] Mattingly said it's feasible for a modern manager to handle, and even punish a Ruth. "The right type of manager. Torre would have handled him great. Joe would have been perfect with him. I think he would have respected him as a player and ask him to follow the guidelines the team sets and treated him fairly compared to the other guys. I've never seen Joe have trouble with a player."[25]

Tosetti is sure of one thing. If her grandfather played today, he'd be paid so much they might as well "give him the franchise."[26] Ruth fans contend he would deserve every dollar he would command today. For such fans, to know Ruth or to simply know *of* him was enough to inspire awe and hyperbole—and that holds true even with today's players.

When David Wells, a huge admirer of the Babe, first reported to the Yankees in 1997, he requested jersey number 3, but when informed that Ruth's number was retired, he settled on number 33. Wells owns a great deal of baseball memorabilia, including a ball signed by Ruth and a hat Ruth wore in games back in 1933. He reportedly paid $35,000 for the cap and showcased it in June 1998, donning it when he took to the mound to make a start for the Yankees.

Julia appreciated that Roger Clemens "always patted Daddy's memorial [in Yankee Stadium's Monument Park] before he went in to pitch."[27] Clemens suggested Ruth's number, like that of Jackie Robinson, be retired in every ballpark in the majors.

The day Sammy Sosa was introduced to the media during a 2005 press conference to welcome him to the Baltimore Orioles, he called Ruth "the man." He added, "It doesn't matter how I'm going to finish in my career, he's still the man in my heart and in this 'land' [Baltimore], too."[28] That "land" truly was Ruth's. In fact, Camden Yards at Orioles Park could have had the name Babe Ruth Stadium. When it came time to give the Orioles facility a name, there was a great deal of sentiment for the name Babe Ruth Stadium to honor the native son.

Julia said, "If you think of baseball today, you say baseball and Babe Ruth comes to mind. He epitomizes baseball. So many people tell me that down the road, as long as there is baseball, his name will never die. I hope that's true because certainly he gave everything that he had to it."[29]

NOTES

1. Ritter, *The Glory of Their Times*, 198.
2. Pirone and Martens, *My Dad, the Babe*, 178.
3. Hoyt, *Babe Ruth as I Knew Him*, 20.

4. From www.baseballalmanac.com.

5. Ritter, *The Babe*, 60.

6. Pirone and Martens, *My Dad, the Babe*, 6.

7. Creamer, *Babe*, 323.

8. Kelley, *In the Shadow of the Babe*, 10.

9. Ibid., 190.

10. Pirone and Martens, *My Dad, the Babe*, 199.

11. Don Mattingly, from interview with author, March 4, 2005.

12. Ibid.

13. Bobby Cox, from interview with author, September 9, 2005.

14. Julia Ruth Stevens, from interviews with author, November 2005.

15. Elrod Hendricks, from interview with author, September 6, 2005.

16. Jim Palmer, from interview with author, September 6, 2005.

17. Don Mattingly, from interview with author, March 4, 2005.

18. Linda Ruth Tosetti, from telephone interview with author, September 23, 2005.

19. Steve Karsay, from interview with author, March 4, 2005.

20. Julia Ruth Stevens, from interviews with author, November 2005.

21. John Olerud, from interview with author, June 21, 2005.

22. Julia Ruth Stevens, from interviews with author, November 2005.

23. Terry Francona, from interview with author, June 21, 2005.

24. Lloyd McClendon, from interview with author, March 4, 2005.

25. Don Mattingly, from interview with author, March 4, 2005.

26. Linda Ruth Tosetti, from telephone interview with author, September 23, 2005.

27. Julia Ruth Stevens, from interviews with author, November 2005.

28. From www.orioles.mlb.com.

29. Julia Ruth Stevens, from interviews with author, November 2005.

Babe Ruth statue at Camden Yards in Baltimore, Maryland. *Courtesy of the author.*

BABE RUTH'S LEGACY

RUTH'S LEGACY: BOOKS AND FILMS

The legacy of Babe Ruth can be scrutinized in two ways: first, by looking at how writers, including screen writers, have portrayed him to the mass public, presenting, in effect, *their* version of the Ruth legacy, and, second, by considering how others—his peers, modern players, and the baseball world in general—today view Ruth.

Regarding the media, there have even been explorations of how it would treat Ruth if he were playing today. In 1995, to celebrate the 100th birthday of the Babe, Hofstra University held a three-day conference to honor Ruth. Numerous panels were held with many scholarly topics discussed. One had the whimsical title *"I Was Babe Ruth's Love Slave" and Other Headlines for the 90s: How the Mass Media Would Cover Babe Ruth Today*. Obviously, the style and the approach of the media have changed greatly since Ruth's era.

Back then, noted Ruth's daughter Julia, Babe realized the press "helped his career along just as the fans did." But how would he have coped with today's paparazzi? Julia continued, "It's hard to say because they are so intrusive. I think he would probably have said, 'Hey, guys, give me a break, will ya'?' He always got along so well with cameramen and newspapermen. He had great rapport with the press. There was never a photographer that didn't always say, 'Just one more, Babe.' He'd say, 'Can I depend on that?' "[1]

As for writers' depictions of Ruth, by and large the writers of Ruth's day and on into the 1960s did not expose players' peccadilloes. Ruth's granddaughter Linda

Tosetti related the time Babe was on a trip and "the car door opened on one end of the train and here comes Babe running through, stark naked, wearing nothing but a towel with a lady running [after him], half-naked with a knife. One reporter says to another, 'It's a good thing we didn't see what we just saw.' It was a different time then. Remember that bumper sticker in Boston [concerning a sex scandal]? 'Don't trade Wade [Boggs] for getting laid.' What do you think they would have done with Babe?" Tosetti believes today's media would "crucify him" for some of his shenanigans. "It's the nature of the new reporter. Hopefully with the easygoing, happy-go-lucky [way] Babe always had with people, he'd probably have his favorite reporters and I'm sure he could cajole some of them. He'd probably still have as many friends. Some [of the media] he would be able to escape and others he wouldn't, but he'd probably still be crucified, but would it stop [his behavior]? I doubt it." Tosetti said that Babe didn't worry too much about what people thought of him other than "what the kids thought of him."[2]

Julia's son Tom Stevens noted that in Ruth's era, "All the travel was by train, they all traveled together, they played cards together. They were friends and they wouldn't have dreamed of writing anything negative about him anyway—they were buddies."[3] Ruth Museum curator Greg Schwalenberg agrees.

> The media was just so different then and they traveled with the team. You can bet that when Ruth was out in the bars having a good time, the writers were probably with him, too. They were friends with him. He enjoyed being around them and liked seeing his name in print a lot.
>
> I'm sure they wouldn't write the stuff a lot of the writers would today. I'm not sure the public was as interested in that stuff. To a certain degree, yes, people were fascinated with the celebrity stuff, but I think there was a little trust between the writers and the players. And, again, if you're going to write something about Ruth, he's going to say, "Hey, don't forget, you were with me doing the same thing." Now, [the members of the media] really do try to keep that distance.[4]

Most biographers presented Ruth as a hero; some even elevated him to the status of a saint, sometimes by writing things that certainly helped build Ruth's celestial image but were either untrue or exaggerated. Some of his biographers were newspaper writers of the day (e.g., Ford Frick and Bob Considine) and were, in fact, Ruth's friends—objectivity was easily blurred at times.

On the other hand, there's no doubt modern journalists have dug up some aspects of Ruth that were kept silent when the Sultan of Swat was alive. Although Robert W. Creamer's *Babe: The Legend Comes to Life* is widely regarded as the best work ever on Ruth, Julia resented it, dismissing tales of "him drinking a pint of whiskey with breakfast. I could not say for a fact that he might not have done that at one time or another before he and Mother got together, but I can assure you he sure didn't do it after they were married and I doubt if he did it before."[5] She also feels some modern biographers also perpetuate falsehoods, some of them quite malicious. The Ruth family also feels some of his misadventures really either don't need to be known by the public—they should, the family contends, remain private—while others should not be for consumption by younger audiences.

However, by the late 1960s, the climate of the country made the protection of Ruth and his image a thing of the past. The decade that gave birth to sit-ins, hippies, and protestors also resulted in the "tell it like it is" atmosphere of the 1970s. Creamer's tell-all approach to his 1974 biography came on the heels of Jim Bouton's *Ball Four* (1970), which violated baseball's oldest rules: "What you see here [in the clubhouse], what you hear here, stays here when you leave here." Bouton exposed Mickey Mantle's mortal transgressions and was vilified for doing so. Likewise, Creamer and others began to reveal, in detail, Ruth's flaws and blemishes. Tom Stevens continued, "Nobody's expecting a saccharine, sweet approach. I mean, he had his foibles and frailties and that's fine. I think in some ways that made him more popular still and more loved because that made him so human—he's just like us. That was a great part of his appeal."[6]

If Ruth played today, the modern press would no doubt delight in his "caught *in flagrante delicto*" situations and not only expose them, but perhaps exacerbate matters. After all, Ruth would expect preferential treatment and would be shocked, outraged, and irate if his image was tarnished, especially in the eyes of children. Brian Roberts of the Orioles believed that the issue nowadays would be, "How would he relate to the media. I think the media's just way more intrusive now than they used to be. I think the media does protect icons in some ways, but there's also a lot of the media that wants to break something big and bad. I think it would be a different relationship."[7]

Yankees great Don Mattingly contended, "I'm sure they'd love him. He'd be fun-loving and as long as he was doing well and was fun-loving, that's great. Then when he did bad and [was] fun-loving, 'He's not taking care of himself.' "[8] Former Yankee catcher Elrod Hendricks said of yesterday's superstars, "These guys knew they were good. I don't think the media could really hurt those guys. They had their own mind and they were hard enough or thick-skulled enough that they didn't let stuff like that bother them they played right through it."[9]

Atlanta coach Bobby Dews said that how the media would treat Ruth would be dependent upon one factor, "I think Babe Ruth would determine that." Dews' father, who played in the minors against Ruth in spring training, told

Bobby that Ruth "was the kind of guy that dictated what went on around him. He might have made you think that you were handling him, but Ruth handled the whole situation. He was just way ahead of his time. He acted like some of the superstars today who are confident and rich and good—and they're good people. People just liked him. He had a quality that just made people like him, and when you do that and you have all the other things going for you, then you dictate whatever atmosphere you want around you."[10]

The "modern" treatment of Ruth has even permeated to the publication of textbooks. Tom Stevens said that when his daughter took American history in high school the "textbook, which was widely heralded and won awards mentioned both Ty Cobb and Babe when it got to the 1920s. They gave Ty a mention, he was a racist and a bigot—they just gave him that little blurb and nothing more. And Babe Ruth was depicted as a drunk and a womanizer, but he hit 60 home runs in 1927. This is in a freaking history book! Well, what the hell purpose does that serve? Why say anything at all? It's that sort of thing that drives me nuts. Or I'll read something on a Web site about how Babe doesn't compare to current day ballplayers and they'll throw out whatever their particular criteria for evaluation might be."[11] It annoys the Ruth family that all of his acts of kindness, generosity, *and* baseball prowess could be reduced to a few lines in a text book.

As for Hollywood's treatment of Ruth, that has also changed over the years. The earliest movies with Ruth as the subject matter featured Ruth himself as an actor. These films include *Speedy*, produced in 1918; *Headin' Home*, a silent picture made in 1920; and *Babe Comes Home*, an early six-reel sound film released in 1927 and now presumed to be lost. According to Stevens, who has never seen one of those films in its entirety, Babe did a nice job of acting in such later films as *Pride of the Yankees*, but "those earlier [films] were almost caricatures, the roles that he was playing."[12] The heavy pancake make-up and poorly conceived, jump-on-the-band-wagon attempt to make a buck off Babe's popularity didn't help the films either. Most baseball and film experts believe the best thing to do with Ruth's earliest movies is to forget them.

Meanwhile, Tosetti believes modern moviemakers aren't content with displaying the positive aspects of Ruth.

> If you take [incidents] and exaggerate them, it makes him look ridiculous. So, Hollywood takes an already fairy-tale life and makes it ridiculous. You don't need to embellish Babe. They always make him look like a buffoon. My mother said he wasn't; he could add and tally numbers in his head. When he first came out of St. Mary's, was he naive? Most certainly. He went from some place very cloistered to "the world was his oyster." So, yeah, he was naive, but he was not a dumb man as they portray him.[13]

Not only has Hollywood shown him as a buffoon, many inaccuracies about Ruth's life have been perpetuated by films. Schwalenberg feels many misconceptions, such as the widely held beliefs that Ruth was an orphan or that his father treated him very poorly, come from Hollywood.

In *The Babe*, the 1992 film starring John Goodman as Ruth, Babe is shown as a blimp-like 19-year-old, which simply wasn't the case. Tosetti says Goodman "looked like Moe Howard coming out of St. Mary's."[14] The movie is full of hyperbole and inaccuracies. For instance, Ruth takes his first cut at a baseball with his hands held awkwardly apart. After swinging and missing wildly, he somehow divines he should put his hands together down at the end of the knob. He then rips a prolific home run and a steady stream of homers follows, climaxed by one that breaks the stained glass window of a distant tower and then strikes a church bell, causing it to resonate dramatically. In a reverential tone, Brother Matthias proclaims the hitting display to be "a miracle."

However, perhaps the most ludicrous occurrence in the movie is Ruth hitting a pop-up so high that all four infielders as well as the pitcher and catcher lose the ball in the sky. It eventually plops to the ground near the third-base foul line about three seconds after Ruth had lumbered by the bag at third en route to a standup, inside-the-park home run. An announcer shouts that it's "the first infield home run in the history of professional baseball." Yes, Ruth did hit them high, but lifting a ball so high that it remained in the air for about seventeen seconds is utterly absurd.

Tosetti felt that "Goodman worked with the material he had. Hollywood seems to have this thing about blowing things out of proportion. My grandfather already had a 'fairy tale' life. Just write [and show] the truth!"[15] For instance, in another scene, intended to evoke tears and pathos but reeking instead of bathos, Ruth hits a home run that he had dedicated to the seriously ill Johnny Sylvester. After crossing home plate, Ruth runs directly to a radio microphone near the playing field and says, "That was for you, Johnny. Now get well." Tosetti rues the fact that the moviemakers "never ask family."[16] Tom Stevens agrees and wishes his family had been consulted by Hollywood; he calls the Goodman film "yet another horrid installment [of Ruth's life story]."[17]

Tom Stevens recalled that for NBC's 1991 Babe Ruth biography, which starred Stephen Lang as the Babe, "Mother [Julia] did get the opportunity to review the script and annotated it; they did put their best foot forward. [In the film *The Babe*] it was clear that John Goodman was not a left-hander, all you had to do was see him swing. Neither was Stephen Lang, but they took the trouble to send him to Rod Carew's hitting camp in California for him to learn how to hit left-handed, at least convincingly. I think they put far more effort into that than they did with the supposed feature film with Goodman."[18] Julia agreed, "They tried harder to portray him right and be accurate and they did ask me about a lot of things: Did he do this or didn't he do that? And I could answer them so that was good."[19]

The 1948 movie *The Babe Ruth Story* with William Bendix is also guilty of many inaccuracies. For instance, it shows Ruth receiving a $5,000 fine and suspension for missing a game because he took a child's injured dog to a hospital for an operation—this is sheer fiction. The film even portrayed the home run Ruth dedicated for Johnny Sylvester in 1926 as the "Called Shot" of 1932. In the maudlin death scene, Ruth is operated on by the same surgeon who saved the life of the dog years earlier, and, Ruth, who had a notoriously poor memory, recalls the doctor's face from almost sixteen years before. The film also inaccurately shows Ruth retiring on the spot just moments after hitting his final three home runs in Pittsburgh, the last of which is actually shown landing in the stands at Yankee Stadium. The filmmakers even failed to get his career home-run total correct, listing it as 725, not 714.

Julia noted that the producers rushed the movie to release it before the rapidly sinking Ruth passed away; they barely met their "deadline," but sacrificed quality in doing so.

> [T]he first [film] with William Bendix—oh, my goodness. To begin with, Bendix was nowhere near Daddy's size. Though, he tried awfully hard to do the job and do it as well as he possibly could. The one thing, even though they did the script from the book that Daddy wrote with Bob Considine [also a co-screenwriter for the film], they still had to go and use their theatrical license and put things in there that were absolutely ridiculous, no question about it.[20]

Dorothy Ruth Pirone wrote in her *My Dad, the Babe* that Bendix once stated it was the worst film he had ever made, although he felt it could have been great. He lamented the inclusion of a scene in which he plays a teenaged Ruth instead of hiring a young actor to portray the young Ruth. "I have to do it with makeup," Bendix recalled. "And I'm thirty-eight years old at the time. The audience laughed. I would have laughed, too, but I felt too bad."[21]

Julia said another flaw of the movie was its exploitation of Ruth before he passed away. "They had to have him over at the opening and he was under sedation and with an attendant on either side of him, holding him up, actually, because he couldn't walk into the theater. That was so sad. When I think of Daddy, I think of him in all the years when he was big and strong."[22]

The films that succeed best with Ruth are documentaries such as HBO's fine 1998 production *Babe Ruth*, which Tom Stevens said his mother "received quite favorably." However, Tom said, "There were a couple of things in there that were a little bit dicey and there was one incorrect quote. The lady, either the one running the candy stand or the one who was talking about Babe paying for her surgery, said he had the most beautiful blue eyes. I mean, where the hell did that come from? He didn't have blue eyes, I think we're pretty square on that [they were brown]. That was one glaring inaccuracy; it's not a big deal, but for the most part I don't recall anything [negative] that jumped out at me."[23]

Even the highly regarded 1994 PBS presentation, *Baseball: A Film by Ken Burns*, wasn't without flaws. Schwalenberg said baseball experts spotted minor inaccuracies in Burns' work. Julia said, "Oh, yes. He never contacted me at all."[24] Tom Stevens found that strange because it seems quite logical to "consult Mother," a great source of information. "That was pretty wild," said Tom, considering Burns devoted a segment "entirely to Babe."[25]

Officials at the Babe Ruth Birthplace and Museum in Baltimore are surprised when writers and documentary makers visit but fail to fact-check 100 percent. It's not unusual to watch a feature on Ruth in which the narrator speaks of his 60th home run while footage is displayed of Ruth drilling a pitch, as if to say, "Here, now, is a clip from that home run." In reality, no such footage exists.

Julia believes that the best movie Ruth ever did was playing himself in the 1942 Samuel Goldwyn *The Pride of the Yankees*, which depicts the life of Ruth's Yankees teammate, Lou Gehrig. "He was good in that, he really was. That was a great, great baseball movie, one of the very few."[26] The movie was, in fact, so good, it garnered nine Academy Awards nominations, though, needless to say, none for Babe in a supporting role. According to Frank Ardolino, Ruth comes off as "a loud, bumptious, well-liked, fun-loving, ebullient phenomenon. In his scenes, he bursts into action and penetrates and dominates our vision, forcing us to concentrate on him." Ardolino quotes Ray Robinson as saying "Ruth looked like a 'truant from an 'Our Gang Comedy.' "[27] Clearly, Ruth remained larger than life, even on a flat screen, and easily managed to upstage the other players.

That shouldn't be surprising because Ruth was playing himself and thus providing a realistic contrast to the more subdued Gehrig. Ardolino believes that the movie was portraying Babe "as an inflated ego who is more interested in promoting himself and satisfying his appetites."[28] In one scene, Ruth celebrates a World Series win by ripping some clothes off fellow Yankees. While the movie was showing his unbridled side, in many ways, Ruth is not so different from today's seemingly jaded, more urbane modern players. Contemporary athletes still play pranks and still lament defeats and revel in victories much like little kids.

Stevens said that both he and his mother felt Babe had "just enough ham" in him to enjoy his antics on the big screen. As Tom commented "ham, but not too much talent in those areas [of show biz]. He made up for it with enthusiasm, I guess."[29] In short, the movie industry has, for the most part, failed to capture Ruth. As Julia noted, "I don't think there will ever be a movie made about him that will truly portray him for what he was." However, the fascination with Ruth in many forms still continues. As Julia observed, "There's scarcely a day goes by that his name is not mentioned some way." Whether it be a new biography or documentary or even "as the answer to a question on a quiz show," the world still hears of the Babe.[30]

RUTH'S LEGACY: HIS PEERS, HIS FAMILY, AND MODERN PLAYERS

Yankees great Don Mattingly said that when he was young, "I always thought Babe Ruth was like a cartoon character, I didn't relate him to a real player."[31] Probably Ruth's exploits seemed too large, too cartoonishly heroic, to be real. Mike Gibbons, executive director of the Ruth Museum, said, "I don't know that we can ever experience anything like that in baseball or in any sport again. When we see Tiger Woods come along and we saw Michael Jordan come along, yeah, it's pretty astonishing to watch, but the, fact is, Ruth was the first athlete ever to take a sport and turn it upside down."[32]

There is no question about it at all, the charismatic Ruth's legacy is as rich as it has been long standing. Even now, well over five decades after his demise, Ruth lives on. People still adore him; they even hunger just to be near his relatives, such as his granddaughter Linda Tosetti—it's as if being with her is as near to the Babe as they can ever get.

> When people find out who I am, [they get] the "Babe Ruth eyes." Their eyes get like saucers and their eyebrows go up—"Babe Ruth eyes," like a double take. And it happens every single time. People can't get enough of the man and that's awesome.
>
> My mother was so shocked the first time she started traveling for my grandfather, when I got older. She was at Yankee Stadium and they introduced her and the roar was deafening. That's when my mother said, "Oh, my God. Linda, your grandfather's name is magic."[33]

Ruth's grandson, Tom Stevens, related what happened when he met Hall-of-Famer Joe Sewell.

> He was wheelchair-bound then, but he played with Babe in the twilight of Babe's career. He had a twinkle in his eye while he was

telling [of the time] he was the last one in the locker room and Babe came, almost stumbling in, late for practice. Sewell was just about to go on the field, and by this time Babe was getting dressed and he said, "Hey, kid, can you give me a hand getting dressed? There's something wrong here and I can't figure it out." He had put his pants on backwards.

What had happened was his knees were so shot by that time in his career he was in continual search for painkillers. With prescription drugs, some of them don't necessarily agree with you too well. Apparently that was what happened in this case.

So he [Sewell] proceeded to tell the story of how he helped him get dressed and then went out onto the field and Babe followed along afterwards. In spite of all that, he put two out and went 3-for-5, I think, and had five or six RBI, not too shabby a day.

At that point [in relating the story] Joe Sewell looked up at me and said, "Son, your grandfather was a baseball god."[34]

In terms of Ruth's impact on the game, start with an act of salvation that, in baseball terms, was nearly tantamount in importance to Biblical acts. Many players, writers, and historians credit Ruth with saving the game of baseball after the notorious "Black Sox Scandal" of 1919. Fans became disgruntled and, more vitally, distrustful of the game once the truth about the fixing of the World Series came out. In such an environment, there existed a very real likelihood that former faithful fans would divorce themselves from the game. That is, until Ruth's one-man outburst began. His 1920 nitro-like explosion of 54 homers helped people forget the gambling fiasco and begin to focus instead on the inherent and enduring beauty of baseball—with an emphasis on a new facet of the game, the dizzying longball.

Noteworthy to baseball historians is a footnote to the scandal featuring Ruth's contention that the actions of the 1919 White Sox may have cost the Yankees the 1920 flag. Several days after they were mathematically eliminated by Chicago in a tight three-team pennant race, a ruling concerning the Series "fix" resulted in eight White Sox players being banned from baseball with two weeks remaining in the season. Ruth believed that if the ban had occurred, say, a week earlier, the Yankees would have played a short-handed, talent-diluted Chicago squad and New York would have emerged as the league champions. Perhaps, but, as it was, the Yankees wound up in third place, one game behind Chicago and three in back of the pennant-winning Cleveland Indians.[35]

Beyond the effect his play had in helping fans forget the Black Sox scandal, Ruth's gargantuan salary hikes helped many players in their pocketbooks.

Teammate Waite Hoyt said that every ballplayer and his wife "should teach their children to pray: 'God bless Mommy, God bless Daddy, and God bless Babe Ruth.'"[36]

Ruth's home-run legacy is monumental. Still, with the media's tendency toward hype, it is often held that the distances his homers traveled were, at times, greatly exaggerated. The first slugger to have his long drives frequently documented was probably Mickey Mantle, beginning after his monstrous 1953 blast in Washington versus Senators pitcher Chuck Stobbs. Yankees Public Relations Director Red Patterson literally took a tape measure to determine the distance the ball traveled. The ball had leaped over the left field bleachers and out of Griffith Stadium onto the streets of the capital. Patterson came up with an ungodly total of 565 feet for that tape-measure homer. Ruth, of course, was long through with his home-run days by then, so the length of Ruth's homers were almost always nothing more than raw estimations. This is not to suggest he didn't propel leviathan homers, but it seems incredulous, for instance, that a ball he ripped out of Tiger Stadium and onto Plum Street was labeled a 602-foot homer. Writers even swore that it didn't stop rolling until it was 850 feet from the batter's box.

Perhaps that's part of the beauty of the legend of the Babe—not all his unbelievable accomplishments were captured on film. Some of the mystique of athletes from the pre-ESPN era lies in the imagination of the fans. Baseball enthusiasts, especially those in NL cities and those in rural areas, relied on radio or the print media to supply them with the "Word According to Ruth." Additionally, because Ruth was larger than life to begin with, the tales of the Babe grew to even more enormous proportions. Writer Shirely Povich related an understated tale featuring Walter Johnson who had been asked which slugger launched the deepest drives. Johnson said he couldn't really say, "but those balls that Ruth hit got smaller, quicker than anybody else's."[37]

To label Ruth a star is tantamount to saying the Grand Canyon is a fairly big ditch. Ruth's name has come to represent excellence in any field of endeavor. Joe Fulks, who revolutionized the game of basketball by introducing the one-handed method of shooting, so impressed one *Saturday Evening Post* writer, he dubbed Fulks "the Babe Ruth of basketball." There was even a "Babe Ruth of Bank Robbers," Willie Sutton. Furthermore, when Lou Gehrig was a standout as a schoolboy, he was called "the Babe Ruth of the high schools." And, before an exhibition game in Omaha, Ruth and Gehrig were introduced to a hen that had laid an egg 171 days running. For such dependability a tie-in with Gehrig seemed logical, but the hen was nicknamed "the Babe Ruth of egg laying."[38]

Adjectives have been created based on surnames of famous men in fields such as the arts and sciences—there's Darwinian and Orwellian. In sports, there's only one parallel, the word "Ruthian." Tom Stevens observed, "That word has made it into accepted lexicon, in Webster's now."[39] Ruth was so unique a word had to be created to encapsulate his aura.

One story that illustrates Ruth's worldwide fame took place during World War II when Japanese soldiers hunkered down on Pacific islands. One version has American soldiers baiting the enemy, "To hell with the Emperor." In return, the Japanese felt the most fitting, equivalent retort, the ultimate affront to the U.S. troops was "To hell with Babe Ruth."

Even in death the Ruth name has earning power. The Curtis Management Group, which represents Ruth's family and estates, reaped a bonanza of roughly $25,000,000 in retail sales 1995, the 100th anniversary of Babe's birth. Ruth's daughter Julia commented that her father would have been amazed and proud. "He is generating more money than when he was playing ball."[40]

Everything involving Ruth seemed large, smacking of exaggeration. Sometimes writers felt his feats required a little spice added to them. Other times his achievements were so singular they could stand alone, without embellishment, but still seemed incredible. Long after he had last seen Ruth on a playing field, Casey Stengel still spoke with reverence and claimed Ruth once raised a pop-up so high that six infielders converged under the ball, nearly colliding as they tried to judge the ball's path. They formed a horde of defenders that resembled a football huddle, yet somehow the ball plopped to the ground and Ruth wound up with a double.

Ruth related a similar, more credible tale of his upper cutting a ball nearly straight up, reaching a height of more than double that of the roof at the Polo Grounds. It finally nicked the fingertips of Jimmy Dykes' glove and allowed Ruth to reach second on an error.[41] In 1919, he once lifted a ball so high to center that when an Athletics outfielder lost the ball, Ruth did wind up on third with a cheap but pleasing triple.[42]

Hype verus stupefying reality aside, people did react to Ruth with a frenzied adulation and awe—and many still do now. A piece in the *New York Daily News* in about 1930 noted that no one could watch Ruth emotionlessly. The writer stated he had witnessed "hundreds of ballplayers at the plate, and none of them managed to convey the message of impending doom to the pitcher that Babe Ruth did with the cock of his head, the position of his legs and the little gentle waving of the bat, feathered in his two big paws."[43]

Once when Dick Williams was managing the Montreal Expos, he ordered that Philadelphia outfielder Bake McBride be intentionally walked with men on second and third, loading the bases for future Hall-of-Famer Mike Schmidt. When Williams was riddled with questions after the game concerning the daring, unconventional move, he defended it, saying, "I don't care if Jesus Christ was coming up, I was going to walk McBride." When a writer asked what if the next batter had been Ruth, not Schmidt, Williams hesitated, then mused, "I don't know about Babe Ruth."[44]

Heywood Hale Broun phrased it another way in an HBO documentary, saying Ruth's existence "enlarges us just by looking at him, thinking about him, because you saw perfection. It was so glorious, it was almost painful." To witness Ruth club a homer was an experience, one that, as he phrased it, allowed fans to comment, "I saw this, I was here, I was in the presence of greatness. And to be in the presence of greatness means that some tiny fleck of it" became attached to the viewer. Such was the emotional impact of Ruth.[45]

Before Lou Boudreau employed a drastic defensive shift on Ted Williams, Mickey Cochrane said his Tigers defended Ruth with their second baseman playing in shallow right field, their shortstop stationed behind second base and the third baseman positioned where the shortstop normally was. Detroit was, in effect, inviting Ruth to guide the ball by third for an easy single (which he occasionally would do), far better than the prospect of a homer. In 1986, Tommy Holmes created a widely quoted observation: "Some twenty years ago, I stopped talking about the Babe for the simple reason that I realized that those who had never seen him didn't believe me."[46]

Teammates of Ruth weren't as reluctant to speak of him. Hoyt concisely commented, "He was the greatest crowd pleaser of them all."[47] Joe Dugan's capsule summation was simply, "To understand him you had to understand this: he wasn't human."[48] Harry Hooper of the Red Sox looked back over the career of the Bambino and commented, "I saw it all happen, from beginning to end. But sometimes I still can't believe what I saw...." He spoke of Ruth's rise from a crude and ill-educated manchild to being "gradually transformed into the idol of American youth and the symbol of baseball the world over.... I saw a man transformed from a human being into something pretty close to a god."[49] As sportswriter Donald Honig is often and widely quoted as saying, "If Babe Ruth had not been born, it would have been impossible to invent him."

Dizzy Dean was coming into his own during the last several great seasons for Ruth. The colorful pitcher was taken with Ruth's power: "No one hit home runs the way Babe did. They were something special. They were like homing pigeons. The ball would leave the bat, pause briefly, suddenly gain its bearings, then take off for the stands." Ruth treated baseballs as if they were a part of the witness protection program, relocating them and doing so with swift dispatch.[50]

It is also revelatory to hear what the players of the past had to say about Ruth and his place in history. Harry Walker saw many of the great ones of the game, but when speaking of Ruth, he gushed, "Babe Ruth was the most remarkable [man ever in baseball]. He's the best ballplayer who ever played the game. He hit .342 for a lifetime average. You know something else he did? He stole 100 bases [123 in all, to be exact, with a personal high of 17 stolen bases in 1921 and 1923]. Nobody knows that."[51] Ruth actually finished in the top ten among stolen base leaders several times.

Walker was correct. Many people think of Ruth solely as a power hitter, but consider his best season ever, 1921: .378 on 204 hits, 44 doubles, 59 homers, 171 RBIs, 177 runs scored (to this day the most runs tallied in a season in the modern era), and a slugging percentage of .846—just .001 off his all-time AL record, but 240 points higher than 1921's second best slugger. He truly was a multidimensional player.

Walker continued his litany of praise, doffing his cap to Ruth because "he won 20 games as a pitcher, and he even went from the outfield to pitching with the Yankees five times [winning all five appearances]. He was unique, different than anybody."[52]

Yet there are misconceptions that remain a part of Ruth lore that irritate his granddaughter, Linda Ruth Tosetti.

> His partying, drinking and carousing. Yes, he could party with the best of them, but he was also a big guy who expended [a lot of] energy and would burn everything off. He was 6' 2" when the average height for a guy was, what 5' 9", 5' 10"? Look at all the team pictures, how he towers over [teammates]. So when he drank, he wasn't like your average guy who partied hardy, he'd suck it up. I'm sure from time to time he got buzzed, but he never was oblivious. He never came to a game drunk.
>
> Obviously in the movies when they portray him as being drunk on the steps of an orphanage, [that was] ridiculous. That riles the living hell out of me because Mom said he was never, never, especially in public, drunk like that. My mother said liquor would never touch his mouth, nothing, when he would visit kids.
>
> That stuff irks the family because [it leads people to think], "Oh, he was a party hardy guy. He spent all his money." They overlook the good works that he did like going back to St. Mary's and building them a gymnasium. What the kids needed, they got. He never forgot where he came from.
>
> "In his later years, when he was sad, yeah, he drank a little bit, but she [Ruth's daughter] said he wasn't a drunk [and he would never] get drunk and go to a game. He couldn't play baseball. As much as he partied, if that was true, he wouldn't have hit a ball at all, he wouldn't have done the feats that he did.[53]

Tosetti believes a lot of the material passed down by former players of days gone by was "locker room stuff. If you think about when you were in high school, how much locker talk was true? When they take the locker room [talk] and make it fact, people print it."[54]

Given the good and the bad of the man, the bottom line is that, for the most part, Ruth *was* immensely likeable. Heywood Hale Broun commented, "He did what he wanted to do. If it got him in trouble, he was always startled."[55] Another writer observed that Ruth "never had any serious thoughts in his head, but you'da liked him." Finally, Waite Hoyt also summed up Ruth the man quite simply when he stated, "God, we liked that big son of a bitch."[56]

Ruth's daughter Julia said, "He treated me as if I had always been his. I just thought, and I still do think, that I was the luckiest girl in the world to have him adopt me; he was just so wonderful. There'll never be another one like him—not ever."[57] Tosetti mused, "Someday when I meet Grandpa—which I will someday—I just want to stand in front of this man and say, "OK, let me just take you in for a minute. Let me just see what type of man you were because it never ends. How'd you do what you did?" He'd probably tell me, "Hey, I don't know—just having fun."[58]

As regards Ruth, Shakespeare had it wrong about 400 years ago when he wrote the words, "The evil that men do lives after them, the good is often interred with their bones." Ruth's legacy, most of what people know of Ruth today, is of epic proportion and the stuff legends are made of. Never frugal with his broad, beaming smile, not only did kids and most teammates take to Ruth, but so did America. It seems absolutely stunning that the boy who was seemingly unloved by his parents grew up to become the man loved by a nation. So, in reality, the words Heywood Broun pounded out on his typewriter almost a century ago are the ones that still hold true today: "The Ruth is mighty and shall prevail."[59]

NOTES

1. Julia Ruth Stevens, from interviews with author, November 2005.
2. Linda Ruth Tosetti, from telephone interview with author, September 23, 2005.
3. Tom Stevens, from interview with author, November 5, 2005.
4. Greg Schwalenberg, from interview with author, September 7, 2005.
5. Julia Ruth Stevens, from interviews with author, November 2005.
6. Tom Stevens, from interview with author, November 5, 2005.
7. Brian Roberts, from interview with author, September 6, 2005.
8. Don Mattingly, from interview with author, March 4, 2005.
9. Elrod Hendricks, from interview with author, September 6, 2005.
10. Bobby Drews, from interview with author, September 9, 2005.
11. Tom Stevens, from interview with author, November 5, 2005.

12. Tom Stevens, from interview with author, November 5, 2005.

13. Linda Ruth Tosetti, from telephone interview with author, September 23, 2005.

14. Ibid.

15. Ibid.

16. Ibid.

17. Tom Stevens, from interview with author, November 5, 2005.

18. Ibid.

19. Julia Ruth Stevens, from interviews with author, November 2005.

20. Ibid.

21. Pirone and Martens, *My Dad, the Babe*, 181.

22. Julia Ruth Stevens, from interviews with author, November 2005.

23. Tom Stevens, from interview with author, November 5, 2005.

24. Julia Ruth Stevens, from interviews with author, November 2005.

25. Tom Stevens, from interview with author, November 5, 2005.

26. Julia Ruth Stevens, from interviews with author, November 2005.

27. Ardolino, "Lou vs. Babe in Life and in *Pride of the Yankees*," 18.

28. Ibid.

29. Tom Stevens, from interview with author, November 5, 2005.

30. Julia Ruth Stevens, from interviews with author, November 2005.

31. Don Mattingly, from interview with author, March 4, 2005.

32. Mike Gibbons, from interview with author, September 7, 2005.

33. Linda Ruth Tosetti, from telephone interview with author, September 23, 2005.

34. Tom Stevens, from interview with author, November 5, 2005.

35. Ruth and Considine, *The Babe Ruth Story*, 83.

36. Widely quoted.

37. Burns, *Baseball*.

38. Eig, *Luckiest Man*, 23, 114–115.

39. Tom Stevens, from interview with author, November 5, 2005.

40. "It's a Babe-O-Nanza," *Sports Illustrated*, February 2, 1995, from www.baberuth.com.

41. Ruth and Considine, *The Babe Ruth Story*, 91.

42. Creamer, *Babe*, 202.

43. From www.baseballhistorian.com.

44. "10 Great Moments in 'The Book' History," *Baseball Digest*, June 2005, 45.

45. HBO Productions, *Babe Ruth: The Life Behind the Legend* (New York: HBO Home Video), 1998.

46. Widely quoted.

47. From Babe Ruth Museum archives.

48. From www.baberuth.com.

49. Ritter, *Glory of Their Times*, 137.

50. From www.baseballalmanac.com.

51. Harry Walker, from interview with author, June 28, 1997.

52. Ibid.

53. Linda Ruth Tosetti, from telephone interview with author, September 23, 2005.

54. Ibid.

55. Heywood H. Broun, from HBO Productions, *Babe Ruth: The Life Behind the Legend*.

56. Waite Hoyt, from HBO Productions, *Babe Ruth: The Life Behind the Legend*.

57. Julia Ruth Stevens, from interviews with author, November 2005.

58. Linda Ruth Tosetti, from telephone interview with author, September 23, 2005.

59. Heywood H. Broun, from *The Fireside Book of Baseball*, edited by Charles Einstein (New York: Simon and Schuster, 1956), 35.

APPENDIX 1: BABE RUTH'S CAREER AND POST-SEASON STATISTICS

CAREER STATISTICS

Year	Club	League	G	AB	R	H	2B	3B	HR	RBI	BA	PO	A	E	FA
1914	Bost. Red Sox	American	5	10	1	2	1	0	0	2	.200	0	7	0	1.000
1915	Bost. Red Sox	American	42	92	16	29	10	1	4	21	.315	17	63	2	.976
1916	Bost. Red Sox	American	67	136	18	37	5	3	3	15	.272	24	83	3	.973
1917	Bost. Red Sox	American	52	123	14	40	6	3	2	12	.325	19	101	2	.984
1918	Bost. Red Sox	American	95	317	50	95	26	11	11	66	.300	270	72	18	.947
1919	Bost. Red Sox	American	130	432	103	139	34	12	29	114	.322	270	53	4	.977
1920	N.Y. Yankees	American	142	458	158	172	36	9	54	137	.376	270	21	20	.948
1921	N.Y. Yankees	American	152	540	177	204	44	16	59	171	.378	357	19	13	.989
1922	N.Y. Yankees	American	110	406	94	128	24	8	35	99	.315	226	14	9	.964
1923	N.Y. Yankees	American	152	522	151	205	45	13	41	131	.393	419	21	12	.975
1924	N.Y. Yankees	American	153	529	143	200	39	7	46	121	.378	340	18	14	.962
1925	N.Y. Yankees	American	98	359	61	104	12	2	25	66	.290	207	15	6	.974
1926	N.Y. Yankees	American	152	495	139	184	30	5	47	146	.372	318	11	7	.990
1927	N.Y. Yankees	American	151	540	158	192	29	8	60	164	.356	328	14	13	.963
1928	N.Y. Yankees	American	154	536	163	173	29	8	54	142	.323	304	9	8	.975
1929	N.Y. Yankees	American	135	499	121	172	26	6	46	154	.345	240	5	4	.984
1930	N.Y. Yankees	American	145	518	150	186	28	9	49	153	.359	266	14	10	.983
1931	N.Y. Yankees	American	145	534	149	199	31	3	46	163	.373	242	5	7	.986
1932	N.Y. Yankees	American	133	457	120	156	13	5	41	137	.341	212	10	9	.981
1933	N.Y. Yankees	American	137	459	97	138	21	3	34	103	.301	222	10	8	.942
1934	N.Y. Yankees	American	125	365	78	105	17	4	22	84	.288	197	3	8	.962
1935	Bost. Braves	National	28	72	13	13	0	0	6	12	.181	39	1	20	.952
Major League Totals		22 years	2503	8399	2174	2873	506	136	714	2213	.342	4787	569	179	.965

POST-SEASON RECORD

Year	Round	Club	G	AB	R	H	2B	3B	HR	RBI	BA
1915	World Series	Bost. Red Sox	1	1	0	0	0	0	0	0	.000
1916	World Series	Bost. Red Sox	1	5	0	0	0	0	0	1	.000
1918	World Series	Bost. Red Sox	3	5	0	1	0	1	0	2	.200
1921	World Series	N.Y. Yankees	6	16	3	5	0	0	1	4	.312
1922	World Series	N.Y. Yankees	5	17	1	2	1	0	0	1	.118
1923	World Series	N.Y. Yankees	6	19	8	7	1	1	3	3	.368
1926	World Series	N.Y. Yankees	7	20	6	6	0	0	4	5	.300
1927	World Series	N.Y. Yankees	4	15	4	6	0	0	2	7	.400
1928	World Series	N.Y. Yankees	4	16	9	10	3	0	3	4	.625
1932	World Series	N.Y. Yankees	4	15	6	5	0	0	2	6	.333
Totals			41	129	37	42	5	2	15	33	.326

A = assists; AB = at-bats; BA = batting average; E = errors; FA = fielding average; G = games; H = hits; HR = home runs; PO = put-outs; R = runs; RBI = runs batted in; 2B = doubles; 3B = triples

APPENDIX 2: A SELECTION OF FAMOUS RUTH ACHIEVEMENTS AND MEMORABLE RUTH HOME RUNS

MEMORABLE ACHIEVEMENTS AND IMPORTANT "FIRSTS"

- On March 7, 1914, in Fayetteville, North Carolina, Ruth annihilated a pitch for a long home run. Thus, he connected in his very first game as a professional.
- His only homer in regulation minor league play came on September 5, 1914, one of his 121 minor league hits over 46 games. It was also his only homer not "born" in the United States; he hit it in Toronto, Canada.
- His first major league home run came on May 6, 1915, at the Polo Grounds off pitcher Jack Warhop of the Yankees.
- His final homer with the Boston Red Sox came on September 27, 1919, victimizing Rip Jordan.
- He owned the first homer ever swatted in Yankee Stadium, which was hit off Howard Ehmke on April 18, 1923. The first of his 60 homers in 1927 also came at Ehmke's expense. One of several men who dished up more than one homer that year included Ernie Nevers, famous for scoring a record six touchdowns in an NFL game.
- The first ever home run in All-Star competition was hit by Ruth in 1933 off "Wild" Bill Hallahan.
- Ruth's final homer, on May 25, 1935, one of three he hit that day, was the first one to clear the right field roof in Pittsburgh's Forbes Field. Because Ruth had also hit three homers in a game once in the AL almost exactly five years before (on May 21, 1930), he became the first player to accomplish this in both leagues.
- Ruth's favorite patsy was Rube Walberg who surrendered 17 of Ruth's homers.
- In 1918, Ruth lost a homer due to the rules of the day. With a runner on first in the bottom of the tenth inning, he destroyed the ball, depositing it into the bleachers, a "walk off" home run by today's rules, but a triple back then.[1]

MEMORABLE LONG HOMERS

- As early as 1917, Ruth drove the first ball ever into the center field bleachers at Boston's Fenway Park.
- In 1919, some sources indicate that Ruth launched the first ball ever over the Polo Grounds right field roof.

- On May 1, 1920, when Ruth generated his first homer in a Yankee uniform, the ball sailed over the Polo Grounds roof; it was said to be the longest homer ever at that park.
- Legend has it a ball Ruth crushed over the right field wall at Detroit's Navin Field, before the park sported an upper roof, bounced off a parked car, continued down Plum Street after already traveling 602 feet, and then rolled to a stop 850 feet from home plate. However, it is almost certain that nobody is capable of homers that travel that far.
- One of his three homers in Game 4 of the 1926 World Series versus the St. Louis Cardinals soared out of Sportsman's Park and broke a car dealer's window across the street.
- After Comiskey Park was remodeled in the 1920s, Ruth was the first man to hit a fair ball completely out of the park, clearing the newly sported right field roof.
- Ruth's final homer—the first to clear the right field roof at Forbes Field—was said to have traveled 600 feet.

OTHER MEMORABLE RUTH HOMERS

Home Run	Date	Pitcher	Team
1	5/06/1915	Jack Warhop	Yankees
100	9/24/1920	Jim Shaw	Senators
200	5/12/1923	Herman Pillette	Tigers
300	9/08/1925	Buster Ross	Red Sox
400	9/02/1927	Rube Walberg	Athletics
500	8/11/1929	Willis Hudlin	Indians
600	8/21/1931	George Blaeholder	Browns
700	7/13/1934	Tommy Bridges	Tigers
714	5/25/1935	Guy Bush	Pirates

NOTE

1. Creamer, *Babe*, 165.

APPENDIX 3: NOTES ON RUTH'S INCOME

In addition to the enormous paychecks Ruth pulled in as a ballplayer, he earned tons more for endorsements and other endeavors. For example, Ruth wrote in his autobiography, *The Babe Ruth Story*, that in 1920, to cash in on his popularity, he appeared in his first movie, *The Babe Comes Home*, which is generally regarded as a terrible film. Ruth said he was promised $50,000 for his part in the movie and got a check up front for $15,000, but after the movie's release, when he tried to cash a second check for $35,000, it bounced.[1]

In 1921, Ruth took on a business manager, Christy Walsh, who was in charge of all Ruth's money-making endeavors beyond the field of play. Ruth admitted he needed someone to handle his business affairs because he was capable of spending money quicker than he could earn it. One case in point was the time his Yankee teammates stayed at a $3-per-night room in Washington, D.C., while Ruth luxuriated in a $100-a-day suite in a much more upscale hotel.

Walsh did well for Ruth as was evidenced by the increase from the less than $500 Ruth was paid for permitting a ghost writer to provide articles for a New York newspaper, to a whopping $15,000 one year.[2] Walsh was definitely a wheeler-dealer with a touch of the con artist in him. When Walsh first contacted Ruth, he seized the slugger's attention with his grandiose ways, handing over a check to Babe for $1,000 up front for nothing more than Ruth agreeing to work with Walsh exclusively. It was $1,000 Walsh didn't even have. He had to scurry to his bank to borrow enough to cover the check.[3] One estimate has Ruth earning around $500,000 in endorsements and other off-the-field activities over his lifetime.[4] Plus, when Walsh got Ruth to invest in annuities, his financial future was set.

Players' salaries averaged $2,500 by 1910 with a high of around $12,000 for megastars. By 1930, the average reached $7,000; if Ruth earned a gaudy $80,000 then, a slew of players were getting paid a whole lot less than $7,000. Due to the Depression, it got worse. In 1933, the average was down to $6,000 "and in 1940 they still lagged behind the 1929 peak of $7,500." As late as 1970, Ruth's salaries from the 1920s still humbled the average major leaguer's pay of $25,000. It's hard to imagine what Ruth would have earned if he had played in the early 1990s when, for the first time, the *average* player earned $1,000,000.[5]

Relying mainly upon figures from his *The Babe Ruth Story,* and with some room for error, listed below is Ruth's salary breakdown for the years of his career from 1914 to 1935:

1914–Ruth's first pro contract was for $600, but Jack Dunn reportedly raised the amount twice, to $1,200 in May then up to $1,800 in June. Later that year, Ruth's first big-league contract called for a salary of $2,500 (or, according to another source, the deal was for $3,500 for part of 1914 and on through 1916).

1915–$3,500

1916–$3,500

1917–$5,000

1918–$7,000

1919–$10,000

1920–The Yankees tore up the contract Ruth had negotiated with the Red Sox and re-signed him at $20,000 in the first of many salary disputes between Ruth and Yankee-owner Jacob Ruppert.

1921–$30,000[6]

1922–Ruth inked a five-year deal at $52,000 per season.[7]

1927–$70,000 per season for a three-year period.

1930–Ruth agreed to a two-year deal at $80,000 per year for the 1930 and 1931 seasons (plus the return of a $5,000 fine that had been levied upon him several years before). Ruth had asked for $100,000, but settled on $80,000. (The $100,000 plateau would not be reached until 1949 when Joe DiMaggio earned that sum.)

1932–Due to the Depression, Ruth took a $5,000 cut to $75,000. The same year also saw Commissioner Landis taking a huge reduction in salary from $65,000 to $50,000.

1933–$52,000

1934–$35,000[8]

1935–Departing the Yankees, Ruth's new deal called for $25,000 and a percentage of the Boston Braves' profits (which amounted to zero).[9]

NOTES

1. Ruth and Considine, *The Babe Ruth Story*, 85. Ruth seems to have his movie titles mixed up in this recollection. *Headin' Home* was made in 1920; *The Babe Comes Home* was not released until 1927.

2. Ibid., 98–99.

3. Eig, *Luckiest Man*, 112.

4. Miller, *The Babe Book*, 94.

5. *The Baseball Encyclopedia*, 6–7, 11–12.

6. The Baseball Almanac Web site lists Ruth's 1921 salary at $39,638.

7. Another source has his five-year deal inked in 1922 as being only a three-year package.

8. The Baseball Almanac Web site lists Ruth's 1934 wages at $43,000.

9. The Baseball Library Web site states Ruth's 1935 salary as $20,000.

Selected Bibliography

Biographies and Autobiographies of Babe Ruth

Broun, Heywood H. *The Fireside Book of Baseball.* Edited by Charles Einstein. New York: Simon and Schuster, 1956.

Creamer, Robert W. *Babe: The Legend Comes to Life.* New York: Penguin Books, 1974.

Gilbert, Brother. *Young Babe Ruth: His Early Life and Baseball Career from the Memoirs of a Xaverian Brother.* Edited by Harry Rothberger. Jefferson, NC: McFarland and Company, 1999.

Harris, Paul F., Sr. *Babe Ruth: The Dark Side.* Glen Burnie, MD: Paul F. Harris Sr., 1998.

Hoyt, Waite. *Babe Ruth As I Knew Him.* New York: Dell, 1948.

Kelley, Brent. *In the Shadow of the Babe: Interviews with Baseball Players Who Played With or Against Babe Ruth.* Jefferson, NC: McFarland and Company, 1995.

Macht, Norman L. *Babe Ruth.* New York: Chelsea House, 1991.

Miller, Ernestine Gichner. *The Babe Book: Baseball's Greatest Legend Remembered.* Kansas City: Andrews McNeel Publishing, 2000.

Pirone, Dorothy Ruth, and Chris Martens. *My Dad, the Babe: Growing Up With an American Hero.* Boston: Quinlan Press, 1988.

Ritter, Lawrence S. *The Babe: A Life in Pictures.* New York: Ticknor and Fields, 1988.

Ruth, Babe. *Babe Ruth's Own Book of Baseball.* New York: G. P. Putnam's Sons, 1928.

Ruth, Babe, and Bob Considine. *The Babe Ruth Story.* New York: Signet, 1992.

Ruth, Mrs. Babe, with Bill Slocum. *The Babe and I.* Englewood Cliffs, NJ: Prentice Hall, 1959.

Smith, Robert. *Babe Ruth's America*. New York: Thomas Y. Crowell Co., 1974.

Stevens, Julia Ruth, with Bill Gilbert. *Major League Dad: A Daughter's Cherished Memories*. Chicago: Triumph Books, 2001.

BOOKS ON BASEBALL HISTORY

Alexander, Charles C. *Our Game: An American Baseball History*. New York: Henry Holt and Company, Inc., 1991.

Allen, Lee. *Cooperstown Corner*. Cleveland: SABR, 1990.

Carter, Craig, editor. *Official World Series Records*. St. Louis: The Sporting News Publishing Company, 1979.

Eig, Jonathan. *Luckiest Man: The Life and Death of Lou Gehrig*. New York: Simon and Schuster, 2005.

Enders, Eric. *Ballparks Then and Now*. San Diego: Thunder Bay Press, 2005.

Fetter, Henry D. *Taking on the Yankees: Winning and Losing in the Business of Baseball, 1903–2003*. New York: W. W. Norton and Company, 2003.

Garner, Joe. *And the Crowd Goes Wild: Relive the Most Celebrated Sports Events Ever Broadcast*. Naperville, IL: Sourcebooks, Inc., 1999.

———. *And the Fans Roared: The Sports Broadcasts that Kept Us on the Edge of Our Seats*. Naperville, IL: Sourcebooks, Inc., 2000.

Gershman, Michael. *Diamonds: The Evolution of the Ballpark*. Boston: Houghton Mifflin Company, 1993.

Gutman, Bill. *It's Outta Here: The History of the Home Run from Babe Ruth to Barry Bonds*. Lanham, MD: Taylor Trade Publishing, 2005.

Harwell, Ernie. *The Babe Signed My Shoe: Baseball As It Was—And Always Will Be*. South Bend, IN: Diamond Communications, Inc., 1994.

Kahn, Roger. *Beyond the Boys of Summer: The Very Best of Roger Kahn*. New York: McGraw-Hill, 2005.

Kalb, Elliott. *Who's Better, Who's Best in Baseball?: Mr. Stats Sets the Record Straight on the Top 75 Players of All Time*. New York: McGraw-Hill, 2005.

Kavanagh, Jack, and Norman Macht. *Uncle Robbie*. Cleveland: The Society for American Baseball Research, 1999.

Koppett, Leonard. *Koppett's Concise History of Major League Baseball*. Philadelphia: Temple University Press, 1998.

———. *The Rise and Fall of the Press Box*. Toronto: Sports Media Publishing, 2003.

Ritter, Lawrence S. *The Glory of Their Times: The Story of the Early Days of Baseball Told by the Men Who Played It*. Macmillan Publishing Co., Inc., 1966.

Schwarz, Alan. *The Numbers Game: Baseball's Lifelong Fascination with Statistics*. New York: T. Dunne Books, 2004.

Stewart, Wayne. *Hitting Secrets of the Pros: Big-League Sluggers Reveal the Tricks of Their Trade*. New York: McGraw-Hill, 2004.

———. *Pitching Secrets of the Pros: Big-League Hurlers Sluggers Reveal the Tricks of Their Trade*. New York: McGraw-Hill, 2004.

Thorn, John, and John Holway. *The Pitcher: The Hundred Year Rivalry Between the Yankees and Red Sox, from the Very Beginning to the End of the Curse*. New York: Doubleday, 2005.

Werber, Bill, and C. Paul Rogers III. *Memories of a Ballplayer: Bill Werber and Baseball in the 1930s*. Cleveland: SABR, 2001.

AUTHOR INTERVIEWS

Bobby Cox, interview in Washington, DC, September 9, 2005.

Bobby Dews, interview in Washington, DC, September 9, 2005.

Bob Feller, telephone interview with author, 1999.

Terry Francona, interview in Cleveland, June 21, 2005.

Mike Gibbons, interview in Baltimore, September 7, 2005.

Tony Gwynn, interview in Pittsburgh, 1992.

Paul F. Harris Sr., telephone interview with author, 2005.

Elrod Hendricks, interview in Baltimore, September 6, 2005.

Steve Karsay, interview in Bradenton, FL, March 4, 2005.

Don Mattingly, interview in Bradenton, FL, March 4, 2005.

Lloyd McClendon, interview in Bradenton, FL, March 4, 2005.

John Olerud, interview in Cleveland, June 21, 2005.

Jim Palmer, interview in Baltimore, September 6, 2005.

Gerald Perry, interview in Bradenton, FL, March 4, 2005.

Charles A. Poekel Jr., telephone interview with author, 2005.

Brian Roberts, interview in Baltimore, September 6, 2005.

Greg Schwalenberg, interview in Baltimore, September 7, 2005.

Julia Ruth Stevens, interview in Sun City, AZ, November 5, 2005, and telephone interview with author, November 18, 2005.

Tom Stevens, interview in Sun City, AZ, November 5, 2005.

Linda Ruth Tosetti, telephone interview with author, September 23, 2005.

Harry Walker, interview in Atlanta, GA, June 28, 1997.

Bill Young, interview in Bradenton, FL, March 4, 2005.

STATISTICAL REFERENCES

Bucek, Jeanine, editorial director. *The Baseball Encyclopedia*. 10th ed. New York: Macmillan Publishing Co., Inc., 1996.

Neft, David S., Richard M. Cohen, and Michael L. Neft. *The Sports Encyclopedia: Baseball*. 23rd ed. New York: St. Martin's Griffin, 2003.

DOCUMENTARY FILMS

Burns, Ken. *Baseball*. Washington, DC, WETA-TV, Florentine Films, 1994.
HBO Productions. *Babe Ruth: The Life Behind the Legend*. New York: HBO Home
  Video, 1998.

MAGAZINE ARTICLES

Ardolino, Frank. "Lou vs. Babe in Life and in *Pride of the Yankees*." *The Baseball Research Journal* (May 2003): 16–20.
Baseball Digest. "10 Great Moments in 'The Book' History" (June 2005): 45.
Costa, Gabe. "Babe Ruth Dethroned?" *The Baseball Research Journal* (May 2003): 102–106.
Fullerton, Hugh S. "Why Babe Ruth is Greatest Home Run Hitter." *Popular Science Monthly* (October 21, 1921): 20–21, 110.
Livingston, Bill. "Whatever Its Shape, a Bat is a Hitter's Best Friend." *Baseball Digest* (November 1979): 85–88.
McMurray, John. "Pitching Great Bob Feller Has Fond Memories of Many Hall of Famers." *Baseball Digest* (July 2005): 68.
Simons, Herbert. "They Pinch-Hit for the Greats." *Baseball Digest* (February 1962).
Vass, George. "Baseball Records: Fact or Fiction." *Baseball Digest* (June 2005): 22–32.
———. "Remarkable One-Season Performances." *Baseball Digest* (September 2005): 22.

WEB SITES

www.baberuth.com
www.baseballalmanac.com
www.baseballhalloffame.org
www.baseballhistorian.com
www.baseballlibrary.com
www.courant.com
www.orioles.mlb.com
www.thedeadballera.com

INDEX

About the Author

WAYNE STEWART has now written 20 books and countless magazine articles. He was born and raised in Donora, Pennsylvania, a town that has produced big-league baseball players, including Stan Musial and the father-son Griffeys. Mr. Stewart now lives in Lorain, Ohio, and is married to Nancy (Panich) Stewart. They have two sons, Sean and Scott. Mr. Stewart has covered the baseball world since 1978 and has interviewed and profiled many Hall of Famers, including Nolan Ryan, Bob Gibson, and Warren Spahn. He has appeared, as a baseball expert/historian on Cleveland's Fox 8 and on ESPN Classic.